AQA English Language and Literature

A2

Exclusively endorsed by AQA

Robert Baldock
Christine Bennett
Heather Coombs
Chris Purple

Series editor
Chris Purple

 Nelson Thornes

Published in 2009 by:
Nelson Thornes Ltd
Delta Place
27 Bath Road
CHELTENHAM
GL53 7TH
United Kingdom

09 10 11 12 13 / 10 9 8 7 6 5 4 3 2

A catalogue record for this book is available from the British Library

ISBN 978 1 4085 1386 6

Cover photograph: Alamy/Design Pics Inc.
Page make-up by Pantek Arts Ltd, Maidstone
Printed in China by 1010 Printing International Ltd

Acknowledgements

The authors and publishers wish to thank the following for permission to use copyright
material:

Georges Borchardt Inc. for the estate of Tennessee Williams for extracts from Tennessee
Williams, *A Streetcar Named Desire*. Copyright © 1947 The University of The South; Faber
and Faber Ltd for extracts from Brian Friel, *Translations* (2000); New York University for an
extract from *Washington Square News*, 4.11.03; HarperCollins Publishers Ltd for an extract
from Patrick O'Brian, *The Surgeon's Mate* (1979). Copyright © 1979 Patrick O'Brian;
Pearson Education Ltd for an extract from the DVD insert from Jeremy Harmer, *How to
Teach English As a Foreign Language* (2007); David Higham Associates Ltd on behalf of
the estate of the author for an extract from Muriel Spark, *The Prime of Miss Jean Brodie*;
Methuen Drama, an imprint of A&C Black Publishers Ltd for an extract from Willy Russell,
Educating Rita, Longman (1991); Palgrave Macmillan for an extract from David Langford,
Analysing Talk (1994); Methuen Publishing Ltd for an extract from *Monty Python's Flying
Circus: Just the Words Volume 1* by Monty Python (1999); *The Spectator* with Brian
Murdoch and Noel Petty for extracts from *The Spectator*, 06.09.08.

Every effort has been made to contact the copyright holders and we apologise if any
have been overlooked. Should copyright have been unwittingly infringed in this book, the
owners should contact the publishers, who will make corrections at reprint.

Contents

Introduction

Nelson Thornes has worked in partnership with AQA to ensure this book and the accompanying online resources offer you the best support for your A Level course.

All resources have been approved by senior AQA examiners so you can feel assured that they closely match the specification for this subject and provide you with everything you need to prepare successfully for your exams.

These print and online resources together **unlock blended learning**; this means that the links between the activities in the book and the activities online blend together to maximise your understanding of a topic and help you achieve your potential.

These online resources are available on  which can be accessed via the internet at **www.kerboodle.com/live**, anytime, anywhere. If your school or college subscribes to this service you will be provided with your own personal login details. Once logged in, access your course and locate the required activity.

For more information and help visit **www.kerboodle.com**

Icons in this book indicate where there is material online related to that topic. The following icons are used:

🔆 Learning activity

These resources include a variety of interactive and non-interactive activities to support your learning.

🔁 Research support

These resources include WebQuests, in which you are assigned a task and provided with a range of web links to use as source material for research.

🔗 Study skills

These resources support you and help develop a skill that is key for your course, for example planning essays.

🔍 Analysis tool

These resources help you to analyse key texts and images by providing questions and prompts to focus your response.

▉ How to use this book

This book covers the specification for your course and is arranged in a sequence approved by AQA. The introduction to the book explains what will be required of you as an English Language and Literature student. The book is divided into two units and each unit into two sections. Each section will prepare you for a certain type of question in your examination.

Unit 3, Section A guides you through the best strategies for dealing successfully with the questions on the set drama texts you will study. This section focuses on close textual study so that you are able to examine the ways in which the dramatist uses literary, linguistic and rhetorical devices within crafted dialogue to create specific dramatic effects. Unit 3, Section B gives detailed guidance on how to respond to and compare a transcript of natural speech and an unseen literary extract in which the writer has created representations of speech. This examination unit also builds on what you have learnt in your study of the extracts in the Unit 1 Anthology and in your coursework task in Unit 2.

Unit 4 guides you through both parts of the coursework unit in which you produce text transformations and associated commentaries on the writing process and the choices you made as a writer. This final unit requires you to bring together all that you have learnt on the course about language and literature, both as a reader and as a writer.

Definitions of all key terms and any words that appear in bold can be found in the glossary at the back of this book.

The features in this book include:

Learning objectives

At the beginning of each unit you will find a list of learning objectives that contain targets linked to the requirements of the specification.

Key terms

Terms that you will need to be able to define and understand. These terms are coloured blue in the textbook and their definitions also appear in the glossary at the end of this book.

Links

Links to other areas in the textbook, or in your experience from GCSE, which are relevant to what you are reading.

Further reading

Links to further sources of information, including websites and other publications.

Think about it

Short activities that encourage reflection.

Background information

Information that will inform your study of a particular text.

Practical activity

Activities to develop skills, knowledge and understanding that will prepare you for assessment in English Language and Literature B.

Critical response activity

Activities that focus on a specific extract to develop skills relevant to your assessment in the examination.

AQA Examiner's tip

Hints from AQA examiners to help you with your study and to prepare you for your exam and coursework.

Commentary

Examples of answers you might give to the activities. These are designed to help you to understand what type of response the examiner is looking for, not to tell you the answer. There are many equally valid responses, so you will find this book most helpful if you try the activity yourself first and then look at the commentary to read another opinion. Not all activities have a commentary.

AQA examination questions are reproduced by permission of the Assessment and Qualifications Alliance.

Web links in the book

As Nelson Thornes is not responsible for third party content online, there may be some changes to this material that are beyond our control. In order for us to ensure that the links referred to in the book are as up-to-date and stable as possible, the websites are usually homepages with supporting instructions on how to reach the relevant pages if necessary.

Please let us know at **kerboodle@nelsonthornes.com.** if you find a link that doesn't work and we will do our best to redirect the link, or to find an alternative site.

Introduction to this book

Integrated study of language and literature

The books in this series are designed to support you in your AS and A2 English Language and Literature studies. What is special about this subject is that it brings together aspects of two other kinds of A Level English course – the separate English Literature and English Language specifications – and there are real advantages in continuing your studies of English Language and Literature in an integrated course of this sort.

English at every level up to GCSE requires both language and literature to be studied as essential parts of the course. How can you study literature properly without being keenly interested in the medium of that literature – the ways in which words, sentences, paragraphs and chapters interrelate to create texts of various kinds? These texts may be novels, short stories, plays, documentary scripts, poems and non-fiction texts of a whole range of types and forms.

Being inquisitive about language in all of its forms and habitats is probably the most important quality that you can bring to your studies. We are immersed in language – it is our medium of communication with other people, it is the medium of entertainment (radio, television, comedy clubs, etc.) and a medium of instruction and information (how to … books, labels on medicines). More than that, my language and your language form essential parts of our identities, our individual personalities.

If you go on to study English at university, you will also encounter a subject which has largely abandoned sharp distinctions between 'literature' and 'language' study as unhelpful oversimplifications. You will inevitably be looking at how writers use language when you study a work of literature, and your knowledge about language and how it is used can help you to appreciate and understand how writers and speakers, readers and listeners can be creative and responsive in their experiences of language.

It is important not to think of A Level English Language and Literature as a mix-and-match course in which you 'do language' in one section of a unit and 'do literature' in another section. The point is that language study and literature study are integrated and you need to think about how your interest in language can extend and enhance your appreciation of literary texts. You also need to think about literary texts as examples of language being used in ways that repay close scrutiny, analysis and reflection. There are four main skills you need to develop during your AS and A2 course:

- You need to show that you are capable of reading texts closely and thoughtfully and writing about those texts in ways that show intelligent engagement and control.
- You need to show that you understand the characteristics of various kinds of spoken language, ranging from spontaneous exchanges between friends or strangers to carefully prepared speeches that are designed to persuade large numbers of people in live events or via television and radio.
- You need to show that you are capable of producing writing that is appropriate to the purpose and audience specified in the task, showing conscious control of your choices of vocabulary, grammar and structure.
- You need to show that you are capable of writing in a focused and analytical way about your own writing – the processes you apply, the choices you make and the evaluation of whether the text works as well as you intended.

All of these activities build directly on the skills you have developed during your GCSE course and in your earlier secondary years, as well as in your primary school and during the pre-school years when you learned language skills by imitating adults and children with whom you grew up. These are skills that many of us continue to develop as the range of our experiences as readers, writers, speakers and listeners expands.

■ The units

This course focuses on a number of literary texts and on particular language topics. Here is a preview of each of the four units that make up the AS and A2 course.

Units 1 and 2 comprise the first year or AS part of the course:

■ Unit 1 (ELLB1): Introduction to language and literature study
Examination: 1 hour and 30 minutes

For this unit you will study an Anthology of thematically linked spoken and written texts. The Anthology covers the three main literary genres of prose fiction, poetry and drama as well as a range of non-literary texts. The theme for the first Anthology (covering examinations in 2009, 2010 and 2011 only) is travel, transport and locomotion. You will answer two questions, the first on an unseen text (or texts) which is thematically linked to the Anthology. The second question is set on the texts studied in the Anthology and will require you to comment on writers'/speakers' uses of language and their attitudes towards a specified theme. This is an open book examination.

■ Unit 2 (ELLB2): Themes in language and literature
Coursework

The aim of this unit is to develop your reading and writing skills through the study of one pair of texts, selected from the six pairs available. Assessment is by a two-part coursework:

- Part A requires you to apply principles of literary and linguistic study to your chosen texts in order to explore the theme specified annually by AQA for each pair of text (1,200 to 1,500 words).
- Part B requires you to demonstrate your understanding of one or both of your chosen texts by producing a piece of creative writing which extends and enhances the thematic discussion you completed in Part A (500 to 850 words).

Units 3 and 4 comprise the second year or A2 part of the course:

■ Unit 3 (ELLB3): Talk in life and literature
Examination: 2 hours

The emphasis in this unit is on the ways meanings are constructed and conveyed in spoken language. You are required to study a choice of four set plays that will include at least one by Shakespeare. You will also be required to apply your literary and linguistic understanding to the study of a variety of transcripts of real-life spoken situations. This is a closed book examination.

■ Unit 4 (ELLB4): Text transformation
Coursework

This unit requires you to choose two literary works from a selection of prescribed authors and use them as the basis for the creation of a new text or texts. It is important to note that you should *not* use any of the texts studied in previous units for this task. The new text or texts must be of a different genre from the original and must be between 1,500 and 2,500 words. You also need to write a commentary or commentaries (1,000 to 2,000 words) in which you reflect on the transformation task in order to demonstrate understanding of the creative process.

Preparation

How should you prepare for approaching your studies in this way? The essential points are that you need to:

- approach your reading and writing in an integrated way, building on both linguistic and literary understanding and methods
- develop your creativity and independence as you encounter both spoken and written language
- think about texts and the relationships between texts, which also requires that you think about the social, cultural and historical contexts of these texts
- develop independent ways of working so that your individual skills as a producer of spoken and written language are extended, and you also become increasingly thoughtful and responsive in your judgements and evaluations of the language you encounter as reader and as listener.

Assessment Objectives

You also need to be clear about the Assessment Objectives (AOs) that underpin all of your studies within this subject. Although the term 'Assessment Objectives' may sound a little remote and forbidding, you do need to understand their importance in order to study effectively and give yourself the best possible chance of achieving high grades. The AOs are set by the Qualifications and Curriculum Authority (QCA), the agency responsible for overseeing the examination system, and they apply to all specifications in this subject (see the table below).

Assessment Objectives	Questions to ask yourself
AO1 Select and apply relevant concepts and approaches from integrated linguistic and literary study, using appropriate terminology and accurate, coherent written expression	Can I write accurately and coherently about a range of texts of various sorts, using specialist linguistic and literary terms and concepts that will help me to be clear and precise?
AO2 Demonstrate detailed critical understanding in analysing the ways in which structure, form and language shape meanings in a range of spoken and written texts	Can I discuss and write about structure, form and language of spoken and written texts in ways that reveal my critical and analytical understanding?
AO3 Use integrated approaches to explore relationships between texts, analysing the significance of contextual factors in their production and reception	Can I use my linguistic and literary understanding to interpret and evaluate texts and to compare different texts and their social, cultural and historical contexts?
AO4 Demonstrate expertise and creativity in using language appropriately for a variety of purposes and audiences, drawing on insights from literary and linguistic studies	Can I use my linguistic and literary understanding to produce written and spoken language appropriately to communicate effectively with a range of audiences and for a range of purposes?

You will have noticed that running through the questions in the table is an insistence on the need to apply your knowledge and understanding of both language and literature, and this is the key to success on this course of study.

■ How to read

The introduction to the AS book referred to three different kinds of reading:

- *Reading the lines*: reading for surface meanings.
- *Reading between the lines*: reading closely so that you are alert to what a text hints at or implies, as well as what is stated explicitly.
- *Reading beyond the lines*: reading creatively so that you relate books to your own experiences and beliefs, challenging and extending your own thinking.

At A2 Level you need to concentrate on developing your analytical skills so that you are able to read between the lines in sophisticated ways, and read beyond the lines so that you can answer questions such as:

- What do I think and feel about this text, and has it affected me and my beliefs and values?
- What do I think about the text in terms of the writer's style and techniques: has he or she won me over as an enthusiastic admirer of the text, or has he or she failed to do so?
- Which other books or real experiences does this text remind me of, and does it make me re-evaluate them and my own responses to them?
- In what ways am I a more effective communicator in my own writing than I was at the beginning of the course?

At this halfway stage of the four-unit course, it is worth reconsidering the quotations that were presented in the introduction to the AS book. Ask yourself whether you respond to them differently now compared with when you first thought about them. If you feel that the implications of each question are a little richer than when you first read them, you are almost certainly working along the right lines as you follow this course.

■ Think about it

Think about the different types of reading in relation to the following quotations about how we read and what the effects of reading can be.

'Some books are to be tasted, others to be swallowed, and some few are to be chewed and digested.'
  Francis Bacon (1561–1626)

'A conventional good read is usually a bad read, a relaxing bath in what we know already. A true good read is surely an act of innovative creation in which we, the readers, become conspirators.'
  Malcolm Bradbury (1932–)

'Reading a book is like re-writing it for yourself … You bring to a novel, anything you read, all your experience of the world. You bring your history and you read it in your own terms.'
  Angela Carter (1940–92)

'There is creative reading as well as creative writing.'
  Ralph Waldo Emerson (1803–82)

'Books give not wisdom where none was before. But where some is, there reading makes it more.'
  John Harington (1561–1612)

'What is reading, but silent conversation?'
  Walter Savage Landor (1775–1864)

Talk in life and literature

This unit covers:

- how to analyse talk in crafted and real texts, using linguistic and literary approaches

- the development of skills needed to do this analysis, using practical exercises and worked examples

- background information on form and structure of crafted texts

- how to approach the examination, together with sample questions, worked examples and examiner's tips.

Key terms

Metaphor: a figure of speech where two things are concisely compared by saying that one thing is the other, e.g. 'Denmark is a prison!'

Simile: an explicit comparison, usually using the word 'like' or 'as', e.g. 'as thick as thieves'.

Introduction

In this unit the emphasis is on spoken language of all kinds, from dialogue in plays to real-life conversations, speeches and sports reports. It builds on the knowledge you will have gained during the AS course when you learnt how to analyse a range of text such as blogs, poems and transcripts. So you should have some knowledge of what linguists call discourse analysis, and you are probably familiar with some literary terms like **metaphor** and **simile**. Such linguistic and literary approaches to texts are used in this unit and its overall aim is to sharpen skills by providing you with a range of tools for analysis. This will help you to better explain how meanings are constructed and conveyed, and how we interpret such meanings in a range of fictional and real-life texts. This is challenging but fascinating work.

The unit has two sections:

Section A

You will have to study one play from a choice of four. The texts offered for study until 2012 are:

- *Hamlet* William Shakespeare
- *The Rivals* Richard Brinsley Sheridan
- *A Streetcar Named Desire* Tennessee Williams
- *Translations* Brian Friel.

Section B

You will have to study transcripts from a variety of situations.

These are the minimum requirements, but obviously the more you read, the more you listen with a critical ear and the more you reflect and write about texts, then the more your skills and enjoyment will grow.

How the unit will be assessed

Assessment is by written examination of two hours and you cannot take the set texts into the examination. You will need to answer two questions, both of which carry equal marks:

- Question 1 is based on an extract from the play you have studied. The focus is on the crafted language of drama, and you will have to discuss how the dramatist uses such language to create **dramatic effects**. This is a key phrase and it reminds us that we are studying a play, not simply a written text – a play which is meant to be heard and seen and to have dramatic impact on the audience.

- Question 2 asks you to show knowledge and understanding of both naturally occurring speech and crafted speech in literature. Natural speech can be anything from a job interview to an impromptu conversation on a bus between strangers. Similarly, crafted speech can be drawn from a wide range of texts: from novels, poems or drama. You will be asked to compare two extracts that you have not seen before, which will be linked thematically. One will be a transcript (for example a conversation between two students planning an end-of-term celebration) and the other a literary extract (for example some dialogue from a novel which takes place at a party). You will be asked to compare the extracts, showing how they reflect differences and similarities between talk in life and in literature. *Compare* is the key word here.

Key terms

Dramatic effects: effects created by the writer to evoke an emotional or intellectual response. For example, dramatic irony is when the audience knows more than the character(s) and so is made to feel helpless, anxious or tense. Suspense occurs when the audience is told something and waits in a state of dread or anticipation for the action to unfold.

Unit 3 of this book is organised in the following way in order to support you in the examination:

- Section A focuses on the study of speech representation and other stylistic features within set texts to create dramatic effects. This should equip you to handle Question 1 of the examination paper as well as providing you with background material on the set texts.

- Section B is concerned with the comparison between naturally occurring speech and crafted speech in literature. A range of stimulating examples is used and the discussions and practical exercises should help to develop your skills so that you will approach Question 2 with confidence.

Assessment Objectives

These can look quite daunting, but it is useful to be aware of how different skills are weighted.

The overall weighting of the whole unit is 30 per cent of the total A Level mark and this can be broken down further into different AO weightings. These are approximate guidelines.

Assessment Objectives	Explanation for Unit 3	Unit weightings
AO1 Select and apply relevant concepts and approaches from integrated linguistic and literary study, using appropriate terminology and accurate, coherent expression	Understand a range of approaches to analysing texts and be able to apply this knowledge to produce well-written discussions of extracts	7.5
AO2 Demonstrate detailed critical understanding in analysing the ways in which structure, form and language shape meanings	Show that you understand how choices such as the kind of **lexis** used, or the way thoughts are organised can affect the meaning. This is a great concern in Unit 3 and underpins everything. How is the meaning of a play or a poem conveyed to us? How does the language we use – say in a transaction in a shop – affect how we are received by the listener?	10
AO3 Use integrated approaches to explore relationships between texts, analysing and evaluating the significance of contextual factors in their production and reception	Understand how important context is in influencing the language choices that people – including authors – make. When and where the 'text' was produced is crucial. In real speech, the environment, whether it is a law court, a school room or a friend's house, together with the audience and the purpose, will all influence language choices	7.5
AO4 Demonstrate expertise and creativity in using language appropriately for a variety of purposes and audiences, drawing on insights from linguistic and literary studies	Adapt your style to suit the question. For example, remember to structure the second essay as a comparison. Creativity in Unit 3 refers to an ability to think independently and critically about issues	5
Overall weighting of Unit 3		30

1 Overview

🔆🔍

You will have to choose only one of the set texts to study; this is the basic requirement of the specification. However, in the following chapters we will look at examples from all four of the texts, but with particular emphasis on *Hamlet* and *Translations*. At first you may be tempted to skip the sections which do not seem directly relevant to your study, but reading and analysing unfamiliar extracts will sharpen skills and provide excellent practice for Question 2 on the examination paper (the unseen exercise). Also, it will broaden your literary experience and provide you with some challenging and enjoyable activities.

■ The question

The wording of the question will vary depending upon the extract. For example, referring to an extract from the climactic closet scene between Hamlet and his mother (Act 3, Scene 4) the question might be:

■ Explore the ways in which Shakespeare uses literary, linguistic and rhetorical devices and conventions to create specific dramatic effects in his portrayal of conflicting relationships in this passage.

Using an example from *Translations* where Lieutenant Yolland and Captain Lancey appear for the first time in Act 1, the question might have a slightly different slant:

■ Explore the ways in which Friel presents issues of communication and miscommunication in this passage by using literary, linguistic and rhetorical devices and conventions to create specific dramatic effects.

The focus in each question is, however, broadly the same: how does the dramatist create dramatic effects? You need to be able to respond to the dramatic impact of an extract/scene and be able to pinpoint how the writer achieves this, by analysing the conventions and devices he uses.

■ Dramatic effects

This refers to what the audience might think and feel in reaction to the performance being viewed. Obviously each performance is different, and some audiences will perceive more humour or more **pathos** in a particular staging. You will also want to reflect on what you understand to be the dramatist's purpose, always accepting that each production or reading will elicit differing responses. Dramatic impact varies according to production decisions made by the director and how actors deliver their lines.

However, we need to make sense of the phrase and below is a list of the kinds of effects which you could consider:

- ■ **Plot**: is the plot being revealed or furthered?
- ■ **Character**: is character being established or revealed?
- ■ **Relationships**: are the relationships between the characters being developed?
- ■ **Mood**: is a particular mood being created or intensified?
- ■ **Ideas and themes**: are thematic issues being presented?
- ■ **Visual and aural effects**: is a scene spectacular, farcical, visually arresting? The focus here is on the staging and its impact.

Key terms

Pathos: originally a Greek word meaning 'suffering', it usually refers to feelings of sadness that a character or scene evokes.

Key terms

Phonology: concerned with studying sounds in languages. It is a broad umbrella term. If you study phonological features you may well include a close look at stress and rhythm, which is where the definition overlaps with prosody.

Verse: language in metrical form, or poetry. Verse builds discourse in a dramatic text by using recurrent syllabic patterns, imposing an order not usually found in spontaneous speech.

Prosody: this is usually applied to the analysis of sounds and rhythm in poetry.

Syntax: a term that refers to the order of words in a sentence: this is normally subject, verb, object (or svo) in Standard English usage. 'The dog (subject) sat (verb) on the mat (object).'

Imagery: this refers to figurative language. An image or picture can be created by imagery, but it can also be created by plainer speaking: 'The grass is green.'

Phonological features: this refers to the sounds in speech: pitch and intonation, speed, stress and volume. Whispering to convey secrecy or using flat tones to suggest depression are examples of how sounds convey meaning.

Hyperbole: exaggeration used deliberately for emphasis: 'Is this the face that launched a thousand ships?'

Reflecting on the closet scene mentioned previously when Hamlet confronts his mother with the differences between the image and stature of his dead father and the new king, the dramatic effects are many. The plot is furthered in a striking way: Hamlet kills Polonius impulsively and shockingly and Hamlet's feigned madness is revealed to his mother, as well as his request for her to avoid Claudius's bed and to keep quiet about his (Hamlet's) plotting. But just to sum up how the plot is furthered is to miss much in this scene. The queen's guilt is revealed, and her fear and sadness; Hamlet's anger and bitterness are graphically conveyed too. There is much about each character which is exposed in this close but tense relationship. With Hamlet's threatening behaviour, and the tension between them, the audience is kept in suspense. The mood fluctuates from tenderness to anger to palpable fear. The appearance of the ghost provides a poignant visual reminder of Hamlet's grief and the rationale for action.

Ideas about mother–son relationships, about Elizabethan views of ghosts and about the morality of revenge all hover around the scene. There is so much to say about the dramatic effects in this scene, and this only brushes the surface.

■ The frameworks needed to analyse these dramatic effects

The specification emphasises that the approach to analysis should be integrated, that both literary and linguistic devices and conventions should be considered. So you do not need to worry about the distinctions between these two areas, which is just as well because you will find different ways of grouping aspects of language study. For example, some might regard investigating **phonology** as the province of the linguist. However, the investigation of the effects of sounds in language, of rhythm in **verse** and a general interest in **prosody** is also regarded as the legitimate area of exploration for those interested in literary techniques. So, analysing sounds in language can involve looking at devices which may not be easily categorised as either literary or linguistic.

However, in the interests of clarity, and to provide a manageable structure for future discussion, the groupings used here are:

■ Linguistic devices: this includes discourse conventions and spoken language features, grammar and **syntax**.

■ Literary devices: these include use of **imagery**, **phonological features**, lexical choice, use of form and structure and the performance element, including the importance of context.

■ Rhetoric: this is concerned with persuasive language and includes techniques such as the use of **hyperbole** or exaggeration.

You will also be concerned with linguistic theories and how they may help your understanding.

To sum up, it is useful to acquire a range of analytical tools or linguistic, literary and rhetorical frameworks, which will inform your thinking and enable you to get to grips with explaining the dramatic effects of an extract. You will then be able to comment with clarity and insight.

2 | Analysing texts: some linguistic tools

This chapter covers:

- linguistic devices and conventions
- the usefulness of theories
- the importance of context and register
- some brief examples of analysing texts using linguistic frameworks
- some suggested activities.

Key terms

Lexis: a unit in the lexicon or vocabulary of a language. Put simply: a word.

Rhetorical question: e.g. 'What time do you call this?' or 'Why am I helping you?' where the intent is to make the listener reflect, rather than expecting them to provide an answer.

Interactional features: features of spoken discourse which are commonly seen when people interact, such as someone being dominant.

Turn-taking: in spontaneous conversation, this is when people take turns to speak, although there can be overlaps and interruptions. Scripted turn-taking is more orderly.

Adjacency pairs: a pair of utterances from different speakers where the second speaker is controlled by the first speaker's utterance. This occurs in a question–answer format, for example, or when one person greets another.

Length of turn: this refers to the length of a participant's speech. The person with the higher status, because of their power or knowledge, will usually have the longest turn; but monopolising turns may well be seen as rude in a conversation when people are of roughly similar status.

🔍 Discourse analysis

The word 'discourse' is so broad that it is often misunderstood. Simply put, discourse is written or spoken language, but it refers to a section of speech or writing which is more than just a single sentence or a short utterance. It could be a few lines from a play or a paragraph from a novel, but a single utterance like: 'What shall I do?' (which the Queen asks of Hamlet in the closet scene) is not very fruitful to analyse unless we see it in context and we hear the preceding speech where Hamlet is pointing to the dead body of Polonius and saying he will 'bestow' the body. The speech which follows the question (interrogative utterance) has Hamlet asking the Queen to keep everything secret and to spurn Claudius. Seeing the question in context, simply expressed, allows us to appreciate the tone of Gertrude's question in all its helplessness and submissiveness.

So, we have just carried out some extremely simple discourse analysis. And, of course, the discourse analysis is focused on talk, on spoken language in fictional texts (and in Section B in real situations). There is no need to analyse written essays or literary texts which contain no speech. Therefore, a useful working definition is:

> the study of conversational exchange, dialogue and interaction between speakers in social contexts.

Susan Cockcroft, Investigating Talk, *1999*

You need to be interested in how participants act, react and interact with each other. At a simple level, this can involve looking at who starts a conversation or who dominates in an exchange, but it will also involve some reflection on how the participants speak, for example how they address each other. What kind of speech do they use?

On the stage the dramatist may well replicate natural speech in order to create a naturalistic feel to his text. Look back at the simple question of Gertrude with its monosyllabic lexis. Or take the opening line in *The Rivals* as Fag the servant meets the Coachman and shouts: 'What! Thomas! sure 'tis he? – What! Thomas! Thomas!' The simple **lexis**, the exclamative utterances, the doubting **rhetorical question** and the hesitation and surprise all give this a realistic quality.

Let us look in more detail at the spoken language features, especially the **interactional features** that might be of interest in a play. Note: this list is not exhaustive and more terms will be used when we look at particular extracts.

- **Turn-taking** features and use of **adjacency pairs** in a dialogue (spoken by two or more participants): the dramatist often makes use of conversational turn-taking, but as in real speech, it is not always neat and tidy. Subverting orderly interaction can create drama. **Length of turn** is of interest too and it is dependent on the relationship of the interactors in the conversation, as well as the amount of knowledge they have and the dramatist's purpose in crafting the character in such a way. Assessing who is dominant and appears to have the power in an interaction is an interesting area to investigate – and, of course, such dominance does not depend simply on length and number of turns. There is much power in conciseness or in silence!

■ **Key terms**

Agenda-setting: this refers to the person who takes the initiative and chooses the topic being talked about.

Topic management: this is to do with how the subject/topic being discussed is handled, i.e. who changes the topic?

Types of utterance: there are four main types of utterance – questions (interrogatives), statements (declaratives), commands (imperatives) and exclamations (though these may be couched in terms of a declarative such as 'Get away!' to indicate disbelief).

Ellipses: the omission of part of a sentence for economy or emphasis, e.g. 'Need any help?', rather than 'Do you need any help?'

Overlaps: where two or more speakers speak at the same time. It is a mistaken belief that overlapping suggests competitive or impatient speech behaviour; it often indicates alignment between participants to show solidarity or cooperation.

Naturalistic theatre: this emphasises the naturalism of everyday speech in order to communicate efficiently. It is not to be confused with Naturalism, a theatre movement in the second half of the 19th century which purported to enact on the stage 'a slice of life'.

Realistic theatre: a movement in the latter half of the 19th century. It intended to make the theatre more useful to society in opposition to the mainstream theatre of the period, which consisted mostly of melodrama, spectacle, comic opera and vaudeville.

■ Discourse markers: both scripted and spontaneous speech, since they are designed to be heard, often use markers to signal that the speakers have finished their turns such as a pause, or words like 'well' or 'so', which can mark boundaries between one topic and the next.

■ Modes of address: what one character calls another is often dramatically significant. For example, Hamlet is often addressed as 'my noble lord' even by his close friend Horatio, reminding us of his royal status. Hamlet also refuses to call Claudius his father.

■ **Agenda-setting** and **topic management**: reflecting on who is controlling an interaction and their possible dominance in an exchange can focus us on a character's role.

■ **Types of utterance**: there are four types of utterance – exclamative, interrogative, declarative and imperative. The kinds of utterance a character makes can contribute to our understanding of their character and role. Manus in Act 1 of *Translations*, is imperative in his orders to Sarah: 'Get your tongue and your lips working' or 'Raise your head. Shout it out.' But we need to know that his intentions are entirely helpful: he is aiming to get Sarah to talk. He is being as Hamlet says 'cruel to be kind'. As you can see, simply categorising utterances will not get us very far; we always have to appreciate the effect of the context.

■ Non-fluency features: these include voiced pauses (for example 'em', 'er', 'oh'), fillers (for example 'you know', 'sort of', 'like'), and false starts (when speakers begin with a topic and then stop and either change direction or restart and often repeat themselves).

The features mentioned above are, of course, common to natural speech, and some of these terms will be used in the analyses in Section B. A dramatist will often attempt to mirror such spontaneous speech, although it is important to remember that the characters are constructs and, of course, the dramatist governs all turns, all thoughts, all viewpoints. Look at the following dialogue from the opening scene of *A Streetcar Named Desire*. Blanche has come to stay (uninvited) with her sister (Stella) and Stella's husband (Stanley). Blanche has just removed some liquor from the closet; she is shaking all over and the bottle nearly slips from her grasp. As Williams says, she is full of 'feverish vivacity'. Stella is concerned:

> **Stella** (*noticing*): Blanche, you sit down and let me pour the drinks, I don't know what we've got to mix with. Maybe a coke's in the icebox. Look'n see, honey, while I'm –
>
> **Blanche**: No coke, honey, not with my nerves tonight! Where – where – where is –?
>
> **Stella**: Stanley? Bowling! He loves it. They're having a – found some soda! – tournament …
>
> **Blanche**: Just water, baby, to chase it! Now don't get worried, your sister hasn't turned into a drunkard, she's just all shaken up and hot and tired and dirty!

This extract mimics real speech with its disjointed utterances, repetitions, pauses, **ellipses**, varied modes of address ('honey', 'baby') and possible **overlaps** or interruptions. Blanche seems to dominate with her requests and exclamations, although Stella also makes some requests. Of course we have to imagine the pitch and tone of their voices, but we can see here that Williams uses the features of conversational interactions and that this helps to create **naturalistic theatre** and **realistic theatre**.

Grammar and syntax

The following is a list of grammatical and syntactical features that might be of interest in a play.

- Types of utterance: already mentioned in the list of interactional features above, these are often grouped with discussions of grammar. How we classify such categories does vary, but as mentioned previously, your main task is to understand and appreciate the usefulness of such terms, and to develop your ability to apply them fruitfully, rather than to fret too much about which 'box' they belong in.

- Standard and non-standard grammar: it is interesting to see how a dramatist will replicate real speech by using less conventional grammatical forms in order to create a character effectively. Look at Jimmy's reply to Manus (the teacher) in Act 1 of *Translations*. Jimmy is 'the infant prodigy' who happily reads Greek and Latin and is steeped in myths. He has just asked Manus which of the three women – Athene, Artemis and Helen of Troy – he would pick, and Manus has evaded the question by asking Sarah which one he should take. Jimmy's reply is: 'No harm to Helen; and no harm to Artemis; and indeed no harm to our own Grania, Manus. But I think I've no choice but to go bull-straight for Athene. By God, sir, them flashing eyes would fair keep a man jigged up constant!' Jimmy has an instinctive mastery of rhetoric with his **triple structure** in the first utterance, and he also uses blunt, colourful language such as 'bull-straight'. But focusing on the grammar in particular we see the use of 'them' instead of the standard 'their'; also the use of 'constant', rather than the adverbial 'constantly'. Where does such analysis get us? It enables us to explain how Jimmy's **idiolect** is put together and how Friel quickly establishes this fascinating character. We have also touched on syntax here.

- Syntax: the word order is important in creating dramatic impact. In Jimmy's speech he structures his ideas by beginning with the choices he would not make and withholds from us his real choice until later in his speech. The first utterance is an incomplete but wonderfully balanced declaration. We have to wait for the climactic final sentence where in **colloquial** lexis Jimmy makes his appreciation clear!

Theory: what is the use?

According to Richard Hudson, in *Invitation to Linguistics* (2000), a theory is a 'testable generalisation'. Theories are meant to help us understand what is going on in discourse. One of the most well known, Grice's cooperative principle, is introduced here and others will be referred to briefly. Studying and applying theories is a broad and fascinating area, but there is only space to touch on a few theories in this book. **Schema** theory is mentioned later together with **pragmatics**. Labov's narrative theory (1972) is also touched upon. This is where a narrative or storytelling is seen as important in much everyday speech, from recounting a meeting with a friend to telling a joke. Labov identified recognisable stages in this storytelling:

- Abstract: the summary of the story.
- Orientation: the context in which the story takes place (who, what, when, where).
- Evaluation: the point of interest in the story.
- Action: what happens.
- Resolution: the outcome, what finally happened.
- Coda: the end of the story.

Key terms

Triple structure: also known as tripling/triplets. Repeating words or longer utterances three times is a common feature in rhetorical oratory: 'Education, education, education!'

Idiolect: an individual's particular way of speaking.

Colloquial: a semi-technical term for the everyday, or vernacular, form of language which is informal and may include slang words.

Schema: a set of expectations in any given situation. For example, in buying and selling there is an expected 'schema' which governs behaviour.

Pragmatics: how we interpret the intentions of the speaker, sometimes defined as the study of 'speaker meaning' in a particular context. For example, 'watch this' can have many meanings depending on the situation.

If you are interested in theory, there is so much to read and digest: from numerous politeness theories to studies of male and female talk. In the Further reading section at the end of the unit there are some suggested useful texts which handle theory (see Pridham (2001) and Cockcroft (1999)).

Paul Grice's cooperative principle is one of the theories most often quoted:

■ Make your conversational contribution such as is required, at the stage at which it occurs, by the accepted purpose or direction of the talk exchange in which you are engaged.

The maxims which support this principle are:

■ Quantity: make your contribution as informative as required.
■ Quality: do not say what you believe to be false, or anything for which you lack adequate evidence.
■ Relation: be relevant.
■ Manner: be clear.

According to Grice we can choose to cooperate or we can deliberately flout one or all of the maxims. If a dramatist crafts a character to deliberately flout a maxim the result is often intriguing and dramatic.

Critical response activity

Look at Polonius's encounter with Hamlet in Act 2, Scene 2 when Hamlet is reading a book:

Polonius: What do you read my Lord?

Hamlet: Words, words, words.

Polonius: What is the matter, my Lord?

Hamlet: Between who?

Polonius: I mean the matter that you read, my Lord.

Hamlet: Slanders, sir: for the satirical slave says here, that old men have grey beards; that their faces are wrinkled; their eyes purging thick amber and plum-tree gum: and that they have a plentiful lack of wit, together with weak hams …

And then a little later in the interaction:

Polonius: Will you walk out of the air my Lord?

Hamlet: Into my grave?

Think about the maxims which Hamlet flouts and reflect on the effect this has on the drama. Write down your own thoughts before comparing your ideas with the commentary that follows.

Commentary

Hamlet chooses to ignore any maxims of quality, relevance and manner. He is impatient with Polonius's silly questioning and spying on him, and so chooses to misunderstand Polonius's questions and give him literal answers. He also gives a long description of the slanders he is reading (flouting Grice's maxim of quantity). There is much conversational implicature here – a phrase coined by Grice. This refers to what is implied rather than clearly outlined. It is clear to anyone in the audience that Hamlet is tired of Polonius and that the slanderous description is of him, although much humour can be extracted from playing the part of Polonius as ignorant of Hamlet's implications.

Politeness theories may also help us to understand what is happening in an interaction. Well-known theories include that of Brown and Levinson about positive and negative politeness (1987). Positive politeness involves avoiding disagreement and trying to be cooperative. The speaker might assume that there is common ground between participants and that they are all on the 'same side'. Hamlet is doing none of this. With negative politeness you often **hedge** a request and say: 'Would you mind opening the window please?' rather than the bald imperative: 'Open the window!' You are being indirect and can sometimes seem apologetic, for example 'Sorry to ask you, but I would be really grateful if you could open the window.'

Politeness is the social glue and we use many strategies, but in a play like *Hamlet* his lack of courtesy for Polonius creates drama. We wonder what actions or words Hamlet will use next. His descriptions may be humorous, but they are particularly offensive and not what would be used in a polite conversation. Polonius, on the other hand, makes a positively polite request, addressing Hamlet with courtesy and asking him to come 'out of the air', i.e. come inside or out of the draught. Hamlet chooses to deliberately misunderstand.

However, this is drama and the conflicts we experience are skilfully crafted.

Context and its importance

In your analysis of real and crafted speech, context is a crucial concept, which can have various meanings. We talk about the context of production: the environment and the era when the play was written (including factors which would have influenced the dramatist), and the cultural milieu of the time (including political and social attitudes and beliefs).

In terms of an individual extract, however, the main concern would be the context of the scene rather than the background information (although this obviously informs your thinking and helps you to understand the play). For example, knowledge of how the Elizabethans perceived ghosts would help you to appreciate the terror that the first scene in *Hamlet* might have evoked. But you will be making judgements about how the particular dramatic context influences the action. Is it a public scene in the hall of the castle with many onlookers, or a private scene with fewer people in a more intimate setting? What has occurred before the scene you are analysing and what happens later? How does the context affect the mood?

Key terms

Hedge: this refers to using a softening phrase to weaken the impact of an utterance, e.g. 'As far as I know, no one has failed this course yet.' It is often a way to avoid being compromised if what you say is later proved wrong. With hedging the speaker avoids directness.

Practical activity

Find a section in the play you are studying where characters are introduced or meet each other for the first time. For example when the players arrive in Elsinore in *Hamlet*. To what extent are politeness strategies used? Are they flouted for dramatic effect?

AQA Examiner's tip

Remember that just quoting a theory for its own sake will not be helpful in your analysis. You need to use and apply the theory.

Critical response activity

Look at Claudius's first very measured and stately speech to the court in Act 1, Scene 2. He addresses them in an appropriate, dominant way, with a very long turn which attempts to explain his actions and to show him in control of the Norwegian situation. It is a polite, coherent statement and what he says is clearly influenced by the very public occasion. He wants to make his mark and to move on.

Here is the opening where we must, however, wait until the sixth line for the main verb. It is carefully crafted and begins with statements about the need to grieve.

King: Though yet of Hamlet our dear brother's death
The memory be green: and that it us befitted
To bear our hearts in grief, and our whole Kingdom
To be contracted in one brow of woe:
Yet so far hath discretion fought with nature,
That we with wisest sorrow think on him,
Together with remembrance of ourselves.

Compare the speech above with a short speech from the opening of Act 4, Scene 1, a much more intimate scene in which he is talking only to Gertrude and his genuine apprehension is conveyed. He has just heard that Polonius has been killed and he is thinking quickly on his feet.

King: O Gertrude, come away:
The sun no sooner shall the mountains touch,
But we will ship him hence, and this vile deed,
We must with all our majesty and skill,
Both countenance, and excuse.

Write down your own thoughts before reading the brief commentary below.

Commentary

This is quite different in syntactical structure and, of course, in tone and lexis, but the context influences the type of discourse which Shakespeare constructs for Claudius. You should be able to pinpoint some of the differences. For example, look at the lexis and compare 'befitted' with a phrase like 'come away'.

■ Register

This is a broad term but one you may find useful. In spoken language, crafted or real, **register** refers to the type of language used, including its level of formality or informality. *Hamlet* ranges from a very elevated register in many of the soliloquies or the courtly dialogue, but it also makes effective use of more **demotic**, colloquial language: a more informal register. Register also refers to a situation as well as the language used. For example, you might talk about the 'register' of a hotel reception area. Some reception areas are welcoming, with comfortable armchairs creating a relaxed mood and informal register, whereas others appear more functional with little furniture and a chillier, more formal register. Lecture theatres imply a more formal register, with all eyes on the lecturer. In an institutionalised context like a courtroom, for instance, the spoken language is expected to be formal. Who is allowed to speak, and when, is also institutionalised in the room's formal layout and the enactment of rituals like standing when the judge enters, which is intended to reinforce his status. Those empowered to speak wear old-fashioned wigs and gowns, but no one laughs! In this context, power resides with the legal profession. They act as **gatekeepers**, deciding which of the participants is allowed a turn and when they are allowed to take it.

The register on stage for the hedge-school in *Translations* is informal and the action is meant to take place in 'a disused barn, hay-shed or byre'. This is very different from the castle ramparts in Elsinore in *Hamlet*, but perhaps not so different from the streets of Bath in *The Rivals*. The claustrophobic, small apartment in *A Streetcar Named Desire* is associated with an informal register, but the dramatist is free to introduce other registers. Blanche is allowed her lengthy lyrical speeches, crafted for dramatic effect.

■ Key terms

Register: the features that are characteristic of a particular type of language or situation, ranging from the informal register of text messages to the formal register of a legal document or a court scene.

Demotic: everyday, ordinary language. The term 'prosaic' is also used to refer to commonplace speech.

Gatekeeper: a person with the power to control the discourse, governing the turn-taking or the ritual.

3 Analysing two examples using linguistic tools

This chapter covers:

■ two worked examples from *Translations* and *Hamlet*, focusing particularly on linguistic devices.

■ *Translations*

Here is an extract from Act 1 of Friel's *Translations*, first presented on the stage in 1980 but set in 1833. Hugh, the schoolmaster, who has a tendency to drink too much, has finally arrived at the Irish hedge-school (a kind of evening class where those who attend vary in age from their twenties to Jimmy, who is in his sixties). His son, Manus, has already begun the 'lesson' in his absence.

Hugh: *Adsum*, Doalty, *adsum*. Perhaps not in *sobrietate perfecta* but adequately *sobrius* to overhear your quip. Vesperal salutations to you all.

(*Various responses.*)

Jimmy: *Ave*, Hugh.

Hugh: James.

(*He removes his hat and coat and hands them and his stick to Manus, as if to a footman.*)

Apologies for my late arrival: we were celebrating the baptism of Nellie Ruadh's baby.

Bridget: (*innocently*) What name did she put on it, Master?

Hugh: Was it Eamon? Yes, it was Eamon.

Bridget: Eamon Donal from Tor! Cripes!

Hugh: And after the *caerimonisa nominationis* – Maire?

Maire: The ritual of naming.

Hugh: Indeed – we then had a few libations to mark the occasion. Altogether very pleasant. The derivation of the word 'baptise'? – where are my Greek scholars? Doalty?

Doalty: Would it be – ah – ah –

Hugh: Too slow. James?

James: 'Baptizein' – to dip or immerse.

Hugh: Indeed – our friend Pliny Minor speaks of the 'baptisterium' – the cold bath.

Critical response activity

■ What are the dramatic effects here? This is not a wildly emotional scene, but it is serving a dramatic purpose effectively.

■ How does the dramatist create these effects? (Remember at this stage to keep the focus on linguistic devices, even though there is much to say here about lexical choices and use of rhetoric.)

Write down your own thoughts before looking at the commentary below.

Commentary

The dramatic effects here are linked with the establishment of character: we are quite taken aback by the drunken (but in control) and very erudite schoolmaster. His relationship with the attendees is shown by his schoolmasterly questioning. The audience would be fascinated to see how he is received by the 'pupils' and there would also be some tension as we wonder how Manus, his son, will respond to his father's late and quietly dramatic entrance. There is also potential humour in the scene, with a mixture of topics and register.

Concentrating particularly on interactional features, we can see how Friel quickly establishes character. The length of turns and the nominating of who is permitted to speak clearly belong to the person who has authority: the Master of the school. His authority is sanctioned in his position as educator: he has the knowledge as well as the socially accepted sanction to gatekeep or control the discourse. Hugh's authority is also shown by the way he monitors who is, or is not, learning successfully by nominating who is allowed to take part in the discourse. Hugh is also empowered to choose or change topic, as when he checks on Doalty's knowledge of the Greek language. The Master also has the power to comment critically on the performance of other characters in the schoolroom (here on Doalty's slowness of recall).

So, Friel has quickly established who is the dominant personality, although he also allows Bridget to ask a question without seeking permission to do so: 'What name did she put on it, Master?'

Though she uses this polite form of address ('Master') to indicate respect, she has been empowered to ignore Hugh's control of the discourse because of the introduction of an informal topic (the christening of the newly baptised baby) outside the realm of the classroom proper. Friel realistically mixes the more formal classroom question/answer discourse method with the informal 'chat' about the christening. Hugh's relaxed authority and his easygoing friendly nature are shown by the mixture of registers. Look, for example, at some of Hugh's utterances: the minor sentence 'Altogether very pleasant' compared with his **Latinate expressions**, for example 'Vesperal salutations'. Such contrasts would be a source of humour to his on-stage audience and the real audience. His easy familiarity with Greek and Latin is clear, just as Doalty's hesitations in his discourse signal his lack of knowledge. A sense of community is established by their shared knowledge of Nellie Ruadh, a community in which Hugh actively participates. This community is later threatened by the casual imperialism of the English map-makers represented by Captain Lancey.

There is certainly more that could be said about this passage. Theory has not been touched on here, although you might have reflected on Hugh's formal politeness, mixed with some quite abrupt and less-than-tactful comments. But you can see that Friel mimics and exploits the typical kinds of interaction which might occur in a schoolroom in order to create humour and to establish character.

■ *Hamlet*

In Act 3, Scene 4, Hamlet, having just arranged the play to discover his uncle's guilt, has been summoned by Gertrude, his mother, to her bedchamber to answer for his actions in upsetting her new husband. If she expects him to be contrite, she is soon disabused by Hamlet's mimicking of her speech when she might have expected him to be apologetic.

■ **Key terms**

Latinate expressions: words which have Latin origins and are often polysyllabic, e.g. circumnavigate, procrastinate.

Hamlet: Now mother, what's the matter?

Queen: Hamlet, thou hast thy father much offended.

Hamlet: Mother, you have my father much offended.

Queen: Come, come, you answer with an idle tongue.

Hamlet: Go, go, you question with an idle tongue.

Queen: Why how now Hamlet?

Hamlet: What's the matter now?

Queen: Have you forgot me?

Hamlet: No, by the Rood, not so:

You are the Queen, your husband's brother's wife,

But would you were not so. You are my mother.

Queen: Nay, then I'll set those to you that can speak.

Hamlet: Come, come, and sit you down, you shall not budge:

You go not till I set you up a glass,

Where you may see the inmost part of you.

Queen: What wilt thou do? thou wilt not murder me?

Help, help, hoa!

Polonius: What hoa, help, help, help.

Hamlet: How now, a rat? dead for a ducat, dead.

Critical response activity

Ask yourself the same questions as for the first extract, remembering to focus mainly on the linguistic devices so far covered.

- What is dramatic about this encounter? This is so much more emotionally charged than the previous Friel extract.
- How does Shakespeare convey the dramatic effects?

Write your own answer in full before looking at the commentary.

Commentary

The repartee in the first four lines is an example of **stichomythia**, or the uttering of single lines by alternate speakers. It creates a rapid pace to this encounter and it is dramatic because it reveals Hamlet's aggressive mood, shows the strength of his feelings, reveals the Queen's fears and, of course, ends with a murder: a violent, impulsive action on Hamlet's part. The tension in the intimate encounter is increased because the audience knows that Polonius is hiding behind the arras, listening in, but the murder is still very shocking.

As for interactional features, initially the balance of power and turns seems equal, when we might expect the Queen to be the participant with more authority by virtue of her rank, and context: it is in her bedchamber. The **parallelism** of the early lines deliberately turns her attention to her own culpability, and the use of repetition gives a chant-like feel to the interchanges. The interaction is full of exclamations and interrogatives, and when a question is answered by a question this also increases the tension. Terms of address are revealing too. Hamlet refers to his mother, but we imagine the tone to be bitter. He also uses 'queen' and the pedantic and laboured 'your husband's brother's wife'. Hamlet always uses the more formal 'you' throughout, although the Queen varies between the intimate thee/thou, and then at times she mirrors

> ### Key terms
>
> **Stichomythia:** a device used in ancient Greek drama; a dialogue in which two characters speak alternate lines of verse.
>
> **Parallelism:** this occurs when utterances are parallel (similar) in form, e.g. 'Our food is rotten; our beds are lousy; our clothes are torn.'

his formality and uses 'you' or his name, all suggesting her confusion and distress. She feels threatened by his challenging behaviour. The distinction between 'thy father' (meaning Claudius, her new husband) and 'my father', which Hamlet uses to refer to his deceased father, is highly significant. Hamlet will not acknowledge Claudius as 'his father'.

In this passage we could also consider how the context creates tension (the audience's knowledge and expectations) and how the register is informal and intimate, but with very deliberate and pedantic formality on Hamlet's part. We can be in no doubt about the strength of his feelings here. Of course, the action of a murder on stage in itself is dramatic. We have touched also on rhetorical devices, and if we were to take the appropriately integrated approach to analysis, of course we would have included comment on lexical choice and phonological aspects.

4 Breaking the rules and dramatic effects

■ Breaking the rules

Having looked at some of the key rules or expectations about how discourse works, let us see what happens when these expectations are ignored or challenged. Keep the following questions in mind when you read the ensuing discussions:

■ What might the observance of normal discourse rules (for example turn-taking, politeness) tell us about the participant?

■ Perhaps more interestingly, what might a challenge to these so-called rules tell us about the person challenging them?

■ Do these factors have any bearing on the ideas the dramatist is conveying (the themes, if you like) and the dramatic effects we assume he is aiming for?

This chapter takes three of the set plays and approaches them in chronological order, analysing the extracts using knowledge of discourse frameworks and with a particular emphasis on whether or not 'rules' are being broken.

Hamlet (1603)

Act 1, Scene 2 opens in 'a room of state in the castle' at Elsinore. The context is important and will affect the register and the expectations of the audience. The previous scene has informed us of the disquieting presence of a ghost who looks like Hamlet's dead father, foreboding some calamity – perhaps an invasion by Norway.

The action takes place in the royal court, so we might well expect the King, Claudius, as the most important character, to initiate the discourse and to have the longest turns to signal his dominant role. Claudius indeed opens with a lengthy speech of 39 lines. The response of the courtiers is restrained and tersely brief: one line of deference reinforces Claudius's importance. The length of this turn establishes his power, dominating for a quite extraordinary amount of time after the more democratically organised speech of the first scene of this act. In that first scene only Horatio gets a lengthy speech because Shakespeare needed to give us some background exposition. It is fitting that such information is given by Horatio and it gives us a sense of his authority. Knowledge empowers Horatio to have a longer speech turn, as it does with Hugh in *Translations*.

Later in Scene 2, when Claudius turns his attention to Laertes, the turns become more equal. A question from the King, in a more powerful register, because it is directly addressed, **nominates** Laertes' right to speak:

■ *King*: And now, Laertes, what's the news with you?

This is responded to in a respectful manner:

■ *Laertes*: Dread my Lord,
 Your leave and favour to return to France.

■ Key terms

Nominates: chooses the next speaker, allocating them a turn in the speech. This may be a direct invitation: 'What do you think …' or by a pause and non-verbal address such as an expectant look.

However, when Claudius addresses Hamlet, the Prince ignores the direct question and refuses to answer respectfully, and instead he interrupts, to offer a face-challenging aside that comments on the question whilst pointedly ignoring the King:

> *King*: But now my cousin Hamlet, and my son?
>
> *Hamlet*: A little more than kin, and less than kind.

This represents a hostile challenge to the king's right to speak at any length, as well as a rebuff in refusing to interact directly when the turn is being offered to him. Conflict is at the heart of all drama and here it is clearly signalled in the discourse. Hamlet's one-line response to Claudius leaves the king exasperated:

> *King*: How is it that the clouds still hang on you?
>
> *Hamlet*: Not so, my lord, I am too much i' th' sun.

Thus the increase in tension is represented: gone are the King's lengthy power-reflecting turns. Gone is the polite nomination of who is to be allocated the next turn. From 'Laertes' and 'Polonius', we now have 'you', used extensively in the play as a distancing form of the prevalent 'thou' (which usually denotes closeness between characters). Even Hamlet's polite form 'my lord' is undercut by the rebuff of being 'i' th' sun' to challenge Claudius's 'in the clouds'.

When Gertrude, his mother, intercedes, he gives her the same one-line brush-off afforded to the King, but then a 12-line length of turn from Hamlet helps to show his relative ease with her. As his mother, despite her 'o'er hasty marriage', she is perhaps deserving of a more personal response. The series of negations and the exclamatory first words still make the speech argumentative in nature:

> *Hamlet*: Seems Madam: nay, it is: I know not seems:
> 'Tis not alone my inky cloak, good mother,
> Nor customary suits of solemn black,
> Nor windy suspiration of forc'd breath.
> No, nor the fruitful river in the eye,
> Nor the dejected 'haviour of the visage …

This heartfelt, poignant appeal would rivet the audience and Hamlet would dominate the stage. However, Claudius responds with a power-driven 30-line turn to attempt to re-establish his authority.

What has happened, in the light of the discourse analysis suggested, is that Hamlet has challenged Claudius's authority in:

- the context of the court, where Claudius should automatically have it
- Claudius's right to speak at length
- Claudius's right to apportion turns by not responding
- Claudius's right to choose the topic, challenged with another refusal to engage
- deliberately engaging at length only with his mother
- showing a lack of politeness by interrupting and ignoring, making a contradictory remark, and finally ignoring Claudius completely again.

All of these features revealed in the discourse analysis are **face-threatening acts** that not only produce tension in the scene but also foreshadow the increase in hostility between Hamlet and Claudius after the murder is exposed. That Hamlet is in terrible danger is a recurrent motif in the play, putting Hamlet under enormous pressure to act in a court that has spies everywhere. Here the discourse reflects just some of those underlying tensions.

Key terms

Face-threatening acts: Brown and Levinson use the terms 'positive face' and 'negative face'. We have positive face needs, which means we want to be liked and valued. Our negative face is a defensive one: we do not want to be imposed on or to be told what to do. Face-threatening refers to when our face needs are flouted, and in drama such flouting creates tension.

Critical response activity

Now choose your own scene for analysis. You could, for example, choose the scene in which Rosencrantz and Guildenstern meet Hamlet for the first time in the play (Act 2, Scene 2). Apply the questions from the beginning of the chapter and reflect on whether 'rules' are being flouted or ignored.

The Rivals (1775)

The approach to discourse analysis with a particular emphasis on whether or not characters ignore or challenge rules is perhaps less obviously fruitful in treating Sheridan's *The Rivals*. Here the characters are more stereotypical, partly in order that the play's wit and plot are **foregrounded**. Turn-taking is more orderly and on the surface there is much politeness. But it is still interesting to track the interactions and to see how there is some subversion.

Look, for example, at Act 1, Scene 2. This is when Lucy Languish greets her cousin Julia. The scene takes place in a dressing-room in Mrs Malaprop's lodgings:

> *Lydia*: My dearest Julia, how delighted am I! (*Embrace*) How unexpected was this happiness!
>
> *Julia*: True, Lydia – and our pleasure is the greater; but what has been the matter? You were denied to me at first!
>
> *Lydia*: Ah, Julia, I have a thousand things to tell you! But first inform me, what has conjured you to Bath? Is Sir Anthony here?
>
> *Julia*: He is – we are arrived within this hour – and I suppose he will be here to wait on Mrs Malaprop as soon as he is dressed.

The exchange is excited, breathless almost with the mimickry of speech pauses, and the liberal use of exclamations. It seems like the normal adjacency pairs 'rule' is being obeyed, but look at how Lydia evades the question and shifts the topic on to Julia. There is no major flouting of politeness strategies here but a little evasiveness. However, this leads to the audience remaining in suspense; we must wait for the details to be filled in. So, looking at linguistic features can alert us to how suspense is created and it allows us to reflect on how the characters relate to each other. The balanced turns and the mirroring of the broken syntax suggest a closeness between the cousins.

 Key terms

Foregrounded: a term used when a writer or speaker brings a topic to the foreground, i.e. emphasises it. Compare this with something in the 'background'.

Critical response activity

Choose another short scene from *The Rivals* and analyse the discourse, reflecting on politeness, etc. For example, look at Acres' arrival in Act 2, Scene 1.
The dialogue follows orderly adjacency pairs, with polite interrogatives. But looking closely at the discourse can alert us to where the drama and the humour occur, for example in Acres' reply to Faulkland's query about Julia's health, when he gives the audience the unexpected comparison: 'she has been as healthy as the German spa'. Hardly face-threatening, but amusing; especially when it was preceded by a typical Acres expression: 'Odd's blushes and blooms'.

Analyse the rest of the initial encounter between Faulkland, Absolute and Acres.

A Streetcar Named Desire (1947)

An interesting variation in the way power is presented is to be found in the following extract taken from Scene 10. However, it would be useful to consider the context of the play as a whole before becoming immersed in the extract. Blanche has attempted to depict herself as a chaste female of high social status with a strict moral code. She has insisted on being wooed by Mitch with the utmost propriety if he wishes to win her hand. However, it transpires that she has virtually been run out of the town she has lived in for being promiscuous. She has also been sacked as a teacher for having an inappropriate sexual relationship with one of the 17-year-old pupils. Mitch, made aware of these facts, has refused to contemplate marrying her and, treating her with contempt, has dropped her.

The scene takes place in the immediate context of her sister Stella's home. Blanche has been left alone with Stanley, Stella's husband. He is a brutish man with little respect for women and none for Blanche, having experienced her flirtatious behaviour and found out about her promiscuous nature. He is a strong male with a violent streak and Blanche is, not surprisingly, frightened of him. He is deeply angry at, and offended by, her assumed airs of respectability and superiority.

The expectation is that there will be a showdown. There may well be violence – Stanley has earlier hit his pregnant wife who is, at this time, in hospital having the baby. It is Stanley's home and he is in control. He is confronting a nervously disposed, frightened woman, and he knows she thinks him an inferior, animal-like being. Now he can get even!

Blanche: A cultivated woman, a woman of intelligence and breeding, can enrich a man's life – immeasurably! I have those things to offer, and this doesn't take them away. Physical beauty is passing. A transitory possession. But beauty of the mind and richness of the spirit and tenderness of the heart – and I have all of those things – aren't taken away, but grow! Increase with the years! How strange that I should be called a destitute woman! When I have all of these treasures locked in my heart. (*A choked sob comes from her.*) I think of myself as a very, very rich woman! But I have been foolish – casting my pearls before swine!

Stanley: Swine, huh?

Blanche: Yes, swine. Swine! And I'm thinking not only of you but of your friend, Mr Mitchell. He came to see me tonight. He dared to come here in his work-clothes! And to repeat slander to me, vicious stories that he had gotten from you! I gave him his walking papers …

Stanley: You did, huh?

Blanche: But then he came back. He returned with a box of roses to beg my forgiveness! He implored my forgiveness. But some things are not forgivable. Deliberate cruelty is not forgivable. It is the one unforgivable thing in my opinion of which I have never, never been guilty. And so I told him, I said to him Thank you, but it was foolish of me to think that we could ever adapt ourselves to each other. Our ways of life are too different. Our attitudes and our backgrounds are incompatible. We have to be realistic about such things. So farewell, my friend! And let there be no hard feelings …

Stanley: Was this before or after the telegram came from the Texas oil millionaire?

> *Blanche*: What telegram? No! No, after! As a matter of fact, the wire came just as –
>
> *Stanley*: As a matter of fact there wasn't no wire at all!
>
> *Blanche*: Oh, oh!

Stanley exercises a strong physical power despite saying very little, but Blanche, though powerless in a physical sense, has the longest turns here, dominating the dialogue at this point. However, in her nervous verbosity she does not dominate Stanley. His terse rejoinders, all threateningly interrogative, and his later accusation, show that he has not just the physical power and presence, which the audience would be aware of, but that he holds the 'cards': information which will reveal Blanche's lies.

Much of what Blanche says is a lie, but as she desperately tries to salvage the fictional, cultured self that she projects on the world, we begin to realise just how damaged she has been. We realise that the man she had loved unequivocally has, in his betrayal of her love, so profoundly damaged her that she finds it difficult to have relationships with any man. We begin to understand what lies behind her promiscuous behaviour. Ultimately this speech gains tremendous power from our dawning understanding of Blanche's predicament. As we see this fragile figure struggling with the disintegration of the face she has presented to the world, we pity her. For this reason, her speech here is profoundly tragic and this feeling of tragedy is compounded by Stanley then committing the violence we had expected, but to a far worse degree than we could have imagined when he rapes her. In the final scene, that follows this one, her personality has disintegrated completely; she is effectively destroyed.

The scene above creates a strong sense of conflict as well as danger because it relies on face-threatening to a shockingly literal degree. It forms a **climax** in the play, leaving the audience feeling bereft and crushed at the more subdued but ultimately terrifying removal of Blanche by impersonal forces to a mental institute.

It is easy then to see what the dramatic effects of this extract are, but it is not enough to focus solely on interactional features (the linguistic devices). The idiolects of the characters, such as Stanley's monosyllables and his grunts, Blanche's more educated speech with her elaboration, and the use of imagery and rhetorical devices all contribute to this overall effect. Finally, Blanche's **narrative discourse** reveals much about her way of thinking and her character generally.

■ Key terms

Climax: an ascending series of events or ideas which intensify, or a moment of decision.

Narrative discourse: a spoken or written account of a linked sequence of events. In other words – a story.

Critical response activity

Look at the opening of Scene 2, as far as Stanley's imperative: 'Let's see the papers.' Analyse the discourse, reflecting particularly on any flouting of politeness for dramatic effect.

To analyse an extract fully and to uncover exactly how the dramatist creates effects, it is essential to use a wider range of tools. So far the focus has been on the interactions between characters and the discussion has touched only briefly on lexical choice and the use of imagery. The next chapter begins to look at literary devices and conventions and the use of rhetoric.

5 | Literary and rhetorical devices and conventions

Key terms

Clichéd: a pejorative term for an over-used phrase that has lost all freshness. For example, 'The pirate fell to the deck with a sickening thud.'

Tropes: words or expressions used in a figurative or non-literal sense.

Personification: giving human characteristics to non-human forms, e.g. 'the waves whispered'.

Literary devices and conventions

Lexical choice

A dramatist has to communicate what is often a complex network of values, ideas and interactions, all in two to three hours or less. In order to do so, the writer has to choose his or her words carefully to create particular characters' idiolects and so provide contrast between characters. Sometimes the language is heightened to lend variety and to stimulate thinking and emotions or to intrigue the audience.

Here is a brief example.

In Act 3 of *Translations*, Owen, the youngest son of the schoolmaster and the one who acts as translator, is accompanying Captain Lancey. The soldier announces to the characters in the schoolroom what the British are proposing to do if Yolland (another soldier) is not found. Look at the formal register of Lancey, with the **clichéd** phrases of authority and the Latinate words.

> **Lancey**: … commencing forty-eight hours from now we will embark on a series of evictions and levelling of every abode in the following selected areas –
>
> **Owen**: You're not – !
>
> **Lancey**: Do your job. Translate.
>
> **Owen**: If they still haven't found him in two days' time they'll begin evicting and levelling every house starting with these townlands.

In *Hamlet* there is a huge variety of lexis: from the exaggeratedly descriptive and artificial verse of the players in their performance, to the 'whirling words' of Hamlet, the down-to-earth prose of the gravediggers, and the poignant, lyrical speech of Gertrude about Ophelia's drowning.

Figurative language

Use of imagery (and some of the commonest **tropes**, such as metaphor, simile and **personification**) can add to the vividness and the dramatic power of crafted speech.

In *Hamlet*, speeches are packed with haunting, memorable imagery. A sustained metaphor of disease and decay runs throughout the play, from Claudius's reference to Hamlet being like a fever in his blood, to Hamlet's reference to Claudius being a 'mildewed ear'. Each page, each scene is rich with detailed, figurative language.

It may seem less obvious in a play like *The Rivals*, but there is much figurative language used for comic effect. For example, when Lydia is trying to dissuade her cousin, Julia, from being so fond of Faulkland, who apparently saved Julia from drowning, she says: 'Believe me, the rude blast that overset your boat was a prosperous gale of love to him.' And later she compares him to a water-spaniel!

Phonological features

These include:

- **Alliteration**: repetition of initial sounds, e.g. 'a miraculous matching of hope and past and present and possibility' from Hugh's lengthy, lyrical speech towards the end of *Translations*.

- **Assonance**: the repetition of vowel sounds, e.g. 'b<u>ur</u>nt and p<u>ur</u>ged away' from a speech of the Ghost in *Hamlet*.

- **Consonance**: the repetition of consonants/consonant groups, e.g. 'a nervou<u>sness</u>, a soft<u>ness</u> and tender<u>ness</u>' from when Blanche is talking about her young lover in *A Streetcar Named Desire*.

- **Onomatopoeia**: when a word sounds like its sense, e.g. '<u>quivering</u>, warm-breathed <u>sighs</u>' from a speech of Faulkland in *The Rivals*.

- **Use of rhyme and other verse forms**: this is discussed at the end of this chapter in the section called 'Additional information on poetry and prose'.

- **Speech in performance**: intonation, pitch and volume, use of stress, and pace and tone of voice.

🔍 Word play

This includes use of **puns** and general playfulness with language. Mrs Malaprop in *The Rivals* is famous for mixing up words, using a similar-sounding word but one with a completely inappropriate sense for the context. Hence, instead of the 'pinnacle of excellence' she talks about 'the pineapple of excellence'.

🔢 Other literary devices

These might include the use of **irony**. **Dramatic irony** occurs when the audience is aware of issues and events of which particular characters are unaware.

Also, literary conventions would include how the author uses the form or **genre** of a play with its internal structure: the conventional use of establishing scenes, developing plot, climactic moments and devices such as the **denouement**.

These include devices such as rhetorical questions, use of listing (**incrementum**), use of repetition and tripling, **antitheses**, hyperbole, parallelism. Such devices help to persuade and give a speech more impact and power. For example, in Act 2, Scene 1 of *Translations*, when Hugh is talking to Yolland, a British soldier, about the Irish language, he uses tripling: 'Yes, it is a rich language, Lieutenant, full of the mythologies of fantasy and hope and self-deception ...'. Also, in Act 1, Scene 5 of *Hamlet* the ghost uses incrementum and hyperbole to create a terrifying picture:

> I could a tale unfold, whose lightest word
> Would harrow up thy soul, freeze thy young blood,
> Make thy two eyes like stars, start from their spheres,
> Thy knotted and combined locks to part,
> And each particular hair to stand an end
> Like quills upon the fretful porpentine:

■ Key terms

Puns: word-play, usually a witty remark that relies for its humour on bringing together two words of similar form but different meaning. For example, 'grave' meaning 'serious' and 'grave' the noun; or where the different meanings of one word are exploited, e.g. cleave can mean 'cut in two' or 'to cling on to something'.

Irony: language that conveys a meaning often the opposite of what the words might literally suggest. For example, 'She was extremely generous and left all her old clothes to her sister.'

Dramatic irony: this is where the character is blind to circumstances of which the audience is all too well aware, creating poignancy as the plot unfurls.

Genre: from the French word (originally Latin) for 'kind' or 'class'. The audience will have expectations of particular genres.

Denouement: this is when the tangles of the plot are unravelled and all is revealed and resolved.

Incrementum: the action or process of gradually increasing. It usually refers to lists which build up to a climax.

Antitheses: constructions in which words are opposed, or contrasted, but balanced, as in 'to live a sinner or to die a saint' or 'Man proposes: God disposes'.

Blank verse: unrhymed verse, usually with 10 syllables to a line, with alternative unstressed and stressed beats.

Iambic pentameter: this is the commonest blank verse metre. An iamb is a metrical foot of two syllables, short then long, first unstressed then stressed. Five of these create a pentameter.

Idiomatic: speech typical of a people or place. The origin of the word is the Greek idios meaning 'one's own, peculiar, strange'. Idioms break the rules semantically and grammatically, e.g. 'jump the gun'. This cannot be understood literally, but it is a colourful idiomatic phrase.

Caesura: another word for a pause or break within a line of verse. Caesuras can occur at the beginning (initial), middle (medial) or end of a line (terminal). Creating a sense of balance, they can be effective in initial and medial positions by drawing attention to a significant word.

■ Additional information on poetry and prose

The following is particularly relevant for those studying a Shakespeare text. One of the remarkable achievements of the Royal Shakespeare Company's treatment of Shakespeare's **blank verse** is to render even this poetic form as if it were actual, heard speech. In fact that is how Shakespeare intended it to sound. How do we know this? Well, blank verse is written in **iambic pentameter** that mirrors the sound patterns of spoken British English, capturing the particular 'signature' or rhythms that distinguish English from other languages with their own particular rhythmic patterns.

Take almost any speech in blank verse from *Hamlet*, for example from Act 1, Scene 1:

> ***Horatio***: Such was the very armour he had on
> When he th' ambitious Norway combated:
> So frown'd he once, when in an angry parle,
> He smote the sledded Poleaxe on the ice.
> 'Tis strange.

Clearly the phrase 'very armour' and the unusual word order (or syntax) of the second line 'he [subject] the ambitious Norway [object] combated [verb]' does not mirror what we would normally encounter in spontaneous speech. The phrase 'the very cheek of the man!' is a more modern **idiomatic** expression that is very close to what Shakespeare does in 'very armour', but the now archaic lexis of 'parle' (conference, which was angry or heated), the verb form 'sledded' (or on sledges) and proper noun 'Poleaxe' (or Polish) are unlikely to be heard in everyday modern speech. Interestingly this mirrors the experience of Shakespeare's age. His audience would have met many such words for the first time because the language was developing apace; the word stock of the English language increased by an astonishing 25 per cent in the Elizabethan period, so many in Shakespeare's audience would have also met such words for the first time, just as we do.

Shakespeare was using the heightened form of poetic blank verse to denote noble or kingly characters with their more elevated lexis and measured speech. They were different in their status, education and understanding from the more prosaic, lower-ranking characters who were given prose utterances as their characteristic form of discourse. Such heightened language might sometimes be found in spontaneous speech, but the underlying rhythm, with the stressed and unstressed syllables, mirrors that of spoken language, echoing the 'lub-dub' of the heartbeat. Shakespeare, of course, uses an organised framework of usually 10 syllables to the line, although part lines are used for effect, as in ''Tis strange'.

Shakespeare was also keenly aware of other features of spontaneous speech. Consider the way that Polonius begins his first line in Act 2, Scene 1 with the regular 10 syllables we expect of iambic pentameter, even though the **caesuras** and the repetition, together with the rhetorical question, give this a less-than-elevated feel. It then falls apart and becomes prose-like:

> ***Polonius***: And then sir does he this, he does: what was I about to say? By the mass, I was about to say something: where did I leave?

Blank verse has been abandoned here, even though the character is a high official in the Royal Court of Denmark but the false starts ('And then', 'he does', 'what was'); the self-interrogation ('what was I about to say?'); and the hesitant pauses mirror exactly what goes on in spontaneous speech.

Hamlet, too, uses prose, often when he talks to Polonius, or the actors, or to his so-called friends, Rosencrantz and Guildenstern. For example, after the players have arrived in Act 2, Scene 2 Hamlet asks Polonius to sort them out and to see that they are 'well bestowed':

> *Polonius*: My Lord, I will use them according to their desert.
>
> *Hamlet*: God's bodykins man, better. Use every man after his desert and who should 'scape whipping? Use them after your own honour and dignity. The less they deserve, the more merit is in your bounty. Take them in.

This is down-to-earth prose with its cursing, its use of 'man', **elision** ('scaping) and its short utterances. However, you will also be aware of the wonderfully balanced and memorable declarative with its antithesis of less and more. Hamlet is still an amazingly sharp speaker, whether it is prose or blank verse.

■ Key terms

Elision: the omission of a sound or syllable, usually marked by an apostrophe, e.g. 'she'd', 'didn't'.

Plays and their form

Key terms

Satire: this aims to bring about correction or reform by means of amusement or ridicule.

How a play's form can affect its dramatic impact

It can be useful to reflect on the form or genre of a text. The A Level Assessment Objectives include an objective which asks you to show understanding of how form shapes meaning (AO2), so it is helpful if you have some appreciation of genre. Within the category of plays, there are obviously further possible subdivisions, for example comedy, romance, **satire** and tragedy. In Act 2, Scene 2 of *Hamlet*, Polonius tediously lists the various permutations of dramatic forms:

> **Polonius**: … for Tragedy, Comedy, History, Pastoral, Pastoral-Comical, Historical-Pastoral: Tragical-Historical: Tragical-Comical-Historical-Pastoral …

The form of a text can suggest particular expectations. An audience approaching tragedy is unlikely to expect a happy outcome. A play billed as a comedy which does not raise any laughs in the audience would be a major disappointment. We anticipate particular dramatic effects if we are aware of a genre, and a dramatist may well fulfil our expectations, but he/she may also cleverly and surprisingly confound them. For an audience, dramatic interest in terms of curiosity, expectations or the confounding of such expectations is part of the intellectual and emotional experience of live theatre. Ask yourself the question: does the writer challenge or subvert an aspect, and what might such an effect have on an audience?

Form and the set texts

For each writer the form of the play will be outlined together with some analysis and comment. Having a broader knowledge and understanding will inform your thinking. You need to be able to appreciate, respond to and develop your own understanding of a play before you can successfully comment in detail on an extract.

Hamlet

Hamlet is usually seen as a revenge tragedy. This genre was hugely popular with Elizabethan audiences with its characteristically gruesome violence, often tinged with black humour. The model is derived from the Roman period, heavily influenced by the dramatist Seneca, who created the formula, typically:

- a secret murder, usually of a good ruler by an evil one
- a ghostly visit from the murdered ruler to a close relative, usually a son
- an interim period of disguise during which the avenger and the murderer plot each other's demise, accompanied by a rising death rate amongst the other characters
- the descent into madness by the avenger, either feigned or actual
- a catastrophic event that disables the avenger
- a climactic and violent finish often accompanied by a festivity, in which many of the characters as well as the avenger die.

Whilst it is interesting to gauge just how much use Shakespeare made of this model, its value lies in what ways Shakespeare used, subverted, or changed the form to meet his purposes.

A secret murder

Look at Hamlet talking to his mother in Act 1, Scene 2, describing the contrast between the noble, dead king and the usurping Claudius, whom he implies is a lecherous drunk:

> *Hamlet*: So excellent a king, that was, to this,
> Hyperion to a satyr; so loving to my mother,
> … my noble father's person

Here Shakespeare makes use of one component of the traditional Senecan revenge tragedy by having a good, virtuous king murdered by a bad one, if not an evil one in our eyes at this stage in the play. He also makes use of classical Greek myth: Hyperion was father of the sun, the moon and the dawn, whereas satyrs were beasts that had a mixture of human and goat-like features. Satyrs indulged in all kinds of sensual pleasure and they loved wine, like Bacchus.

A ghostly visit

Consider what purposes the ghost serves in the play. It may be seen that Shakespeare uses him to deepen the philosophical debate; in Act 1, Scene 4 he acts as a prompt to make Hamlet reflect on the nature of life and the afterlife, and the nature of ghosts:

> *Hamlet*: Be thou a spirit of health or goblin damn'd,
> Bring with thee airs from Heaven or blasts from Hell,
> Be thy intents wicked or charitable,
> … So horridly to shake our disposition,
> With thoughts beyond the reaches of our souls…?

There is mounting tension, apprehension and excitement caused by the appearance of a ghost in the stage darkness. It affects the audience as well as Hamlet, who is clearly in a state of dread as to the intent of the spirit.

The ghostly visitation component of the revenge tragedy is used to enable Hamlet to exhibit a Christian belief in a New Testament Heaven and Hell. Also, the audience is reminded of the role of some ghosts: to spread evil and contaminate our souls. Shakespeare's use of these genre conventions establishes some motivation for Hamlet's hesitation in sweeping to revenge, and so deepens the psychological plausibility of his character.

The ghost, in making demands on Hamlet, might be seen as a device to represent a thematic conflict between Roman values of martial heroism set against Christian values of humility and acceptance of fate. Such acceptance is called into question by the idea of revenge. In Act 3, Scene 4 Hamlet visits his mother in her bedroom when the ghost appears:

> *Hamlet*: Do you not come your tardy son to chide,
> That laps'd in time and passion, lets go by
> Th'important acting of your dread command?
> Oh say.

And here the ghost is used to highlight Hamlet's slow-moving ('tardy') action towards revenge, for which he reproves himself for letting opportunity ('time') and passion slip away. However, 'dread' implies reverence yet horror too at the consequences of such an act, in a Christian belief system where only God may judge.

A period of disguise

The audience questions whether Hamlet is mad by cunning (the disguise element) or genuinely mad. Certainly these elements intrigue and create suspense, for we wonder if Claudius will then stop plotting and scheming against Hamlet. Also, we pity him – if indeed we believe that such a fine intellect is reduced by despair to madness.

The descent into madness

Shakespeare uses this theme, but subverts it by making us always unsure about his real mental state. Is he always just 'mad in craft'? The ambivalence is fascinating. We have a well-rounded, psychologically intriguing character, interpreted differently in every production. This is far removed from any stereotypical, clear-cut descent into insanity.

A catastrophic event

After Hamlet kills Polonious, he is temporarily disabled when Claudius banishes him to England. This is combined with a plot device to force a change in Hamlet's character: he becomes a hero, charged with a will to resolve matters by revengeful action. The feature moves the action towards the resolution and climax of the play.

A violent climax

Knowing a little about revenge tragedy and the **Greek tragic model**, how might we see the exciting yet appalling climax, and what significance is there in the death of the **protagonist**?

From a structural perspective the play's climax follows the Renaissance revenge form with the absence, significantly, of the revel, or celebration (unless we count the player scene as such).

What Shakespeare intended, from this most thoughtfully philosophical play, was that his audience be encouraged by the sombre ending to react as Aristotle's Greek tragic model would have expected: with a chastening sense of terror at the casual way that evil can disrupt and devastate human lives. The Greek term **catharsis**, which such a tragedy was intended to produce, means to experience purgation, or a cleansing of the emotions of overwhelming awe and wonder that we feel at the power of human evil that can cause the loss of so much goodness.

Perhaps our sense of relief that the force of evil has been swept away is **mediated** by the prospect of the warlike, rash Fortinbras carrying the day. This squashes any hope for a future governed by a fine-natured, Renaissance prince. Such a prospect may encourage us to contemplate that even though evil is finally vanquished, it badly debilitates virtue.

Summary

An awareness of the components of revenge tragedy may help you to appreciate how Shakespeare used traditional forms. There may be some elements of predictability about the tragedy – especially its climax – but the journey Shakespeare takes us on is anything but straightforward. The main characters are psychologically interesting and convincingly rounded and there is much ambiguity.

The Rivals

The Rivals is regarded as a comedy of manners, which was a very popular form in the Restoration period. The comedy of manners is concerned with the question of whether its characters meet commonly accepted social standards, standards which may themselves appear to us as morally trivial. This form of theatre followed a model first developed by the Greek dramatist Menander. The model, typically, has:

Greek tragic model: put simply this includes the notion of a noble hero with a character flaw which leads to his/her downfall.

Protagonist: the main character in a play, poem or novel.

Catharsis: the outpouring of emotions and the relief of tension that the audience feels at the climactic moment in a play.

Mediated: when someone or something has intervened in a situation, e.g. a disagreement can be 'mediated' by a teacher.

- stock characters, rather than fully rounded ones with a believable psychology
- skilfully constructed, elaborate plots
- an upper-class world setting
- mockery of pretension, superficiality and materialism
- deflation by use of satire of people who consider themselves superior
- exploration of relationships between the sexes
- witty dialogue
- truth and virtue triumphing over vice and hypocrisy.

From the above it is clear that there are two major thrusts in a comedy of manners:

- pretentious upper-class characters are mocked and deflated in a witty way, in order that
- truth and virtue can triumph.

Stock characters

Stock characters can be traced back to the Italian **commedia dell'arte** of the 16th and 17th centuries. They themselves imitated the characters and stock situations of Roman and Greek plays before them, and may be tracked forwards to the TV sitcoms of today. These consist of familiar types, instantly recognisable to an audience, i.e. a pair of young lovers; a cheating servant; a pair of old men – one lecherous, the other pompous; and a clown figure.

Sheridan uses stock characters with names that describe their types, a language device known as an **aptronym**. Lydia Languish does just that: she languishes or pines, a suitable name for the attitude of a romantic heiress. Lucius O'Trigger is a suitably descriptive appellation for an impetuous belligerent; Bob Acres is a country bumpkin. Mrs Malaprop's name has entered the dictionary (**malapropism**) as denoting all humans with the foible of misusing words in the way she does. However, her name comes from the French *mal à propos*, or 'inappropriate', an appropriate name for a woman who seldom says exactly what she means. For example, in 'I am sorry to say, Sir Anthony, that my affluence over my niece is very small' she means 'influence', but the misuse suggests, wittily, that she is tight-fisted with money.

The characters, then, are stock comic caricatures of human folly, aptly named. Most of them lack self-knowledge. Sir Anthony Absolute imagines he is a very kind father and a good friend though he is neither; Mrs Malaprop imagines herself an intellectual but talks nonsense. Most of the characters are either of the gentry or servant class and the setting is an upper-class one, fulfilling one aspect of the commedia.

Elaborate plot

The plot is complex but not overwhelmingly intricate. There are mistaken identities, scandalous servants and slapstick, duels and weddings, all components of several of Shakespeare's comedies.

> The play satirises sentimentality and sophisticated pretensions but it blessedly lacking in the heavy-handed moralising component of many plays of the time. Marrissa Harris, an American critic, wrote of the New York, 2003 production of the play that it was 'light-hearted, fabulous fluff'. She writes: '*The Rivals* does not challenge you to think, analyse or change the world. It is a comedy in its purest, most concentrated form, free from politics, vicious satire and the evils of mankind.'

Key terms

Commedia dell'arte: meaning 'the comedy of artists', this is a form of improvisational theatre that began in Italy in the 16th century.

Aptronym: a term used for stock characters whose names embody their characteristics.

Malapropism: using the wrong word, but one which sounds similar. For example, Mrs Malaprop says, 'It gives me the hydrostatics' instead of 'hysterics'.

The Rivals explores conformity and deviation in the young characters to suggest that men and women are often led by their hearts rather than their heads. The play questions how far money and class are important elements in choosing a spouse and it establishes that genuine love is founded on virtue, honour, a similarity of taste and sympathy of souls. So, in exploring relationships it reveals a more serious intent, light-hearted, witty comedy though it is.

Summary

It might then be argued that *The Rivals* fulfils most of the descriptors of its genre as a comedy of manners which amuses and diverts. It uses stock situations, but these are universal. Love thwarted is a common theme: being in love and having an obstacle to overcome is timeless. That is why the form has appealed over such a long time period and still appeals today. The play also has a deeper, more profound objective, as Shakespeare's comedies do, and shares several of their features. Though Sheridan was often accused by his biographers of plagiarising character and incident, in his defence what needs to be seen is how far he used the existing genre conventions to serve his own purposes. So, knowledge of the form helps us to understand the dramatist's intentions and to appreciate the context and the traditions which influenced his approach.

A Streetcar Named Desire

A Streetcar Named Desire fits less easily into any genre category; although some critics see it as a modern American tragedy. According to the Greek paradigm, or model, a tragedy needs to have:

- a protagonist who has a major flaw or flaws
- a weakness in character that leads to what the Greeks termed **hubris**, which is commonly translated as 'overweening (i.e. excessively presumptuous) pride'
- a protagonist punished as a result of hubris, resulting in a fall from grace.

Blanche Dubois may be seen to be a tragic heroine in that she refuses to let go of her past and clings to her former grandeur, providing us with the flaw and the hubris. Eventually her punishment is rape, and with her fall from grace she is incarcerated in a mental institution. However, some critics point out that Blanche is not a wholly sympathetic character. Should we then view Blanche or Stanley as the tragic protagonist? You can see that classical Greek drama, although hugely influential, has been adapted and refined as a model. This play borrows some of its motifs, but it goes its own way too. The problem is partly whether we view the play as a social conflict or a personal one.

Some modern criticism focuses on a **dualism** in the play, which causes conflict:

- The idea of the play having a binary conflict has resulted in some seeing Stanley as representing flesh and Blanche as spirit, much as the mediaeval morality plays used one-dimensional characters to represent a vice or a virtue.
- Critics who see the play as a social drama have seen it as a dramatisation of Darwinian natural selection with a clash between two creatures of the same species (Blanche and Stanley) fighting for survival of their kind with Stella as the prize, rather than a struggle between the forces of good and evil.

■ Key terms

Hubris: a Greek term meaning arrogance and pride. In classical tragedy, a protagonist will defy the laws of the gods (a flaw of character known as hamartia), leading to an inevitable downfall. Hubris is the common example of hamartia in tragedy.

Dualism: in philosophy, this is the view that the world comprises two opposing entities such as mind and matter; in psychology, this is the view that the mind and body function separately; in theology, this is the concept that the world is ruled by the opposed forces of good and evil, and the concept that humans have two basic natures – the physical and the spiritual.

■ In terms of personal psychology, Freudian critics suggest that there is a binary struggle between the id (represented by Stanley's raw, animalistic passionate nature) and the ego (represented by Blanche's cultured, reasoning temperament). This psychologically dualistic view of the play can be tracked back to links between Williams's knowledge of Nietzsche's *The Birth of Tragedy* where restraint battles against passion, which Nietzsche saw in terms of Greek mythical figures, with Apollo embodying restraint and order and Dionysus characterised by passion and metaphysics. In this paradigm Blanche is Apollonian and Stanley is Dionysian. The problem with this is that whilst Nietzsche believed the conflict would result in chaos, Williams takes a different line and seems to be showing that passion overwhelmed restraint.

■ It has been suggested that the play is ambiguous and deeply flawed in its resolution. Is this perhaps because Williams was unsure whether he was writing a dark comedy or a tragedy? Or is he blending both in a disturbing, thought-provoking way? Nothing with Williams is ever simple or straightforward.

■ Those who perceive the play as a gender conflict have regarded it as **symbolising** the struggle between feminine 'culture' and masculine 'libido'. Stanley is the masculine character: aggressive, lustful and economical with words compared with Blanche's vulnerable, sensitive and loquacious character.

It is clear that there is diverse opinion as to the form of this play and how we understand it, but some knowledge of the common feeling that it has a conflict of opposing forces – whether social, psychological, or moral – may help us in our appreciation of how Williams creates dramatic impact.

Translations

Friel suggests his play is 'about language and only about language', but it also addresses cultural imperialism. It focuses on British decisions about imposing uniformity of language and how this affects the community. Seamus Deane, Professor of Irish Studies at the University of Notre Dame, suggests that it is a tragedy of English imperialism and it may be seen as a political play.

Some features of post-colonial (or post-imperial) literature are that it:

■ questions colonial power structures and hierarchies

■ is concerned with cultural identity in the colonised society and how that identity is shown and celebrated

■ reconsiders ideas of racial superiority/inferiority

■ questions how the coloniser has justified views of the colonised as inferior.

The play deals with how the consciousness of an entire culture, embodied in its language and place names, is fractured by the translation of one landscape (Gaelic and traditional) for another (Anglo-Saxon and colonialist) with the subsequent loss of Irish language, tradition, social and cultural heritage. In doing so, it uncovers a rich and diverse, well-educated culture which draws on Classical Greek and Roman as well as Gaelic Irish languages and cultural influences, which contests the **monoglot** Lancey and Yolland and undermines their power structure by acts of subversion. Their social hierarchy is partly undermined by Friel setting in place a humane and rich social network amongst the colonised Irish community, but only allowing us to see the rigid military structure of the colonisers.

■ **Key terms**

Symbolising: made to represent something else, e.g. a river symbolising life.

Monoglot: a person who knows one language only (noun); something written in one language only (adjective).

Language as a means of cultural, social and personal identity is at the heart of a play which explores not only that central function of language, but also seeks to question its significance. Friel deals not just with identity but with the idea of the possibility of communication. Only when Maire and Yolland move beyond language are the two able to establish a more profound form of communication.

Identity is also addressed by the idea of the Irish having their geographical space violated by being explored, mapped and brought under English control with locations rendered into the language of the colonisers. They are to lose the geographical identity of their place names as well as the cultural history that accompanies them.

Friel encourages us to question Lancey's assumption that English represents a superior culture with its military might (and assumed right) to rename Irish place names. Friel invites us to view Lancey's ignorance in the following exchange. Here he patronises the Irish characters whom the audience has seen to be knowledgeable in Gaelic and Classical languages:

> **Lancey**: I see. (*He clears his throat. He speaks as if he were addressing children – a shade too loudly and enunciating excessively.*) You may have seen me – seen me – working in this section – section? – working. We are here – here – in this place – you understand? – to make a map – a map – a map and –
>
> **Jimmy**: *Nonne Latine loquitur?*
>
> (*Hugh holds up a restraining hand.*)
>
> **Hugh**: James.
>
> **Lancey**: (*to Jimmy*) I do not speak Gaelic, sir.

The irony that Lancey thinks Latin is Gaelic, in which he shows his ignorance of both, is compounded by the fractured way he speaks. In thinking that the Irish are like children, he shows overweening arrogance – but his own rendition of language is itself childlike in its long pauses, its simplicity of expression and in its inappropriate loudness of delivery.

However, a different view is offered of the coloniser through Yolland who wants to create a kind of paradise, a 'new Eden' in his romanticised view of Ireland, its language and people. Friel is careful not to show that all colonisers share Lancey's acceptance that English cultural norms have to be imposed on this community.

The play questions whether one can identify a coherent imperial project to subjugate people or whether what is going on is the inevitable influence of commerce. It makes us reconsider categories such as notions of racial superiority/inferiority by questioning the significance of renaming places.

Friel suggests that the coming national schools, which will teach in English, will replace their hedge-schools and destroy their language at a stroke. Renaming their places will, likewise, destroy historical knowledge; their culture is being subsumed and ignored.

7 How structure can affect meaning and dramatic impact

This chapter covers:

■ a discussion of how structure shapes meaning in particular scenes or extracts

■ a discussion of how structure shapes meaning in the play as a whole.

Structure in a play is concerned with:

■ how utterances and larger sections of discourse such as whole scenes are combined by the writer to create drama

■ how individual scenes contrast with each other to create variety in mood and atmosphere

■ how the whole play is structured: how the plot is revealed and developed; where dramatic climaxes occur; and how the different issues are resolved.

A range of linguistic and literary devices which are used for dramatic effects have already been dealt with in this book, but a further look at the general idea of structure should help to reinforce your understanding of all the techniques used to create powerful drama.

■ Looking at an individual scene or extract

Using *Hamlet* as an example, the analysis which follows looks closely at how the interaction is structured and reflects on what is revealed in Act 2, Scene 2. Polonius has been reading a love letter from Hamlet to Ophelia, and the King has asked him how Ophelia has received it:

> *King*: But how hath she receiv'd his love?
>
> *Polonius*: What do you think of me?
>
> *King*: As of a man, faithful and honourable.

The very simplicity of the utterance by Polonius is remarkable from so loquacious a character, drawing attention to (or foregrounding itself) because it is so unusual when we are used to Polonius's verbose, rambling sentence structures. When it is put into direct contact with the preceding question from Claudius concerning Ophelia's response to Hamlet, something else even more remarkable happens.

Think back to what you have learned of discourse conventions. The King has asked a direct question and, given his royal status, we expect an answer – but not only does Polonius refuse to engage in the normal adjacency question–answer pattern, he answers a question with another question. In fact, he almost overlaps the King's question as well as initiating a topic switch. The effect of this is to create a character so excited by his plotting, by having stolen a private love letter from Hamlet to Ophelia and reading it aloud to Claudius and Gertrude, and so full of himself, that he completely forgets his position.

In Act 2, Scene 1 of *Translations*, Yolland says: 'I had moved into a consciousness that wasn't striving nor agitated, but at its ease and with its own conviction and assurance.' This declarative sentence lends Yolland an air of thoughtfulness here, signalled by the complex structure together with the lexical complexity in the abstract nouns: 'consciousness', 'conviction' and' assurance'.

These aspects create the impression of a serious character, thoughtful and intelligent enough to have complex thought patterns. The lexical choices of 'striving nor agitated' lend the character a poetic quality as well as a sense of balance in his thought processes.

■ Looking at a whole play

The overall structure of a plot can help us to appreciate where a section of discourse fits in with the whole and how we can interpret it. The plot is the basic sequence of events that we call the story. Narrative discourse is concerned with the way the story is sequenced, of how causal factors are put together and what effects these have on an audience. For example, there may be flashbacks or parallel scenes that interrupt the sequencing. Short, comic scenes may interrupt the action to break the tension in order to then subject an audience to even more tension. Such scenes also serve as a contrast, so the blissful moments of comedy might make an audience feel that the world of the play is not such a bad one after all, only to have that belief squashed when the next scenes increase the tense or tragic atmosphere of the play.

In terms of the play as a whole, as opposed to the more particular juxtaposition of scenes, it is useful to look to Aristotle's enormously influential *Poetics*, where he believed that there should be a unity created by a beginning, middle and an end. In dramatic tragedy this basic configuration was seen to comprise:

■ peripeteia: a reversal of the hero's fortunes from good to bad
■ agnorisis: a recognition of a change in relationship between characters
■ catastrophe: the punishment following a sin or moral flaw in the hero's character.

More recently, plays have tended to be of five acts often structured in this way:

■ introduction
■ complication
■ climax
■ resolution
■ catastrophe.

So, an awareness of overall structure can help you to appreciate and anticipate particular dramatic effects. But, of course, you need to be aware that drama is not formulaic. Dramatists adapt and use conventions to suit their purposes.

8 | Sample extracts: an integrated approach to analysis

This chapter covers:

- sample examination extracts for all the set texts
- suggested activities using linguistic, literary and rhetorical frameworks for analysis
- discursive commentaries on the examination extracts.

Key terms

Soliloquy: a form of monologue that allows the character to speak their internal thoughts out loud, to offer an audience self-revelation or motive or self-uncertainty. What is said can always be regarded as the truth as it appears to that character.

You have now acquired a range of 'tools' which you can use to analyse extracts, looking at everything from lexis and rhetorical devices to discourse features such as turn-taking. You have also gained some background knowledge about genre, form and structure which should inform your thinking. You also know that you need to use this information to explain the dramatic effects in a scene. Each scene needs to be responded to differently, for example the dramatic impact of a fight scene is very different from that of a poignant **soliloquy**.

Each of the following extracts is followed by analysis of the kind you would be expected to produce. These are *not* model answers, but the commentary takes you through the process of analysis and explains what is needed. Consequently they are fuller discussions than you would be able to produce in a timed examination.

Hamlet

Critical response activity

Consider this question on *Hamlet*:

- Explore the ways in which Shakespeare uses literary, linguistic and rhetorical devices and conventions to create specific dramatic effects in Act 1, Scene 1.

Read the following extract through very carefully at least twice. Make a copy of it and annotate it, then read the discursive commentary which follows. Next put that to one side and write your own essay, which is likely to be shorter than the commentary. You will have only one hour in the examination, so there is a limit to the amount you can say!

> *Barnardo*: Who's there?
>
> *Francisco*: Nay answer me. Stand and unfold yourself.
>
> *Barnardo*: Long live the King.
>
> *Francisco*: Barnardo?
>
> *Barnardo*: He.
>
> *Francisco*: You come most carefully upon your hour.
>
> *Barnardo*: 'Tis now struck twelve, get thee to bed Francisco.
>
> *Francisco*: For this relief much thanks: 'tis bitter cold,
> And I am sick at heart.
>
> *Barnardo*: Have you had quiet guard?
>
> *Francisco*: Not a mouse stirring.
>
> *Barnardo*: Well, good night.
> If you do meet Horatio and Marcellus,
> The rivals of my watch, bid them make haste.
>
> *(Enter Horatio and Marcellus.)*
>
> *Francisco*: I think I hear them. Stand: ho, who is there?
>
> *Horatio*: Friends to this ground.
>
> *Marcellus*: And liegemen to the Dane.

> *Francisco*: Give you good night.
>
> *Marcellus*: O, farewell honest soldiers, who hath
> reliev'd you?
>
> *Francisco*: Barnardo has my place: give you good night.
>
> (*Exit Fransisco*)
>
> *Marcellus*: Holla Barnardo.
>
> *Barnardo*: Say, what is Horatio there?
>
> *Horatio*: A piece of him.
>
> *Barnardo*: Welcome Horatio, welcome good Marcellus.
>
> *Marcellus*: What, has this thing appear'd again to-night?
>
> *Barnardo*: I have seen nothing.
>
> *Marcellus*: Horatio says, 'tis but our fantasy,
> And will not let belief take hold of him
> Touching this dreaded sight, twice seen of us;
> Therefore I have entreated him along
> With us, to watch the minutes of this night,
> That if again this apparition come,
> He may approve our eyes, and speak to it.
>
> *Horatio*: Tush, tush, 'twill not appear.
>
> *Barnardo*: Sit down awhile,
> And let us once again assail your ears,
> That are so fortified against our story,
> What we two nights have seen.
>
> *Horatio*: Well, sit we down,
> And let us hear Barnardo speak of this.
>
> *Barnardo*: Last night of all,
> When yond same star that's westward from the pole
> Had made his course t'illume that part of heaven
> Where now it burns, Marcellus and myself,
> The bell beating one –
>
> *Marcellus*: Peace, break thee off:
>
> (*Enter Ghost*)
>
> Look where it comes again!

At around 40 to 50 lines, this is approximately the length of extract you can expect in the first part of the examination.

Commentary

Dramatic effects and context

Initially it is useful to sum up the dramatic effects in the scene and to comment on the context (in this case, the setting and the characters who gather here). This is a frightening, confusing and fast-paced opening. The soldiers are on watch and the guard is being relieved, but it all happens so quickly and not even the participants can recognise each other in the dark. There are challenges about identity and the audience feels as if they have been introduced mid-action. This is a deliberate dramatic effect: we are intrigued and startled by the start. Characters are introduced quickly and then the most powerful dramatic effect is the sudden entrance of the ghost.

The opening scene shows what Frank Kermode suggests in *Shakespeare's Language* (2000) is 'continuous and deliberate reluctance' to provide the necessary exposition we might expect at the beginning of a play. The tense, short questions, many simple sentences or one-word utterances and exclamations increase the pace to create a sense of urgency reflecting the uncertainty as to who or what is there. A palpable sense of fear is conveyed, reinforced by Francisco's evident thankfulness and Barnardo's urgent desire to know if the guard had experienced any disturbance, and for his companion on the watch to 'make haste'.

The audience sees the fear as arising from two sources, the first being uncertainty as to identity (even Horatio laconically refers to himself as only a 'piece' of himself rather than a whole) and the second being from a more frightening source (the 'it' or 'thing' referred to with the adjective 'dreaded'). This 'it' then dramatically appears on stage – a terrifying opening!

We do not hear of its hero until *Hamlet* has run for 10 minutes at line 170, still less see him until 65 lines into the next scene. The play deliberately delays such an introduction, and the fast pace of the opening discourse concentrates instead on the production of an atmosphere of raw fear and uncertainty, an atmosphere Kermode sees as 'seething with menace'.

Devices used to create the dramatic effects

In order to comment on the devices used to create these dramatic effects, it is necessary to look at the text in more detail. As mentioned, the fast pace is brought about by the short utterances and the brief, challenging questions in the first few lines. The comment on the weather – not just cold, but 'bitter cold' – together with the expressive 'sick at heart' adds an ominous touch. As confidence in identity begins to grow, however, so the sentences lengthen and the homely image 'not a mouse stirring' creates a reduction in the initial tension and a greater sense of normality.

The turns are evenly distributed until Marcellus has a seven-line speech that fleshes out Horatio's character. When Marcellus says 'Horatio says 'tis but our fantasy', the use of the collective pronoun 'our' establishes Horatio as separate and a man who thinks differently to others. His confidently colloquial exclamation 'Tush, tush' reinforces him as the voice of scepticism. Shakespeare quickly establishes character: there is a self-possession about Horatio and a respect shown to him by the others. Marcellus, too, appears to be someone who is clear-thinking: the syntax is straightforward and the information given concise. Although iambic pentameter is used, here it delivers information in a simple register. Barnardo's character is established, fleetingly, using a more poetic, heightened language form, possibly to indicate respect for Horatio. He personifies a star, creating a poetic image in the heavens. His elision 't'illume' makes the line flow, perhaps helping to create a sense of majestic sweep in the star's movement. Things seem more natural until a series of **plosives** interrupt with their dead beat: 'bell beating … Peace, break'. The imperative to 'break thee off' destroys the brief poeticised harmony and marks the entrance of the ghost.

Throughout this opening the register switches, as it will do so often in this play, from simple, everyday lexis, including the greetings and challenges, to the more measured blank verse of Marcellus and the poetic narrative of Barnardo. This is finally interrupted by Marcellus's monosyllabic imperative, and tension is raised with his performative exclamation: 'look where it comes again'. Visual shock increases the excitement and fear felt by the audience as the ghostly figure enters the stage.

Summary

This opening effectively establishes characters, creates tension and suspense and introduces the ghost. The fast interaction and the shrill, loud voices at the beginning of the scene create dramatic interest and the small amount of information given away about the 'apparition' engages our interest instantly.

> ### Key terms
>
> **Plosives:** sounds such as b, p, t, k; consonants which are produced by stopping the air by the lips, teeth or palate. Other sound labels include fricative (f) and sibilant (s).

The audience is made well aware that something very much out of the ordinary has happened but is kept waiting to find out what it is. When we find out more, much later in this act, we have the source of Hamlet's peripeteia (his reversal of fortune) as he is forced to assume the role of an avenger. According to Aristotle, this is the first element of a dramatic tragedy.

■ *The Rivals*

■ Critical response activity

Consider the same question on *The Rivals*:

■ Explore the ways in which Sheridan uses literary, linguistic and rhetorical devices and conventions to create specific dramatic effects in Act 1, Scene 1.

Read the following extract through very carefully at least twice. Make a copy of it and annotate it, then read the discursive commentary which follows. Next put that to one side and write your own essay, which is likely to be shorter than the commentary. You will have only one hour in the examination, so there is a limit to the amount you can say!

(*Scene – A street.*

Enter Thomas; he crosses the stage; Fag follows, looking after him)

Fag: What! – Thomas! – Sure 'tis he? – What! Thomas! Thomas!

Thomas: Hey! – Odd's life! – Mr Fag! – give us your hand, my old fellow-servant.

Fag: Excuse my glove, Thomas: I'm devilish glad to see you, my lad: why, my prince of charioteers, you look as hearty! – but who the deuce thought of seeing you in Bath!

Thomas: Sure, Master, Madam Julia, Harry, Mrs Kate, and the postillion be all come!

Fag: Indeed!

Thomas: Aye! Master thought another fit of the gout was coming to make him a visit: so he'd a mind to gi't the slip, and whip we were all off at an hour's warning.

Fag: Aye, aye! hasty in everything, or it would not be Sir Anthony Absolute!

Thomas: But tell us, Mr Fag, how does young Master? Odd! Sir Anthony will stare to see the Captain here!

Fag: I do not serve Captain Absolute now –

Thomas: Why sure!

Fag: At present I am employed by Ensign Beverley.

Thomas: I doubt, Mr Fag, you ha'n't changed for the better.

Fag: I have not changed, Thomas.

Thomas: No! why didn't you say you had left young Master?

Fag: No – well, honest Thomas, I must puzzle you no farther: briefly then – Captain Absolute and Ensign Beverley are one and the same person.

Thomas: The devil they are!

Fag: So it is indeed, Thomas; and the *Ensign* half of my master being on guard at present – the *Captain* has nothing to do with me.

Thomas: So, so! – what, this is some freak, I warrant! Do, tell us, Mr Fag, the meaning o't – you know I ha' trusted you.

Fag: You'll be secret, Thomas?

Thomas: As a coach-horse.

Fag: Why then the cause of all this is – LOVE – love, Thomas, who (as you may get read to you) has been a masquerader ever since the days of Jupiter.

Thomas: Aye, aye; I guessed there was a lady in the case: but pray, why does your master pass only for an Ensign? – now if he had shammed General indeed –

Fag: Ah! Thomas, there lies the mystery o' the matter. Harkee, Thomas, my master is in love with a lady of a very singular taste: a lady who likes him better as a half-pay ensign than if she knew he was son and heir to Sir Anthony Absolute, a baronet of three thousand a year.

Thomas: That is an odd taste indeed! – but has she got the stuff, Mr Fag; is she rich, hey?

Fag: Rich! – why, I believe she owns half the stocks! Zounds! Thomas, she could pay the national debt as easily as I could my washerwoman! She has a lapdog that eats out of gold – she feeds her parrot with small pearls – and all her thread-papers are made of bank-notes!

Thomas: Bravo – faith! – Odd! I warrant she has a set of thousands at least: – but does she draw kindly with the Captain?

Fag: As fond as pigeons.

Thomas: May one hear her name?

Fag: Miss Lydia Languish – but there is an old, tough aunt in the way; though by the by – she has never seen my master – for we got acquainted with Miss while on a visit in Gloucestershire.

Thomas: Well – I wish they were once harnessed together in matrimony. But pray, Mr Fag, what kind of a place is this Bath? I ha'heard a deal of it – here's a mort o'merry-making, hey?

Fag: Pretty well, Thomas, pretty well – 'tis a good lounge. In the morning we go to the pump-room (though neither my master nor I drink the waters); after breakfast we saunter on the parades or play a game at billiards; at night we dance: but damn the place, I'm tired of it: their regular hours stupefy me – not a fiddle nor a card after eleven! – however Mr Faulkland's gentleman and I keep it up a little in private parties; I'll introduce you there, Thomas – you'll like him much.

At around 40 to 50 lines this is approximately the length of extract you can expect in the first part of the examination.

Commentary

Dramatic effects and context

This opening scene is very humorous and takes place in a public setting in a street. Two well-acquainted servants meet, and we would expect greetings and exchange of gossip and information. The dramatic effects include the all-important establishing of characters and their relationships; the beginning of plot development and the introduction of a theme which will dominate the action; and, of course, the mood created: jocularity.

Devices used to create the dramatic effects

Fag's character is quickly established through the dialogue and the actions. He is well-mannered (he apologises for shaking hands with his glove on), friendly and down-to-earth with his mode of address, using 'my lad' and the modifier 'devilish'. He is openly judgemental (or opinionated) with a fellow servant when he says 'hasty in everything, or it would

Key terms

Choric: taking on the role of a 'chorus', and commenting and reflecting on the action.

Clauses: constructions that consist minimally of a subject and a verb, e.g. 'I sang'. Or a clause may be within a larger construction and coordinated with another clause, e.g. 'I sang on Saturday and you can sing next week'. Or it can subordinate to another clause, e.g. 'they asked whether I would sing'.

not be Sir Anthony Absolute', but apparently discreet and able to keep a confidence: 'You know I ha' trusted you' says Thomas. He also has a **choric** role, informing us about other characters: their characteristics ('old, tough aunt in the way'), how ridiculously rich some of them are, and their geographical and social movements. In this sense he is a plot device, uncovering the romantic attachment of Lydia and Ensign Beverley who is actually the rich Captain Absolute.

The idiolect of each character is well established. For example, Fag's numerous elisions and ellipses, ('tis, he'd, g'it, o't, h'a'nt) help to create an impression of simplicity or directness in the character, as does the use of colloquial expressions ('the deuce', 'the stuff', 'by the by'), minor blasphemies ('Odd's life', 'zounds') and oaths ('devilish glad', 'damn the place'). These suggest lower-class speech traits, but of course these servants are devilish cunning. In terms of structure, at sentence level Fag's closing speech is a compound sentence; its coordinated **clauses** build up to convey a busy social scene but the majority of sentences are simple, aiding their informational purpose.

The discourse is primarily a series of questions, exclamations and statements designed to inform the audience. The adjacency pairs would suggest equality in status between the two participants, each having roughly the same length. Some of Fag's turns are slightly longer because he has more knowledge than Thomas, giving him a little more power in this respect; though, in reality it is more to do with his expositional role than any mismatch in status.

The pace of the interaction is fast and humorous. For example, Fag, credited with the aptronym that denotes a servant, is surprised to see his fellow servant and friend, Thomas, whose personification of the gout creates humour: 'master thought another fit of the gout was coming to make him a visit: – so he'd a mind to gi't the slip'. Humour is maintained in this light-hearted opening by Fag's punning on the disguise of Captain Absolute as an Ensign-being only 'half on guard', and his hyperbolic claims about Lydia's wealth: 'Thomas, she could pay the national debt as easily as I could my washerwoman! She has a lapdog that eats out of gold – she feeds her parrot with small pearls – and all her thread-papers are made of bank-notes!' The rhetorical list of four extravagant claims serves to underline her great wealth and this would provide the audience with hilarious visual images.

The introduction of themes could be construed as a dramatic effect, and here the audience is informed that love between two members of the upper social class is, supposedly, not influenced by money. The servants' views on this are clearly declared: Fag talks about such lack of interest in money as being a 'mystery'; Thomas, too, reflects that this is 'an odd taste'.

Love is elevated in importance though by its capitalisation into a proper noun, and in performance the tone would be sarcastic and the volume loud. The homely simile about the young lovers who are 'as fond as pigeons' amusingly undercuts any seriousness and adds to the semantic field of birds and animals (lapdog, parrot), which provides a ludicrous range of visual stimuli for the audience.

Sheridan also sustains the use of a semantic field linked with horses, entirely appropriate for the characters concerned. Dotted throughout the extract are the nouns: 'postillion', 'whip', 'coach-horse', and the metaphor 'harnessed together in matrimony', which all convey a fairly realistic portrait of a servant's concerns and help to create believable characters as well as providing amusement. 'Harnessed together' suggests anything but a romantic view of marriage!

Summary

This opening provides us with an amusing, riveting start with the portrayal of two wily servants. It is dramatically important too because the audience quickly learns much about some of the other characters, admittedly filtered through the eyes of these interesting servants. It also adds a complication with the reference to the aunt.

This intrigues the audience, as does the talk about Lydia Languish and Captain Absolute. We wonder whether these characters will be as besotted and romantic as the servants imply and, of course, we wonder about the aunt's role. This is certainly a fascinating, very amusing opening.

■ *A Streetcar Named Desire*

■ Critical response activity

Consider this question on *A Streetcar Named Desire*:

■ Explore the way in which Williams presents the relationship between Blanche and Stanley in this passage from Act 1, Scene 2 by using literary, linguistic and rhetorical devices and conventions to create specific dramatic effects.

Read the following extract through very carefully at least twice. Make a copy of it and annotate it, then read the discursive commentary which follows. Next put that to one side and write your own essay, which is likely to be shorter than the commentary. You will have only one hour in the examination, so there is a limit to the amount you can say!

(*Stella goes out on the porch. Blanche comes out of the bathroom in a red satin robe.*)

Stanley: That's good.

Blanche: (*drawing the curtains at the windows*): Excuse me while I slip on my pretty new dress!!

Stanley: Go right ahead, Blanche.

(*She closes the drapes between the rooms.*)

Blanche: I understand there's to be a little card party to which we ladies are cordially *not* invited.

Stanley (*ominously*): Yeah?

(*Blanche throws off her robe and slips into a flowered print dress.*)

Blanche: Where's Stella?

Stanley: Out on the porch.

Blanche: I'm going to ask a favour of you in a moment.

Stanley: What could that be, I wonder?

Blanche: Some buttons in back! You may enter!

(*He crosses through drapes with a smouldering look.*)

Blanche: How do I look?

Stanley: You look all right.

Blanche: Many thanks! Now the buttons!

Stanley: I can't do nothing with them.

Blanche: You men with your big clumsy fingers. May I have a drag on your cig?

Stanley: Have one for yourself.

Blanche: Why, thanks! ... It looks like my trunk has exploded.

Stanley: Me an' Stella were helping you unpack.

Blanche: Well, you certainly did a fast and thorough job of it!

Stanley: It looks like you raided some stylish shops in Paris.

Blanche: Ha-ha! Yes – clothes are my passion!

Stanley: What does it cost for a string of fur-pieces like that?

Blanche: Why, those were a tribute from an admirer of mine!

Stanley: He must have had a lot of – admiration!

Blanche: Oh, in my youth I excited some admiration. But look at me now! (*She smiles at him radiantly.*) Would you think it possible that I was once considered to be – attractive?

Stanley: Your looks are okay.

Blanche: I was fishing for a compliment, Stanley.

Stanley: I don't go in for that stuff.

Blanche: What – stuff?

Stanley: Compliments to women about their looks. I never met a woman that didn't know if she was good-looking or not without being told, and some of them give themselves credit for more than they've got. I once went out with a doll who said to me, 'I am the glamorous type, I am the glamorous type!' I said, 'So what!'

Blanche: And what did she say then?

Stanley: She didn't say nothing. That shut her up like a clam.

Blanche: Did it end the romance?

Stanley: It ended the conversation – that was all.

At around 40 to 50 lines this is approximately the length of extract you can expect in the first part of the examination.

Commentary

Dramatic effects and context

Stanley, only just informed of Blanche's intention to stay, is angry because he believes she has stolen his wife's (and he supposes his) share of their inheritance from Belle Reve: the sisters' home. He believes money has been squandered on the expensive clothes, furs and jewellery he has just found in her trunk. Blanche has just bathed and needs to get dressed, but the situation is awkward: she is in a home that is not her own and wearing only a bathrobe in the presence of a stranger. The context is private, domestic and the only participants are Blanche and Stanley. Stella is outside and they are alone. Stanley is now able to confront Blanche and there are no witnesses.

It is an intense, uneasy scene with much implied between the lines (implicature is important here). Blanche is nervous by nature, but even more so in Stanley's aggressive, strongly masculine presence. The tension is palpable and such a mood is clearly an effect which Williams wanted. He is also establishing character, slowly revealing aspects of each and showing us how opposite they are. Such contrast – both in language and physical presence – is, in itself, dramatic. This is a scene full of anger, but also smouldering sexuality.

Devices used to create the dramatic effects

Williams is here establishing character and relationship. Stanley's opening comment on her robe is face-threatening, challenging in its inappropriate sexual undertone. He hardly knows her, yet offers approval that she is barely dressed. Closing the curtains is her overt indication

that Blanche needs privacy, reinforced by her direct request: 'Excuse me.'
Stanley's challenging response is sexually voyeuristic: 'Go right ahead.'
The adjacency pair of her ambiguous promise and his question sustains
this mood of sexual tension:

> **Blanche**: I'm going to ask a favour of you in a moment.
>
> **Stanley**: What could that be I wonder?

And the tension is maintained by her request for a man she hardly knows
to help button her dress.

The tension between the characters is not just sexual. Twice Blanche
challenges Stanley: that he has not included her in the card game
invitation and that her trunk has been interfered with. She also attempts
to provoke him into a closer relationship by direct questions calling for
approval: 'How do I look? … Would you think it possible that I was once
considered to be – attractive?'

There is coyness here in a woman her age that might suggest a naivety
or neediness in her character. She wants to be thought attractive still; she
wants to appeal to a male both in her looks and her show of vulnerability
(not being able to fasten her dress buttons).

Stanley is revealed to be something of a sexual predator. He offers
approval only when Blanche is partially dressed in her robe and bluntly
invites her to dress in front of him: 'Go right ahead.' Blanche responds to
this undercurrent of sexual suggestion, slipping into a different register
to indicate an attempt at closeness: 'May I have a drag on your cig?' in
what is called downward **convergence**. Her use of the colloquial term also
helps to indicate a certain coarseness in her character that periodically
emerges from the genteel façade: the use of the polite term 'may' in the
same sentence, rather than the usual (grammatically incorrect) 'can',
structurally reinforces this refined aspect of her character.

Stanley's utterances match Blanche's in their curt simplicity, perhaps
indicating a similarity in character as well as expression, so it is
interesting that the only extended expression is from this rather blunt
character. In outlining his attitude to women's vanity, Stanley launches
into an extended utterance that reveals by its very length that he needs
Blanche to understand him.

Their final statements show an interesting difference in perspective
in their lexical choices. Blanche, with her starry-eyed use of the term
'romance' contrasts with Stanley's more pragmatic observation 'It ended
the conversation'. The disparity in outlook here might cause some
humour in an audience as indicating gendered viewpoints.

It is interesting to single out idiolects here to show how characters
are possibly being defined by gender differences in language use. His
statement, 'That's good' and command, 'Go right ahead' help to convey
Stanley's directness. They also have the appearance of cliché, as does his
one simile, 'like a clam'. These phrases suggest he is an unimaginative,
unresponsive man.

Blanche attempts to slip into this clichéd form only once, as mentioned
above, but turns the cliché 'cordially invited' to: 'I understand there's
to be a little card party to which we ladies are cordially not invited',
suggesting a more creative mindset; as does the lexis 'romance', which is
perhaps a stereotypically female view of relationships that is reinforced by
Blanche's desire for approval and praise, reflected in her curious inclusion
of the adjective 'pretty' to describe her dress when she is, self-consciously,
having to dress in Stanley's proximity. Stanley refers to the female as a

■ Key terms

Convergence: when a speaker
wants to show orientation with
another speaker they may change
their normal speech, perhaps
by adopting a more formal or
higher prestige form (upward
convergence) or by adopting an
informal register (downward
convergence). The opposite is
divergence, where a speaker wants
to isolate themselves from another
speaker and ensure differentiation.

'doll', again a cliché, and a noun stereotypically presenting the female as an object or toy.

Blanche's code is rather more elaborate with the use of the **modal auxiliary verb** '*would* you think' inviting a personal response when Stanley refuses to respond on a personal level with his non-committal statement: 'your looks are okay'. He asks only one question: 'What could that be I wonder?', which is more of a rhetorical question with its sexual innuendo. 'What does it cost for a string of fur pieces like that?' is designed to elicit information rather than an invitation for there to be open communication in the discourse.

However, the main impact of the scene is in its intensification of tension. This arises from the conflicting undercurrent of Stanley's suspicion of being cheated and Blanche's anger at the invasion of her personal space and possessions, though both are only indirectly hinted at. Williams's explicit stage directions as to how he wants the actors to interpret the characters, ('a smouldering look', 'drawing the curtains ... she closes the drapes', 'she smiles at him radiantly') as predatory male and vulnerable (yet flirtatious) female also help to create tension.

In terms of the play as a whole, structurally the scene also provides some **proleptic irony** since it establishes a degree of sexual chemistry between the two that will later develop into the act of rape for which the extract provides some motivational credibility.

Summary

This extract shows the tensions in this incipient relationship: Stanley's disapproval and wariness, together with his aggression and Blanche's nervous, dangerous, flirtatiousness. Blanche's view that he is very much her social inferior is conveyed by her contrasting register, her attempts at convergence and Williams's depiction of Stanley himself as the near monosyllabic but very macho man. This is a skirmish, in a psychological drama, between two characters of apparently different social class and linguistic codes. As well as the well-crafted dialogue, the use of pauses together with the **paralinguistics** and the actions would all help in a performance to create immense tension.

Thematically, Williams is introducing aspects of a conflict between old-world values, embodied in the faded splendour of Blanche and Stella's past and the emergent 'values' of the New America, a democratised land of (immigrant) opportunism; a land where male and female sexuality is more open, where there is less romance but also less pretence in sexual relationships.

■ *Translations*

■ Critical response activity

The question here would be:

■ Explore the ways in which Friel uses literary, linguistic and rhetorical devices and conventions to create specific dramatic effects in his presentation of characters and issues of communication in Act 1.

Read the following extract through very carefully at least twice. Make a copy of it and annotate it, then read the discursive commentary which follows. Next put that to one side and write your own essay, which is likely to be shorter than the commentary. You will have only one hour in the examination, so there is a limit to the amount you can say!

■ Key terms

Modal auxiliary verb: e.g. can, could, might, may, shall, should, will, would, must. Using modal verbs can create tentativeness or emphasis.

Proleptic irony: that irony which arises from an event, speech or thought which goes on to actually happen later in the drama.

Paralinguistics: a broad term used to refer to aspects of talk that are non-lexical, but which convey meaning. For example, sounds made which are meaningful but are not usually recognised as words, such as grunts or affirmative noises like 'umm'. It can also refer to facial expressions or intonation which all help to convey the sense of an utterance.

Maire enters, a strong-minded, strong-bodied woman in her twenties with a head of curly hair. She is carrying a small can of milk.

Maire: Is this all's here? Is there no school this evening?

Manus: If my father's not back I'll take it.

(*Manus stands awkwardly, having been caught kissing Sarah and with the flowers almost formally at his chest.*)

Maire: Well now, isn't that a pretty sight. There's your milk. How's Sarah?

(*Sarah grunts a reply.*)

Manus: I saw you out at the hay.

(*Maire ignores this and goes to Jimmy.*)

Maire: And how's Jimmy Jack Cassie?

Jimmy: Sit down beside me Maire.

Maire: Would I be safe?

Jimmy: No safer man in Donegal.

(*Marie flops on a stool beside Jimmy.*)

Maire: Ooooh. The best harvest in living memory, they say; but I don't want to see another like it. (*Showing Jimmy her hands.*) Look at the blisters.

Jimmy: *Esne fatigata?*

Maire: *Sum fatigatissima.*

Jimmy: *Bene! Optime!*

Maire: That's the height of my Latin. Fit me better if I had even that much English.

Jimmy: English? I thought you had some English?

Maire: Three words. Wait – there was spake I used to have off by heart. What's this it was?

(*Her accent is strange because she is speaking in a foreign language and because she does not understand what she is saying.*)

'In Norfolk we besport ourselves around the maypoll.' What about that?

Manus: Maypole.

(*Again Maire ignores Manus.*)

Maire: God have mercy on my Aunt Mary – she taught me that when I was about four, whatever it means. Do you know what it means, Jimmy?

Jimmy: Sure you know I have only Irish like yourself.

Maire: And Latin. And Greek.

Jimmy: I'm telling you I know one English word.

Maire: What?

Jimmy: Bo-som.

Maire: What's a bo-sum?

Jimmy: You know (*He illustrates with his hands.*) – bo-som – bo-sum – you know – Diana, the huntress, she has two powerful bo-sum.

Maire: You may be sure that's the one English word you would know. (*Rises.*) Is there a drop of milk about?

(*Manus gives Maire his bowl of milk.*)

Manus: I'm sorry I couldn't get up last night.

> *Maire*: Doesn't matter.
>
> *Manus*: Biddy Hanna sent for me to write a letter to her sister in Nova Scotia. All the gossip of the parish. 'I brought the cow to the bull three times last week but no good. There's nothing for it now but Big Ned Frank.'
>
> *Maire* (*drinking*): That's better.
>
> *Manus*: And she got so engrossed in it that she forgot who she was dictating to: 'The aul drunken schoolmaster and that lame son of his are still footering about in the hedge-school, wasting people's good time and money.'
>
> (*Maire has to laugh at this.*)
>
> *Maire*: She did not!

At around 40 to 50 lines this is approximately the length of extract you can expect in the first part of the examination.

Commentary

Dramatic effects and context

The scene occurs early in the play. Previously, we have been introduced to Manus, the schoolmaster's lame son who has managed to get Sarah to speak her name. Since she has such a bad speech defect the locals consider her to be dumb, but he kisses her for joy because she has finally spoken: a dramatic start. Jimmy, 'the infant prodigy' though in his sixties, has meanwhile been comfortably reading Greek. The setting is the hedge-school and so our expectations would be of a schoolroom atmosphere, which makes the kiss between master and pupil consequently startling. Maire is then introduced for the first time and we are intrigued by her actions and the ensuing amusing discussion of language. The dramatist plunges us straight into a scene which asks us to engage with questions about communication, introduces a strong and fascinating character and contains humour and ironic comment.

Devices used to create the dramatic effects

This is the audience's first sight of Maire, and Friel intends to focus us on her character. We are intrigued when she ignores Manus who has been caught kissing Sarah. Her ambiguous comment leaves us considering whether or not she morally disapproves because he has apparently taken advantage of Sarah, or whether she is jealous: 'Well now, isn't that a pretty sight … How's Sarah?' Is she referring to the flowers or the kiss or both? We do not know. Such ambivalence is dramatically effective. She then ignores his attempt to initiate conversation and instead seems to flirt with the older man with the question 'Would I be safe?', leaving Manus entirely out of the discourse. There is then another refusal to engage after he corrects her pronunciation: 'Maypole', followed by a brief, dismissive 'doesn't matter'. This is the first time she has not spoken in **Standard English** grammar, omitting the subject word 'it' as if she cannot be bothered to talk to him in the correct form. It is only finally when he manages to make her laugh by a narration which initiates a new topic that she responds. Maire has kept the loquacious and fairly confident Manus out of the discourse and this reveals her power, maintained by her final, humorously dismissive ejaculation: 'She did not!' In structuring the dialogue this way, Friel ensures that the audience's interest is aroused. What is the relationship between Manus and Maire? How is it that she can ignore him in this way? What authority, if any, does he have? Questions are raised: essential in sustaining attention.

■ Key terms

Standard English: the 'educated' variety of English recognised in British society as the prestigious form, free of regional dialect, with uniform spelling and grammar in its written form, sometimes called the Queen's English.

What Friel also does, and very skilfully, is to use an **alienation** technique. So far the audience has taken it for granted that English is the native language of the characters, as this is recognisably what they are speaking. Also, we have previously heard Jimmy talking in Greek, then he and Maire in Latin, but when she says: 'That's the height of my Latin. Fit me better if I had even that much English', we begin to realise what the dramatist is doing. And, in case some members of the audience have not twigged, Friel makes Jimmy ask: 'English? I thought you had some English?'

We are suddenly confronted with a paradox: we thought it was English that the characters are speaking much of the time and so we are made to consider the concept that they are actually speaking Irish, a language we apparently understand as well as our own. We are forced to consider one of the play's major concerns: what role does language play in our lives? Maire's ignoring of Manus removes him from the social aspect of language as well as preventing him from communicating ideas. Friel then does several clever manipulations of actual English to make it sound alien to us, to make us complicit with his Irish characters who regard English as a foreign language. He achieves this in a number of ways.

Firstly, Maire uses the wrong form of 'speak', rendering it in an archaic past tense. Next, Friel changes the syntax. The normal subject + verb + object order: 'What was it?' becomes 'What's this it was?' (to subject + determiner + object + verb). Maire is then made to recite, in a strangulated accent, an idiomatic expression containing the archaic form 'we besport ourselves' and a mispronounced noun, 'maypoll'. These factors create a stilted form of English that, plainly, fails to communicate much about anything.

From a thematic viewpoint, Friel has introduced two key ideas: that language creates social identity and that it communicates meanings, here in Latin and Irish but not, tellingly, English. Focusing the audience on ideas about language so early in the play, and doing this with humour and creating character interest and suspense, are all very specific dramatic effects. There is playful humour in Friel's clever piece of theatrical manipulation, when the audience is made to feel more at one with the Irish. Jimmy splits the syllables of 'bo-som' to make the word sound strange and to emphasise his sexual appreciation of the opposite sex. Maire's wry observation: 'You may be sure that's the one English word you would know' is a neatly humorous way of telling the audience about Jimmy's interests.

The small mistakes in the text also draw attention to what is to become a central aspect of the play: what is lost when one language is rendered into another. Later in the play Owen is continually translating from 'Irish' into 'English', so the idea of processing language becomes a key aspect of the play's dynamic. Language is integral to identity and culture and these issues are raised early in the play, here in the humorous, fast-paced interaction.

Summary

The audience's curiosity about the characters and their relationships is aroused in this extract, together with some interesting issues about communication. Friel uses a range of linguistic and literary devices, from the flouting of politeness in the interaction to the careful choice of lexis and utterance to create a powerful introductory scene which has humour and tension. We are aware of contrast in characters and impending conflicts.

Key terms

Alienation: a theatrical technique developed by the dramatist Bertolt Brecht where a commonly held belief is challenged and the audience is made to reconsider its validity.

Approaching the examination

■ An integrated approach

The earlier examples in this book concentrated on finding ways of explaining how linguistic devices created dramatic effects. Next, the focus was on some examples which showed the dramatist flouting conventions, for dramatic effect. Finally, Chapter 8 provided some detailed working ideas on each of the set texts, taking the essential integrated approach by referring to both literary and linguistic devices in their analysis of dramatic effects. This is what you will have to do in the examination: use all of the analytical tools you have acquired to answer the question fully. You will need a working critical vocabulary, and the key words pinpointed in the main text (and collated in the glossary at the back of the book) should be useful but not exhaustive.

■ The dangers of feature spotting

Once you have an extensive knowledge of linguistic and literary features, there is sometimes a tendency to get carried away with feature spotting: identifying and listing devices whether or not you can say anything constructive about the features. For example, just to spot that a character uses many interrogatives is not very helpful unless it is followed by a comment about their quizzical nature, or the way they are perhaps deliberately avoiding answering another character's question. Also, just saying that a writer uses imagery is less than helpful unless some analysis is made: what does the image evoke and how does it contribute to the mood and atmosphere?

Knowledge of the devices and conventions needs to be 'internalised'. Just displaying that you know, for example, all about Grice's theory, is not useful unless it leads you to say something pertinent about the dramatic effects in the scene. If Grice or Labov or knowledge of rhetorical features does not seem relevant for the given extract, then do not force these points into your writing. Each extract has to be responded to differently.

> **Link**
>
> Look back at the explanations of the theories of Grice and Labov in Chapter 2.

■ The examination

Preparatory work

■ Read the given extract carefully: you should go through it at least twice.

■ Reflect on the context: consider what has happened before and what comes afterwards. Placing the scene is essential.

■ Think about what the dramatic effects are: stand back from the extract and decide what its impact is; is this a tense scene, a climactic one, a quietly humorous extract, a visually spectacular scene? It is useful to have some general idea in your mind about its impact before you get down to the detail.

■ Pay attention to the detail: it is helpful to write about the text as you go through it, observing interactional features, types of utterance, use of lexis, rhetorical devices, etc. This will provide you with the practical examples you can use to support points about what makes the scene dramatic.

■ Think again about the dramatic effects: having annotated the extract you will have some more ideas about the characters and the mood, which will inform your thinking.

Writing the essay

■ Introduction: do not spend too long on this. Some candidates are tempted to retell the whole plot, which is completely unnecessary, but do show that you know where the scene occurs and that you are aware of the context and its influence on the kind of action we see. Also, a brief summary of the dramatic impact of the scene is useful.

■ The meat of the essay: you need to show how the writer achieves specific effects. There are different ways in which you can organise your thoughts:

– The chronological approach: going through the text in the order in which it occurs, analysing and commenting on features. This can work well, but can also seem a little mechanistic, and it is easy to end up doing a line-by-line job and feature-spotting and forgetting the question.

– Using literary and linguistic frameworks to provide a structured approach: for example, you might begin by looking at interactional features in the whole extract; then move on to an analysis of lexis and semantic fields. However, there will always be some overlap: looking at lexis can lead you into some reflection on syntax and grammar and rhetorical devices. That is fine. As mentioned above, the emphasis is on an integrated approach, and literary and linguistic frameworks overlap.

■ Allusions: alluding to (that is referring to) other scenes in the play, or to critics, or to other writers when it seems relevant and helpful can illuminate and enrich what you are saying. But make any reference work for you; that is, make it link in with what you are talking about. Just because you happen to know a lot, for example, about the Elizabethan views on ghosts, this will not necessarily be helpful if you were trying to analyse the dramatic effects in the final fight scene in *Hamlet*, but it might be extremely interesting if you were analysing a scene in which the ghost appears.

■ Conclusion: make it brief. Some reiteration of points is useful and should include reference to 'dramatic effects'. Do not peter out. Remember this is the last piece of your writing that the examiner reads; the final impression can be important.

A final word about complexities. The best essays acknowledge that there is often ambiguity in a text and that a scene can be interpreted in many different ways. If you see difficulties and issues, then mention this. The examiner is looking for a thinking response and often the more you reflect and analyse, the more complex an issue can become. Do not dodge this, confront it; have confidence in your own response and judgement. The examiner is looking for a clear, well-argued analysis which uses evidence to support points, but there is no single, right, definitive answer.

■ Sample question and answer with examiner's comments

Sample question

Read the following extract from Act 5, Scene 1 of *Hamlet*, and explore the ways in which Shakespeare depicts Hamlet and his relationship with Horatio in this passage by using literary, linguistic and rhetorical devices and conventions to create specific dramatic effects.

First clown: This same skull sir, this same skull sir, was Yorick's skull, the King's Jester.

Hamlet: This?

First clown: E'en that.

Hamlet: Let me see. Alas poor Yorick, I knew him Horatio, a fellow of infinite jest; of most excellent fancy, he hath borne me on his back a thousand times: and now how abhorred in my imagination it is, my gorge rises at it. Here hung those lips, that I have kiss'd I know not how oft. Where be your gibes now? your gambols? your songs? your flashes of merriment that were wont to set the table on a roar? Not one now to mock your own jeering? quite chop-fallen? Now get you to my Lady's chamber, and tell her, let her paint an inch thick, to this favour she must come. Make her laugh at that: prithee Horatio tell me one thing.

Horatio: What's that my Lord?

Hamlet: Dost thou think Alexander look'd o' this fashion i' th' earth?

Horatio: E'en so.

Hamlet: And smelt so? puh.

Horatio: E'en so, my Lord.

Hamlet: To what base uses we may return, Horatio. Why may not imagination trace the noble dust of Alexander, till he find it stopping a bung-hole?

Horatio: 'Twere to consider too curiously, to consider so.

Hamlet: No faith, not a jot. But to follow him thither with modesty enough, and likelihood to lead it; as thus. Alexander died: Alexander was buried: Alexander returneth to dust; the dust is earth; of earth we make loam; and why of that loam (whereto he was converted) might they not stop a beer-barrel?
Imperial Caesar, dead and turn'd to clay.
Might stop a hole to keep the wind away.
O, that that earth, which kept the world in awe,
Should patch a wall, t' expel the winter's flaw.

Sample answer

The examiner's comments are shown alongside the essay, with a summary of the strengths and weaknesses at the end.

A useful start with some details about the context.	This scene takes place not long after Hamlet has returned from his enforced voyage to England. The ship was attacked by pirates who allowed him to escape, leaving his one-time friends Rosencrantz and Guildenstern to continue to England, unbeknowingly to their deaths. The setting is a graveyard, and Hamlet and Horatio have come across a grave being dug, which leads to the discussion about mortality.
Sensible reference to the dramatic aspects: good focus on dramatic irony. Apt points about Horatio. Discourse features: makes some points, not just feature spotting.	It is a quietly dramatic scene, both amusing and full of dramatic irony. Hamlet is unaware that the grave being dug is for Ophelia, but the audience knows this and this lends a great poignancy to the scene, and his bemused and apparently relaxed musings on death. Horatio, the loyal friend and confidante, listens and responds to Hamlet's long turns. Hamlet obviously has the most status here and he is the agenda-setter, although the clown's initial declarative, showing Hamlet the skull, triggers the philosophical thoughts. The clown, however, still addresses him as 'Sir' and Horatio acknowledges him as 'my Lord'. Hamlet

dominates the scene and the hierarchy is maintained, as the audience would expect.

Horatio's short rejoinders lend a cooperative air to the discourse: 'E'en so my lord.' He agrees with Hamlet's statements and questions, but towards the end the audience is reminded of his thoughtful and cautious character: ''Twere to consider too curiously to consider so'. This is his reply to Hamlet's question about tracing 'the noble dust' of Alexander. However, the dominant Hamlet ignores his advice and carries on with his thoughts. This is a close relationship, shown by the way Hamlet opens up to Horatio, but status and power are still clearly with Hamlet.

> More on Horatio's character and their relationship, with textual evidence.

The informality of the scene and the friendly relationship with Horatio are shown also by Shakespeare's use of prose. There are everyday expressions like the elided 'e'en that' and much deixis: 'this' (referring to the skull). The audience, of course, would have much to watch: the skull would provide dramatic focus and the scene is packed with pathos. Hamlet's reflection that the skull is of someone he knew well leads to some happy/sad reminiscences. Hamlet's speech about Yorick shows a mixture of emotions. He is shocked: 'Alas poor Yorick' and he uses strong words such as 'infinite', 'abhorred' and 'excellent' together with the hyperbolic 'a thousand times' to show his strong feelings. Rhetorical devices such as tripling or tripartite listing: 'gambols … songs … flashes' show the Hamlet who is a master of words. The positive semantic field of 'kiss'd', 'excellent' and 'merriment' also show an aspect of his character: the amiable qualities and regard for other people. There is a mixture of emotion in this speech though. Hamlet's use of rhetorical questions: 'Not one now to mock your own jeering? quite chop-fallen?' seem to show that he is trying to recover his cool in the face of his shock. The mood towards the end of this speech changes again, however, and Hamlet is dramatically sharp about women painting their faces. The audience is reminded of Hamlet's bitterness and anger about his mother's remarriage. It is also a poignant moment because the woman he loved is about to come to 'this favour': death.

> Identifies prose and register of the scene: leads in to performance element and then to dramatic effects.

> Good point about pathos.

> Detailed, well-supported discussion of lexis and rhetoric. Well linked with points about the mood conveyed and Hamlet's character.

> (No need to give alternatives such as 'tripling' or 'tripartite listing'.)

> Perceptive point about mood change and a reminder about dramatic irony (implied).

Hamlet's thoughts then turn to Alexander: someone who died a long time ago. He 'bounces' his ideas off Horatio, almost as though he is thinking aloud. He then plays with the idea of a logical argument and leads Horatio and the audience bit by bit to the conclusion that even Alexander could end up as a bung in a beer barrel. The dramatic effect here is both humour and a touch of sadness, mixed with fatalism. Hamlet's cleverness and his way with words is shown again by the playful, rhyming poem. This mixture of light-heartedness with the serious undertones would have the audience holding its breath. How will Hamlet react to what is about to happen: the burial of Ophelia?

> Another perceptive point about Hamlet's rhetoric: playing with the structure of an argument.

> Good, explicit focus on audience and dramatic effects.

This is a touching and dramatic passage which is sad, amusing and fascinating. Hamlet is clear-thinking, musing in an interesting way about the theme which dominates this tragedy, and Horatio, as ever, is the loyal companion. This is the quiet but serious and perhaps ghoulish scene before the storm of emotions in the scene which follows.

> Clear summing up, although the ending 'begs the question'. It would be useful to briefly mention the ensuing scene and the fight with Laertes.

Examiner's summary

The candidate clearly addresses the question and handles a range of literary, linguistic and rhetorical features. There is more that could have been said, for example about the range of lexical choice from the familiar, everyday language such as 'things' or 'Let me see' to phrases

■ **Key terms**

Bathetic: anticlimactic speech or situation. It occurs when there is a change from a serious mood to a more trivial or down-to-earth mood. This often leads to humour. Bathos is the noun.

conveying horror and physical disgust ('gorge rises'). Also, the final poem with its connotations might have been further explored, as well as the exact nature of the **bathetic** humour in the Alexander example. Also, phonological features like the simple alliterative 'borne me on his back' with its touching, simple image and the graphic detail of 'Here hung those lips' might have been mentioned. But, in an examination situation the candidate has provided well-supported examples and throughout they have remembered to mention dramatic effects (implied and explicit). They have also shown understanding of Hamlet's mood and his relationship with Horatio.

The candidate writes clearly and fluently. There are some less succinctly expressed sections (for example overuse of the vague 'strong', but the meaning is conveyed) and some mixing of registers (from the colloquial 'cool' to the more elaborate, formally expressed comments such as 'provide dramatic focus'). However, this is a lively, thoughtful response which takes an integrated approach. This is not a mechanistic listing of features, but the candidate is using their knowledge, the analytical 'tools' they have acquired to get to grips with the question.

This is not a perfect answer – and there will be better – but this candidate is analysing, exploring and reflecting. This would merit the top band.

10 Overview

■ The examination question and its key terms

The question

The focus of the question is on the differences and similarities between talk in life and talk in literature (prose fiction, drama or poetry). Two previously unseen texts are used:

■ Text A will be a transcript of real speech: anything from sports reporting to a job interview, an informal chat between friends or a request for help in a library. Any real situation.

■ Text B will be an extract from either prose fiction (such as a novel or a short story), drama (which might be a television or theatrical script) or poetry.

The extracts will be linked thematically. For example, two encounters in a train, one real and one fictional, or an extract from a debate about legalising euthanasia alongside a literary extract.

The question will ask you to compare the two texts, showing how they reflect differences and similarities between talk in life and talk in literature, including the relationship between *context* and *purpose*, and the ways in which speakers' *attitudes* and *values* are conveyed.

Context and purpose

Talk in life

In real talk, the context refers to where the talk occurs, whether it is a speech or a casual conversation. Who is involved can also be viewed as part of the context. This context is hugely significant in influencing the way someone speaks. If, for example, you have the job of thanking a speaker who has talked to college students about his travels in Guatemala, you may well have prepared some thoughts and followed a schema for thank you speeches. But you would probably also have to think on your feet and respond with some spontaneous comment to what you had just heard. The situation is probably quite formal and you might be nervous, all of which would affect fluency and lexical choices. It is obvious that the real talk here would be very different from an informal discussion which might take place afterwards between students who know each other well. The register would then be relaxed, the lexis might include more **slang** and colloquialisms, in-jokes and social **dialect**, and the interactional features of conversation would be apparent.

The purpose of talk is inextricably linked to, and influenced by, the setting and the intended audience(s). The purpose of a thank you speech is clear, although the level of formality needed would depend upon the context and audience expectations. The purpose of the ensuing interaction mentioned above may be just phatic, establishing and reinforcing social relationships. If the discussion were in a classroom, however, and mediated by the teacher, its purpose and nature would differ; the presence of an authority figure might influence the content of the discussion, the tone and lexical choice.

You might find it useful to know the following terms which can be helpful when describing the purpose of some talk:

Key terms

Slang: non-standard language often used to create and reinforce group identity. It is influenced by fashion and is ephemeral. Words like 'cool' and 'wicked' have replaced an earlier generation's 'hip' and 'far out'.

Dialect: a variety of language where the regional or social background of the speaker can be identified from non-standard variations in their vocabulary and grammar.

- **Expressive**: revealing feelings and emotions as varied as 'What a great song!' to phrases like 'I'm really fed up.'
- **Phatic**: the kinds of phrases used to oil the wheels of interaction, such as 'Lovely day, isn't it?' or 'How's it going?', but without necessarily imparting much meaning except to be polite and express some interest in the other person.
- **Transactional**: language used to obtain goods, services or ideas. As Brown and Yule say, it is language used to convey 'factual or propositional information.' For example: 'What's the quickest way to the O2 centre?', 'Well, get the tube to … ', etc.
- **Evaluative**: a comment like the one above – 'What a great song!' – can be both expressive and simply evaluative. Another example is a phrase like 'I think the Mini performs much better than the Peugeot.'
- **Expository**: explaining ideas or theories, e.g. 'The philosophy of utilitarianism is concerned with creating the greatest happiness for the greatest number.'
- **Instructive**: giving clear instructions, such as: 'Always turn off the light before changing the bulb.'
- **Persuasive**: an example might be 'You're really the best person to play Joseph. No one sings as well as you,' where the speaker is using flattery to persuade.
- **Collaborative**: agreeing and showing solidarity and cooperation. For example: 'I agree. Let's all go in fancy dress – then we can all be in it together.'
- **Performative**: some utterances can be treated as the performance of an act. For example: 'I am so sorry for eating all the chocolate'. The apology is 'performed'.

Hint: utterances and interactions will not necessarily fall neatly into one category. For example, a student going to a computer centre to ask for help with some internet research might be expressive ('this is so irritating'), evaluative ('but it's fascinating to look at Google Earth, it really helps') and persuasive ('you're so much better at tracking things down than I am. Could you help me with this programme?).

Talk in literature

The context is a little more complex when we refer to crafted texts. Take, for example, the opening of *The Hound of the Baskervilles* by Arthur Conan Doyle, in which the context or setting is the living room of Sherlock Holmes's house in Baker Street. Holmes and Watson are present, and a conversation occurs after breakfast. It is more of an interrogation of Watson: Holmes is testing his powers of deduction, asking him what he makes of a stick that has been left behind by a visitor. Their relationship is politely formal and, of course, we need to understand the Victorian context of the novel's setting and production to appreciate the register. So, there is more than one context: the immediate fictional setting; and the context when it was produced which obviously influences the language and ideas.

The author, of course, can be mocking or parodying the ideas and beliefs of the time. For example, Arthur Miller wrote the play *The Crucible* in the 1950s, but he set it in the context of 17th-century New England. However, he clearly uses the story of Salem witch-hunting to question the validity of the 1950s McCarthy Communist witch-hunts.

As with real talk, purpose and context are linked. The purpose of the Doyle opening is to establish character and alert us to an issue which will play a role in the ensuing plot. So, Doyle chooses a relaxed domestic context to show us how Watson and Holmes interact. But with crafted talk there is another dimension: authorial purpose. Here, Conan Doyle shows us how important, fascinating and essential such deductive powers are for a detective. We sense the author's admiration for the superior intellect of Holmes and immediately we detect the author's ironic touches: Watson is oblivious to Holmes' quite cruel testing of his powers of thinking; his naive self-belief is quite endearing. So, there is much going on in this opening.

It is useful to sum up generally the purpose of crafted talk, bearing in mind that the overall purpose of a crafted work is to 'entertain' in the broadest sense. We can be amused, saddened, intrigued and puzzled, to name but a few effects of what we might call 'entertainment'.

Depending upon the extract, the purposes could include:

- creating or revealing character
- advancing the plot or narrative
- describing a place or situation
- conveying mood and emotion or creating atmosphere
- expressing opinion or feelings
- addressing the audience and inviting empathy/sympathy and some involvement.

We also have particular expectations of a text, depending upon its genre. It might tentatively be suggested that the purpose of poetry is usually to convey emotions or ideas concisely. Within a condensed format, the poet often uses figurative language to convey a complex array of meanings. In a novel, however, the expectation is to have some characters and a plot which develops, no matter how bizarre or unconventional the plot and the inhabitants of the novel may be. Its function is usually to take us on a slower journey than a poem, and it may also set us thinking about life issues. In drama, a comedy sketch has the clear function of amusing the audience, although it may also have a satirical purpose with more serious underlying values being addressed. Serious drama may seek to address fundamental issues, such as the nature of a good king. Its purpose is not simply to entertain, but to encourage us to examine our beliefs and ideas.

Attitudes and values

These two words are often conflated, i.e. used interchangeably. The word 'values' really refers to the deep-seated beliefs that someone holds, whereas attitudes are the outward signs and expressions of these beliefs. So, we might say that Jane *values* reliability and her *attitude* towards this is one of impatience: she tends to condemn people who do not turn up when they say they will, or who do not keep their promises. For the examination question, you need to discern what attitudes and values are revealed in the given texts.

Talk in life

In the real speech extract, you will need to look closely at how the discourse is organised, what is being talked about and how it is expressed. This will help you to discern attitudes and values. It is not always easy in a transcript because you only have the language to go by, and so much is missing. Therefore, commentators might disagree about the tone, and interpretations of attitudes and values will vary.

Talk in literature

With crafted talk, you need to be aware of the attitudes and values expressed by the speakers, and also the underlying attitudes and values of the author (as far as you can appreciate them). It may seem easier to appreciate attitudes in a novel, where the author is giving a fleshed-out context, than in a transcript. In a play, too, there is the visual context which helps you to appreciate the interaction. However, tone can still be differently interpreted, and not everyone will agree about the attitudes and values revealed.

🔍💡 Talk features

Talk in life

Many talk features were discussed in Section A, but it would be useful to look in more detail at some of these features:

Structure in conversations

The principle of agreement

Natural talk is often governed by what is termed the principle of agreement. Speakers in life, though they may agree or disagree on the subject matter of their conversation, have to agree to participate in that conversation, even reluctantly, since it could not proceed if they did not.

Observe the following:

> A. It's a lovely day isn't it?
>
> B. Typical. Sun shines so you have to comment on it.

B flouts one aspect of the principle of agreement by refusing to provide the normal response to the phatic opener about weather, such as 'Yes, it's lovely.' However, they do respond and so are agreeing to some interaction.

The principle of cooperation and types of exchanges

Having tacitly agreed to have a conversation, according to Grice this principle suggests that we need to respond to the other speaker cooperatively. In a clear adjacency pair a question would not usually be followed by another question, but by an answer.

> A. What time is it?
>
> B. Six o'clock.

However, there might be an insertion sequence:

> A. What time is it?
>
> B. Why do you want to know?
>
> A. 'Cos I've got to catch a train soon.
>
> A. Six o'clock.

Another example of an insertion sequence is:

> A. What time is the next bus?
>
> B. What, to town, or …?
>
> A. To Newcastle.
>
> B. Six o'clock.

IRF (initiation, response and then feedback) is another common sequence in a conversation:

A. Would you text me when you get to Billericay?

B. Yes, will do.

A. Thanks a lot. I just need to know you've arrived.

Does it help to apply theory to a selection of exchanges?

▪ Relation/relevance: when a speaker chooses a topic, it is usual for the other speaker to keep to that topic:

> A. Do you enjoy curries?
>
> B. I enjoy sunbathing.

We assume that A's question was genuine and they wanted to know about B's opinion of curries. The answer seems less than relevant, but we do need to know the context to understand the tone and implication. They may be lying on a beach and B is tired of A's questions. B may be deliberately flouting this so-called rule. So, be careful about judging a short interchange without knowing more.

▪ Quantity: according to Grice, a speaker's interaction with another should be of roughly the same quantity, as much or as little as is appropriate. Consider two students:

> A. I'm going to the pub, do you want to come?
>
> B. Well I've got to finish cooking this fish, after which I'm intending to cut the lawn, tidy my bedroom and then do my homework. There's a match I want to watch on TV. Then I'll come.

B gives too much information here. A would not want to hear all these details. Pragmatically, however, it may be that B is joking and being ironic.

▪ Quality: In conversations Grice suggests that an utterance has to be truthful. Truthfulness, of course, can be taken too far:

> A. Does my bum look big in this?
>
> B. No it looks enormous.

This appears to be flouting politeness rules. But, again, we need to understand the context to understand the implicature. The relationship between A and B could be close, with such a comment meant to be teasing or ironic. However, if A were asking an assistant in a shop, such a response would be rude, even if truthful. A politer exchange might be:

> A. Does my bum look big in this?
>
> B. I don't think the style does much for you.

▪ Manner: Grice suggests we need to be clear in our meaning. Look at this exchange:

> A. The rain tips down like puppy tails.
>
> B. What?

This might be clearer if A had said: 'It's raining hard' (or the clichéd 'It's raining cats and dogs'). B's response would have been something like 'Yep. We're going to get wet.' But, as with all of the above examples, pragmatics is important in how we understand the exchanges. A could be being deliberately odd and obscure, or this could be the opening line of a joke.

Though much conversational patterning takes the adjacency-pairing format simply because of the cooperative principle, we do find that

Link

Look back at the explanation of Grice's theory in Chapter 2.

Think about it

Which of these rules are being flouted in these pairings?

▪ A. My mother saw you in the supermarket yesterday.
  B. Supermarkets are cheap places to shop in.

▪ A. How time flies.
  B. How much is that doggy in the window?

▪ A. How long do you have to boil an egg for it to be soft done?
  B. About two hours.

▪ A. It's hot today!
  B. The azimuth extends its benignity tangentially at noon.

overlaps (where another speaker speaks simultaneously), interruptions, pauses (for thinking time or as a signal to let the other speaker take a turn), and topic switches occur for a variety of reasons in normal conversation. These are often fascinating areas of investigation because they can usually tell us something about the relationships between speakers.

Speakers also indicate by feedback that they are following the conversation, or they may show support by such means. Stubbs (1983) observed how speakers signal **alignment** with the other speaker by using 'yeah', 'uhuh' and 'mm'. Acceptance is indicated by 'yeah', 'okay' and 'yeah, I know'.

Endorsement is the explicit acceptance of an utterance, such as: 'Yes, that's right.' These are all markers of speaker solidarity.

Other talk features

■ Deixis or the use of deictics: when words are used which refer backwards or forwards to something said or about to be explained. For example, 'Pass that to me. It looks full already so we'll need to take it over there. He'll deal with it tomorrow.' This is typical of the way we abbreviate. It would be cumbersome to spell it out, and unnecessary if the person we are talking to can see and understand what is being referred to: 'Pass that box to me. The box looks full of books already so we'll need to put it out of the way in the corner. Dad will sort it and take it to the charity shop tomorrow.'

■ Use of contracted verb forms: 'I can't play the flute' or, 'Jack's invited us all'.

■ Use of phrases rather than complete sentences: 'Can't get there in time' or 'Not hungry'.

■ Conjunctions: frequent use of 'and' or 'but'.

■ Lexis: use of simpler and often less abstract vocabulary (however, this would not be true if a formal lecture were the given example). Use of fillers or hedging devices such as 'like', 'you know', 'sort of'.

■ Tag questions: these are commonly used at the end of an utterance to alert or prompt the audience. For example, 'He's a brilliant musician, isn't he?'

■ Repetition: we often repeat ourselves for emphasis.

■ Reformulation: making an utterance and then rephrasing it is common. For example, 'What do you think about euthanasia, I mean, what are your views on mercy killing?'

■ Back-channel features: these signal our responses to utterances. They can be as diverse as a grunt or 'Yes, absolutely', etc.

The principle of register

Register is concerned with the kind of language used according to:

■ the person(s) addressed

■ the situation or context the speakers are in.

In a debating chamber you would expect the language used to be formal, close to Standard English and using an elevated **repertoire**, whereas in a pub the language used tends to be informal, with a number of colloquial or slang words and other non-standard features. Terms of address are more likely to be first names, or 'mate', rather than 'the Right Honourable Member'.

■ Key terms

Alignment: this is indicated by repetition of a speaker's phrase.

Endorsement: where a speaker wishes to endorse another speaker's view or statement to indicate solidarity by reinforcement, though it might also be used to bid for a turn such as: 'Yes, you're right there, I feel there is also …'.

Repertoire: a person's word stock or vocabulary range.

Some brief theories and final thoughts

Language and situation are inseparable; the social context determines how things are said and also governs what they mean. Stubbs (1983) points out that 'it is principally through conversational interaction … that social roles are recognised and sustained.' The relationship between speakers and their situation together with the purpose of the interaction provide the parameters for the kind of conversational rules which the speakers will observe.

Interestingly, the first few words we utter can indicate much according to Sinclair and Coulthard's (1975) concept of orientation which assumes 'that we are forever signalling our orientation in our latent patterning and that the most important place to look for the signals is the first few words of an utterance.' If, for example, someone begins an utterance with 'Well, I never', you would be aware that the speaker's orientation is probably one of surprise or amazement.

Talk in literature

An author will make use of many of the talk features mentioned above in order to replicate or mimic real speech. However, they will adapt the features, otherwise the reader or audience might be at a loss to make sense of what is happening. Even in more experimental novels, when we are not sure who is speaking and about what – conversational mayhem is perhaps being recreated – there will be some ordering of speech, otherwise the reader might become totally lost.

Here is a brief summary of some of the main and obvious differences between crafted and real talk.

- Real speech is much more likely to have overlaps and interruptions; written speech would lose clarity if it had much of this. Even in a play there will be a limit to the naturalistic overlaps used.

- Real speech is influenced by the other speakers and listeners and can be modified to help them understand during the discourse. A written text is unchanging, with speakers having to ask for qualification or explanation on their turn.

- Real, spontaneous speech is rarely in completely Standard English, unlike written speech which is mainly standard for ease of communication with the reader, though of course it may replicate real speech with dialect forms and elisions, some hesitation and interruption, but these will probably be limited for readability. A dramatist might use dialect more freely, but using a broad Geordie accent and dialect words might limit the reach of the play as some audiences would not be able to follow the speech.

- Real speech does not contain full details of action and setting since the speakers are already aware of these. In this respect the context is a shared one; with a written text the context has to be imaginatively constructed by the writer. In a play the context can obviously be created visually as well as established through language.

- Real speech, especially in a transcript which is minus paralinguistics, is often difficult to interpret. In a novel, however, we can be privy to the thoughts and feelings of characters, either revealed through authorial comment as in a **third person narrative**: '"Ouch," she said *crossly*' or, 'spoken in a *hoarse shout*', or a longer section of description of a character's features and behaviour. In a play, the author can indicate preferred tone and actions in the stage directions and characters are often given lengthy self-revelationary speeches: unrealistic, but suiting the play's purpose.

Key terms

Third person narrative: this is when the author (or omniscient narrator) sees and knows everything, all actions and thoughts of the characters. The 'third person' is used: he wrote; she cycled; they danced.

Some final thoughts on graphology. Transcripts can be punctuated, or not, depending on the style of transcription. However, pauses are usually indicated and stressed words are often italicised. Overlaps and interruptions are indicated precisely where they occur by vertical lines. On the other hand, a novelist, poet or dramatist can be very exact about punctuation, the purpose of which is to convey the sense clearly. Some writers may ignore the traditional conventions of using inverted commas to indicate speech, or even separate short paragraphs for each speaker, but the text is usually laid out in such a way that we are aware of different speakers and their turns.

AQA Examiner's tip

- Provide evidence from texts to support your conclusions: it is not useful just to say that a character is very pompous in attitude without giving a brief example of how you reached that conclusion. Or to say that the speaker in a real piece of discourse is very surly in attitude without explaining how you assessed this. You must refer to the ways in which these attitudes and values are conveyed. Therefore, you need to look closely at the talk features in each text, and with a novel or poem to look at the supporting authorial comment and description.

- Remember it is a comparative question: the question is about comparing crafted and real language, so do not just do two separate analyses. You can organise the essay in several different ways, for example:
  - Introduction: refer to both texts with a brief overview of context and purpose.
  - Body of the essay: either deal with Text A first, working your way through points about context and purpose, attitudes and values, then handle Text B and make comparative points as you work your way through the analysis. Or the more sophisticated approach is to handle the texts alongside each other, so that when you deal with context and purpose, for example, you look at both extracts and compare them.
  - Conclusion: sum up the main comparative points.

- Do not forget to handle the *differences* between real and crafted talk in the given extracts. This is the heart of the question!

11 Sample extracts: some typical pairings

This chapter covers:

- a sample pairing with a commentary
- a second pairing for you to write about (hints are given).

Pairing 1

Here is an example of a pairing, followed by a commentary. This is not a model answer, but it takes you through the kind of thinking and analysis you would carry out.

The question

Compare the two texts, showing how they reflect differences and similarities between talk in life and talk in literature, including the relationship between context and purpose, and the ways in which speakers' attitudes and values are conveyed.

Text A

Context: two girls (B and C) and two boys (A and D) and, initially, their teacher (T) who leaves the room after briefly focusing the pupils on a task: to discuss Edwin Brock's poem 'Five ways to kill a man'.

Key
(.)	Short pause
(3)	Length of longer pause in seconds
<u>Underlining</u>	Stressed word or syllable
[	Overlap/interruption

T. Just – consider the first point about this – idea – of the <u>methods</u>
of killing a man [he made it cumbersome

A.   Yes [cumbersome

T. Have a think about that, I'll sit down

5 A. It's the listing of everything it makes it look as if you need so
many – things – [to   <u>kill</u> these [people

D.   [It's like

C.   [It's more
[like talking about [going to the supermarket

10 D. [It's like I said

B.   Yeh it [

C. And buying y – weeks [food not killing somebody –

B.   [Or <u>how to make</u> jam tarts or how to

C.   [Unless the pe…

15 B. buy make jam tarts [or something like that [

C.   unless [the people [are there

A.   [It all (.)
looks too difficult doesn't it, too much of the stuff to

B. He makes it sounds like it's so inconvenient y'know he
20 Could do this <u>but</u> he needs this, this, this and this [

A.   [In a way
I mean it it's it it <u>tells</u> you if you like how to kill
People but in a way it's – puttin' you off because

B. (*laugh*)

25 A. Y' know

c. Yeh hu

A. Y wouldn't particulluly go round collectin' English trees
An' men with bows and arrows an ⌐

B.   umph ⌊

30 D. Makes you seem how silly it is dunnit?

A. Yeh

B.   Yeah

A.   I don't think I could find a prince ⌐ anywhere

C.   ⌊ who said he wa…

35 A. With a castle to hold y' banquet in

B. Yeah

C. (*low laugh*) Says the many ways that people were killed ⌐

A.   very ⌊
cumbersome (3) well like he says it's a long list of
40 ingredients – how to make this fruit cake ⌐

B.   Yeh ⌊ (*laugh*) (*mumble*)
only he don't – fruit – it very quickly innit y'know – you think
wouldn't think he was talking about death

D. Killing people yeh

45 B. Mmmm he, you'd think he was saying oh you put the currants in
(mumbles) well ⌐ you huh

A.   ⌊ Yes down to Marks and Sparks for uh – for
ingredients for your cake

B. Yeah well s y'know (*mumbling, tails off*)

50 C.   Hah

A. It's a bit weird

B. It's a bit ⌐

C.   A ⌊ definitely a strange poem ⌐ (laugh)

B.   Yeh ⌊ yeha ⌐ a – a just

55 C.   ⌊ Not normal

B. Wonder what 'e was thinkin' of when 'e was writin' this (giggle)

A. In a way though it it's very – it's funny

B. ⌐ Yeah

C. ⌊ Yeh

60 A. In it ⌐ he makes a mockery ⌐

B.   ⌊ Yeh

D.   Yeh ⌊

A.   of all these various ways of ⌐

B.   Yeh ⌊

65 D. It's gone through 'istory annit like from – first one and –

A. That's right all the way.

Lines have been numbered for ease of reference; though will not be so
indicated in your examination text.

Text B

The following is taken from Patrick O'Brian's novel *The Surgeon's Mate*
written in 1979 and one of a series of novels set in the Royal Navy of the
early 1800s about the adventures of Captain Jack Aubrey and the ship's
surgeon Stephen Maturin. As a surgeon he is not part of the crew but
has accompanied Aubrey on many voyages as a personal friend as well as
intelligence agent.

Britain is at war with France and the Danish are, at this time, a belligerent power. At present they are sailing up the Baltic Sound between Sweden and Denmark in the warship Ariel, passing the site of Elsinore Castle where Shakespeare's tragedy *Hamlet* is set.

'Were you ever in Elsinore, Mr Jagiello?' asked Jack.

'Oh, many a time, sir,' said Jagiello, 'I know it well. I believe I could show you Hamlet's grave from here.'

'I was really wondering whether they were ten – or thirteen – inch mortars on the upper terrace,' said Jack, 'but I should be very happy to see Hamlet's grave as well.'

'Both ten and thirteen, sir. And if you go a little to the right from the furthest turret, there are some trees: and among those trees is the grave. You can just make out the rocks.'

'So there he lies,' said Jack, his telescope levelled. 'Well, well: we must all come to it. But it was a capital piece, capital. I never laughed so much in my life.'

'A capital piece indeed,' said Stephen, 'and I doubt I could have done much better myself. But, do you know, I have never in my own mind classed it among the comedies. Pray, did you read it recently?'

'I never read it at all,' said Jack. 'That is to say, not right through. No: I did something better than that – I acted in it. There, the upper terrace fires. I was a midshipman at the time.'

'What part did you play?'

Jack did not answer at once: he was watching for the fall, counting the seconds. At the twenty-eighth it came, well pitched up but wide to starboard. 'Port your helm, there,' he called, and then went on, 'I was one of the sexton's mates. There were seventeen of us, and we had real earth to dig, brought it from shore; it played Old Harry with the deck, but by God it was worth it. Lord, how we laughed! The carpenter was the sexton, and instead of going it in that tedious way about whose grave it was he made remarks about the ship's company. I was Ophelia too: that is to say, one of the Ophelias.'

Another salvo tore up the sea, true in line this time, but short: and as he watched Jack caught the flash of a single mortar. Again the line was true and he saw the shell soar to its height, soar until it was no more than a small black ball against the pale sky, then curve down, racing down, growing fast, to burst well astern. 'Judging from the height,' he said. 'I fancy they have reached their full elevation and their full charge.'

The next salvo confirmed his judgement; the last hundred yards had carried them beyond the battery's malice; and he suggested that they too should have breakfast. 'The smell of that fish is more than I can bear,' he said privately to Stephen.

At the breakfast-table, with a fine view of the narrows and the now silent Elsinore, Stephen said, 'So you were Ophelia in your youth Captain Aubrey.'

'A part of Ophelia. But in this case the part was greater than the whole: I was called back three times, and the other fellows were not called back at all, even the one that was drowned in a green dress with sprigs. Three times, upon my honour!'

'How did the poor young lady come to be divided up?'

'Why, there was only one midshipman in the flagship pretty enough for a girl, but his voice was broke and he could not keep in tune neither; so for the part where she has to sing, I put on a dress and

sang with my back to the audience. But neither of us was going
to be drowned and buried in real earth, Admiral or no Admiral, so
that part fell to a youngster who could not defend himself; and that
made three of us, do you see.' Jack smiled, his mind going back to
the West Indies, where the performance had taken place, and after a
while he sang:

> 'Young men will do't
> An they come to't
> By Cock they are to blame.'

'Yes, alas; and it all ended unhappy, as I recall.'

'So it did too, said Stephen, 'the pity of the world. I believe I shall
go upstairs again, if there is no more coffee left. I should be sorry to
miss any of the Baltic's wonders, they being, as you might say, some
compensation for all the grief there is by land.'

Commentary

General points

It is useful to have a brief introduction which summarises the main
and obvious differences. Text A is an unsupervised discussion in a
classroom between pupils who know each other and who are engaged in a
discussion about a poem. Text B is a novel extract designed to entertain,
further the plot and reveal character. It is obviously a much more
contrived and orderly piece of discourse with descriptive detail to help the
reader imagine the scene.

Hint: it is helpful to mention (very briefly) the differences initially, just to
establish that this is going to be a comparison.

Context and purpose

In Text A, the purpose is to discuss a poem and to provide practice for
the GCSE oral examination. A video is being made of the discussion; this
is likely to influence the behaviour of the pupils. However, they are in a
familiar classroom setting and the participants all know each other, so
we may expect a more relaxed, informal manner of speech, perhaps with
some use of technical terms since they are discussing poetry. There is
no teacher present, so any discussion has to be initiated by the students.
Therefore, we do not find the normal question, answer, feedback form
encountered in most classrooms.

The context in Text B is quite different: it is set on a warship near to a
hostile country and the dialogue is mostly between Captain Jack Aubrey
and the surgeon, Stephen Maturin, with some initial interaction between
the Captain and Jagiello. As professional men, the Captain and Maturin
might be expected to employ some elevated lexical choices and complex
structuring. Jack Aubrey, as Captain, would be spoken to deferentially.
Although Maturin is a friend and may address the captain directly, he still
has to adopt a respectful form of speech because they are on deck amongst
officers and crew. The discourse then would have to be reasonably formal.
As they are in a war situation, the reader might expect the dialogue
to be terse, so the surprisingly lengthy and humorous discussion of a
Shakespearian tragedy would intrigue and amuse the audience. It is crafted
for effect. The discussion of *Hamlet* mixed with talk of the enemy lends a
surreal air to the extract. The purpose of the text is to engage the reader's
interest and entertain them whilst providing some back-story to lend
realism and to reveal aspects of character in action.

Part of what is entertaining here is the comic element. The Captain is
under the impression that *Hamlet* is a comedy because he had such fun in
taking a part. Comedy, which counterbalances and lightens the tension of

their being fired at in enemy waters, is also subtly introduced in the belief by Jagiello that a character in a play can actually be buried in a real grave.

The humour takes on a different form when we learn that the Captain played Ophelia, one of three boys who portrayed different aspects of the character. We are reminded of the extreme youth of the midshipmen in Nelson's time with the account of bullying the youngest who was, in a comically literal interpretation of the role, to be actually buried. Readers are provided with the intriguing insight that entertaining the crew is an historical aspect of naval life, then as now.

So, the context and purpose in each case are very different. It is now useful to look in more detail at the texts and reflect on the way the interaction is structured, so that crafted and real talk can be compared. The following provides a far more detailed, blow-by-blow account than you would need in an examination. The analysis is rather mechanistic, but the detail might help you to see how much could be said about these extracts.

A more detailed look at the relationship between speakers, context and purpose

For Text A, the following points would provide you with notes and ideas which would then need to be reshaped and edited.

Look at the behaviour of the speaker A. At line 5 he makes an initiation:

> T. Have a think about that, I'll sit down
> A. It's the listing of everything it makes it look as if you need so many things to <u>kill</u> these | people.

The others bid for entry into the discourse but are blocked by A (6) who increases loudness 'kill these people' to drown them out. All are talking at once with considerable overlapping. B sets up a repetitive and loud (13) monologue about jam tarts but cannot get the initiative. A regains control at (17) by using a long pause as if he is about to summarise (much as a teacher would, to give feedback) but in actuality he has nothing to add to the discourse and, because he is floundering, he makes a statement which expects a response. Much of the discourse is dominated by a male speaker, but there is an element of competitiveness, a desire on the part of all the participants to be heard. As they are meant to be simulating an examination process they are all likely to be eager to contribute. The context is affecting behaviour.

An endorsement signals directly when speakers think they are on the same wavelength, which Stubbs (1983) believes indicates social solidarity, claiming that it is principally through conversational interaction that social roles are recognised and sustained. There is one at (3) and a second one at (66), both by the boy A:

> A. 'Yes [cumbersome'
> A. 'That's right all the way'

Spotting such features is the starting point in your essay. What is revealed here is far more important: they are cooperating and agreeing with each other. There is some convergence, in the form of echoing, which indicates that the speakers want to be aligned with each other's ideas.

From lines 51 and 52:

> A. It's a bit weird
> B. It's a bit [

These aspects of the discourse may be a conscious effort to be supportive, as this element is mentioned in the exam criteria. So the context and purpose are very important in influencing the course of the interaction. This supportiveness may also be a marker of real friendship or group solidarity.

An interesting example of such social solidarity is in the references to cake baking. Pupil A observes that the poet lists the things needed to kill a man (5). C picks up the idea and links it arbitrarily to a supermarket list (lines 8 and 9).

> c. 'It's more
>   like talking about [going to the supermarket

B tries to link it to a list of cake ingredients (13) and insists on this, cutting in by repetition. A eventually echoes the idea (39) by saying 'how to make this fruit cake'. B laboriously prolongs the idea (45) 'You'd think he was saying, "Oh you put the currants in,"' to which A responds with the ludicrous line, 'Yes down to Marks and Sparks for … ingredients for your cake.' The idea has nothing to do with ways of killing a man, bearing no relationship at all to the poem they are supposed to be talking about. Pupil D, hardly getting a word in anywhere does make an intelligent comment with: 'It's gone through 'istory annit.' (65).

In addition to the cooperation, there is an element of competitiveness in the interaction, which we mentioned above. But A is definitely dominant, with the others often falling into line with his viewpoints. For example, he declares that it is very funny and then B and C agree.

In comparison the interaction in Text B is orderly, beginning with a question from the Captain, and the discourse progresses mostly in adjacency pairs, although the topic of the play and the enemy artillery emplacement are interwoven. But the reader can understand what is happening because we are told details like 'his telescope levelled'. The writing is plain, however, and information about tone is limited to 'said' and 'asked' and the occasional detail such as 'Jack did not answer at once'. The action moves from the deck to the breakfast table and it is the Captain who initiates this move. Maturin has obviously been listening (politely) because he asks further about the acting and this leads into Jack holding the floor in an amusing way – explaining why and how he played Ophelia. The Captain dominates, as we might expect in the context.

Comparing the language used

In Text A there is quite a lot of non-standard English, as you would expect in actual speech, and between pupils who all know each other and so can freely use informal language. Dialect forms like 'dunnit' (30) and 'annit' (65); the omission of the aspirant ''istory' (65), elision 'y'know' (49) and cliché 'Marks and Sparks' are all features of informal spoken language, and there appears to be some regional accent in 'particulluly' and dialect grammar: 'Makes you seem how silly it is dunnit? (30) all reflecting how relaxed they are in their familiar environment and, presumably, with friends.

■ **Key terms**

Field-specific: this refers to a particular semantic field, such as language linked with war, or with flowers, or with horse-racing; words that are connected in meaning or range of reference.

Comparing this with the crafted piece, the language is more formal ('compensation'; 'I should be sorry to miss'; and **field-specific** ('salvo'; 'inch mortars'). The sentences are also mostly complete, which compares with the broken utterances and the overlaps in Text A. However, there is some mimicking of real speech in lines like 'I never read it at all', 'That is to say, not right through'. Here he reformulates which is a little like A in Text A when he says: 'In a way I mean it it's it it tells you if you like how to kill.' Such stuttering and repetition, however, would become tedious in the crafted piece. But the writer does make use of other talk features such as discourse markers ('So') and tag questions ('and that made three of us do you see') and deixis ('There, the upper terrace fires').

The speech characteristics or **argot** of the period are skilfully captured in several ways. For example, O'Brian captures the 'voice' of the 18th century by altering modern syntax: 'Port your helm, there', 'so there he lies'; using archaic lexis: 'Pray, did you read it recently?'; altering verb agreement: 'it all ended unhappy', 'his voice was broke'; and by using the additional prepositional use of 'up' in: 'How did the poor young lady come to be divided up?'

It would make decoding the text difficult had O'Brian decided to indicate dialect and accent, as Lawrence attempted in his plays and Emily Brontë with Joseph in *Wuthering Heights*. The author skilfully and aptly crafts the speech to create a convincing scene designed to entertain.

Attitudes and values

It is more difficult to extract the attitudes and values from the transcript, but we have already touched on this above. However, we can see by their comments and laughter that they find the topic weird and their attitude to the poem is one of disbelief that leads into possibly nervous joking. They mostly cooperate with each other, suggesting they have a positive attitude to the group social situation. There is much agreement: 'Yeh', 'Yeah', and they allow everyone to have a turn, although every time D voices a view he is usually interrupted or cut across, until near the end. The group's attitude to A is one of respect: he is allowed to dominate and there is some deferring to him. As to any deep-seated values being revealed, we would need to see more of the transcript to appreciate whether or not they really do get to grips with ideas of the poem. In this extract they seem amused and a little bewildered and there is little poetic analysis of the text taking place.

It is much easier to discern attitudes and values in the fictional piece. The characterisation of Captain Aubrey is well conveyed, revealing his attitudes. He is cheerful in the face of enemy fire and highly competent: guiding the ship, keeping a keen look-out and gauging the danger with a high degree of equanimity that suggests calm courage. His enthusiasm, even affection, for naval life and its lighter side is clear. His attitude to his men is one of friendliness, but the modes of address ('Sir') and the deference shown suggest that the naval hierarchy is clearly adhered to.

We learn also about the attitudes of Maturin whose deference and politeness is shown by the face-saving device: 'I have never in my own mind classed it among the comedies'. His tactful question about how recently the play had been read gains the response: 'I have never read it at all', which is downright funny in its disarming honesty. Clearly Aubrey is confident enough in his friendship to speak truthfully without the least show of overbearing authority.

Skilfully woven into this comic discourse is a contrasting unfolding of action, or exposition, as O'Brian details the threat posed by the Danish artillery bearing on the ship. This begins with a simple insertion: 'There, the terrace fires', the omnipotent novelist showing that Jack Aubrey is watching the battery. This is followed by a refusal to respond to Maturin's question: 'What part did you play?' This alerts the reader to the centre of Aubrey's consciousness and indicates he is preoccupied with the mortar shell. The second topic is expounded, the active verb 'tore' hinting at the danger in 'another salvo tore up the sea.' An order to evade is briskly given before the topic is 'straightway resumed'. Aubrey and the others are not at all intimidated by being fired upon. The novelist has shown us the danger; the characters, remarkably, make no comment, but then O'Brian is showing us their bravery under fire. This is the British Navy and the authorial attitude is clearly revealed: admiration for such coolness under fire. There is a sense of bravery and adventure associated with the navy.

> ■ **Key terms**
>
> **Argot:** special vocabulary used by a particular group and often not understood by outsiders.

Summary

Both texts are concerned with discussion of a work of literature, but their purposes and contexts are entirely different. The novel entertains us and provides some details about the characters and their attitudes, together with the authorial view. The transcript shows us a group discussion, with natural rather disjointed speech, very different from the crafted text. The purpose here is to discuss a poem, but this seems to be subverted to create a social event with only a modicum of analysis. It is more difficult to decode the transcript, but attitudes to each other are revealed through the discourse features and the roles the speakers seem to play. The crafted text has the advantage of giving the reader not just the polished dialogue, but explanatory detail and scene setting, which help us to draw conclusions about attitudes and values.

■ Pairing 2

■ Critical response activity

Here is a similar pairing in that the first extract is from an educational setting and the second piece is from a novel. Both texts deal with interactions between pupils and teachers. However, the first context (Text C) is from an English lesson where the teacher is very much in control, quite different from the previous Text A. Text D is an extract from *The Prime of Miss Jean Brodie* by Muriel Spark. These two extracts are shorter and more manageable than the previous pairing, more like the length you will see in the examination.

■ Compare the two texts, showing how they reflect differences and similarities between talk in life and talk in literature, including the relationship between context and purpose, and the ways in which speakers' attitudes and values are conveyed.

Read the following extracts through very carefully at least twice. Make a copy of each and annotate them, then write out your answer in full, remembering to compare and to handle those key points in the question; the link between the setting/context and the purpose of the talk and how attitudes and values are conveyed. Throughout your discussion highlight differences and similarities between the crafted extract and the real one.

There are some hints and questions at the end of the extracts to focus your thinking.

Text C

The following is a transcript of an English language lesson provided by Bill, a teacher working for Embassy CEL. This is an English for Foreign Students centre which teaches English as a second language.

> BILL. Hi everybody, good morning!
> CLASS. (*together*) Morning. Good morning.
> BILL. How are you today?
> CLASS. Fine
> BILL. The weather today? Mm, mm, or mm?
> (*He is putting his thumb up, sideways and down.*)
> FEMALE STUDENT. Awful.
> OTHER STUDENTS. Awful.
> (*Bill indicates with his hand that the students should try the pronunciation again.*)
> STUDENTS. Awful.

BILL. Ok. Look at my five faces.

(*He turns towards the whiteboard, where there are five yellow paper faces, each with a different expression, from happy to sad.*)

BILL. Number one.

(*He points at the top face.*)

BILL. Number five.

(*He points at the bottom face.*)

BILL. Awful. Which number?

(*He opens his hands wide.*)

CLASS. (*together*) Five.

BILL. How do you spell it?

CLASS. A, dou –

BILL. Ok. One person.

(*He points at a female student.*)

BILL. Go ahead.

STUDENT. A W F U L

(*Bill is writing the word on the whiteboard as she says it.*)

BILL. Ok. Pronunciation.

(*He puts his hand to his mouth and gestures outwards.*)

STUDENT. (*with a bit of an accent*) Awful.

BILL. Ok. Everybody say it. Speak!

(*He gestures to include everyone.*)

STUDENTS. Awful. Awful.

BILL. Very good? Or very bad?

STUDENTS. Very bad.

BILL. Ok.

(*He raises one finger.*)

BILL. One minute. With your partner, think …

(*He gestures to the faces.*)

BILL. Adjectives. Ok go!

Text D

This is an extract from the novel *The Prime of Miss Jean Brodie* by Muriel Spark and first published in 1963.

Six years previously, Miss Brodie had led her new class into the garden for a history lesson underneath the big elm. On the way through the school corridors they passed the Headmistress's study. The door was wide open, the room was empty.

'Little girls,' said Miss Brodie, 'come and observe this.'

They clustered round the open door while she pointed to a large poster pinned with drawing pins on the opposite wall within the room. It depicted a man's big face. Underneath were the words 'Safety First'.

'This is Stanley Baldwin who got in as Prime Minister and got out again ere long,' said Miss Brodie. 'Miss Mackay retains him on the wall because she believes in the slogan "Safety First." But Safety does not come first. Goodness, Truth and Beauty come first. Follow me.'

This was the first intimation, to the girls, of an odds between Miss Brodie and the rest of the teaching staff. Indeed, to some of them, it was the first time they had realized it was possible for people glued together in grown-up authority to differ at all. Taking inward note of this, and with an exhilarating feeling of being in on the faint smell of a row, without being endangered by it, they followed dangerous Miss Brodie into the secure shade of the elm.

Often, that sunny autumn, when the weather permitted, the small girls took their lessons on three benches arranged about the elm.

'Hold up your books,' said Miss Brodie quite often that autumn, 'prop them up in your hands, in case of intruders. If there are any intruders, we are doing our history lesson … our poetry … English grammar.'

The small girls held up their books with their eyes not on them but on Miss Brodie.

'Meantime I will tell you about my last summer holiday in Egypt … I will tell you about the care of the skin, and of the hands … about the Frenchman I met in the train to Biarritz … and I must tell you about the Italian paintings I saw. Who is the greatest Italian painter?'

'Leonardo da Vinci, Miss Brodie.'

'That is incorrect. The answer is Giotto, he is my favourite.'

Some days it seemed to Sandy that Miss Brodie's chest was flat, no bulges at all, but straight as her back. On other days her chest was breast-shaped and large, very noticeable, something for Sandy to sit and peer at through her tiny eyes while Miss Brodie on a day of lessons indoors stood erect, with her brown head held high, staring out of the window like Joan of Arc as she spoke.

'I have frequently told you, and the holidays just past have convinced me, that my prime truly has begun. One's prime is elusive. You little girls, when you grow up, must be on the alert to recognize your prime at whatever time of your life it may occur. You must then live it to the full. Mary, what have you got under your desk, what are you looking at?'

Mary sat lump-like and too stupid to invent something. She was too stupid even to tell a lie; she didn't know how to cover up.

'A comic, Miss Brodie,' she said.

'Do you mean a comedian, a droll?'

Everyone tittered.

'A comic paper,' said Mary.

'A comic paper, forsooth. How old are you?'

'Ten, ma'am.'

'You are too old for comic papers at ten. Give it to me.'

Miss Brodie looked at the coloured sheets. '*Tiger Tim's* forsooth,' she said, and threw it into the waste-paper basket. Perceiving all eyes upon it she lifted it out of the basket, tore it up beyond all redemption and put it back again.

'Attend to me girls. One's prime is the moment one was born for. Now that my prime has begun – Sandy, your attention is wandering. What have I been talking about?'

'Your prime, Miss Brodie.'

Hints

Here are some notes and questions that might help your thinking.

Purpose and context

Text C

What is Bill's aim in this lesson?

How does the context affect the purpose? (Think of the nature of the group and their level of expertise, and look at the language Bill uses, together with the visual aids.)

Text D

What are the contexts here and how do they affect Miss Brodie's behaviour and the behaviour of the girls? Our usual expectations of a teaching situation are subverted.

What do you think Miss Brodie's main aim is?

Look at the kinds of language used by Miss Brodie, her terms of address ('Little girls') and the way she turns every topic to her personal likes and dislikes and her own philosophy, and the descriptive detail given by the author to create the setting and mood. Miss Brodie dominates and the girls' eyes are not on their books but on her.

Moving to authorial purpose, can you discern Muriel Spark's interests and sympathies?

Remember that the crafted purpose includes creation of character and the sustaining of our interest in these characters and their relationships.

Attitudes and values

Text C

There is not much to go on here, but look at how purposeful and simply focused the lesson is. Also, look at how the teacher greets the class.

Are the students responsive?

Does Bill question them to draw them in?

What kind of lexis does he use?

Text D

There is much more to say on this extract.

What kind of a relationship does Miss Brodie have with the girls and the other staff? Look at her persuasive, dramatic approach and how her revelation of a different opinion from the head teacher is quietly shocking to the girls. Her language is direct and clear: there is no room for doubts in her statements.

How do we detect what the girls' attitudes are? Look at the authorial comment and Sandy's linking of her with Joan of Arc; also how Sandy obediently repeats back her key phrase about 'Your prime'.

Also, focus closely on the crafted language. For example, Miss Brodie's speeches dominate. There is some mimicking of adjacency pairs towards the end, but it is an orderly controlled interaction with Miss Brodie asking the questions and being imperative: 'Give it to me.' The lexis is a mixture of simple phrases like the previous order together with somewhat grand oratory: the tripling, for example, of 'Goodness, Truth and Beauty'. Also the formal register of 'Attend to me' and the use of the impersonal 'one' help to create the clear voice of this apparently charismatic character.

12 More examples of examination-type pairings

This chapter covers:

- another sample pairing with commentary

- two further examples for you to work through.

Pairing 3

These two texts are linked with education. The first text is similar to Text A in that students are practising for their GCSE examination. However, the second text is taken from a play.

The question

Compare the two texts, showing how they reflect differences and similarities between talk in life and talk in literature, including the relationship between context and purpose, and the ways in which speakers' attitudes and values are conveyed.

Text E

The following is a transcription of two 16-year-old girls discussing a short story by Doris Lessing: *Flight*. Their teacher had asked them to give evidence to support their views while exploring the meaning of the text. The teacher and their classmates watch them practising for their oral GCSE examination. They have a prompt sheet with questions they should address.

It is worth noting some of the paralinguistic features to assist analysis. Although their seats had been arranged so they could sit side-by-side, A has turned so she is facing her partner. Both smile often, sometimes to acknowledge points, sometimes in unison. A listens intently. There is constant eye contact. This is, of course, additional information which will help in the analysis – but it would be possible to draw conclusions without this extra detail.

Key

(4)   Length of pause in seconds

[Overlap/interruption

B.   I think the old man loves his birds.

A.   Umm I think he loves them because – he knows that they can't answer him back or betray him like his daughters have. His granddaughters have and he finds that – the birds are a place to retreat to because he knows the birds need him. They depend on him unlike his granddaughters.

B.   So …

A.   Dunno, where it says 'symbol' look.

B.   They – represent his granddaughters, yeh?

A.   Yes, yeah, in comparison with his granddaughters there.

B.   What about his favourite birds because I think his favourite birds are, what's it called represent Alice because – I dunno why – it's just the way he treats Alice because as if he's coveting her sort of thing isn't it?

A.   [Mmm

B.   [And, um, (4) I dunno, erm, he's coveting her he, he protects his birds his his favourite birds just as much as he protects Alice. (2) Yeh? Um – um – just (2) Talk to me Trace (*both girls laugh*)

72

A. Oh, um, (reading) 'How does the writer make his surroundings attractive?'

B. Oh

A. Um, ⌈umph

B.   ⌊I think really in the way he uses his language

    ⌈because

A. ⌊Oh

B. He just way he's describing it. He's just making it really nice and trying making it sound pretty and beautiful and ⌈er

A.   ⌊Yes

B. and that's the way he describes it really

A. Way he says 'The trees mark the course of the valley. A stream of rich green grass around' – it's as though – he gives it a bare, idyllic – erm – description in the places where there is perfection. Well it's just the language he uses really

B. ⌈Yeh

A. ⌊Places

B. and where he's describing er his granddaughter swinging under the – the tree, and er and her hair falling ⌈back

A.   ⌊Mm

B. Just making. It adds to, er, the beauty really, doesn't it? (1) Well, ⌈um

A.   ⌊Tuh

B. Well. And about the, it says here 'She's gazing past the pink flowers past the railway and cottage where they lived.' Sounds nice doesn't ⌈it?

A.   ⌊Mm mm well um

(reading)

Text F

Willy Russell's play *Educating Rita* is about a 26-year-old, unqualified, Liverpool hairdresser who enrols in an Open University course to better herself by gaining a university degree. The comedy centres on Rita's relationship with her tutor, Frank, a drunkard who has lost the will to teach, loathes his students and is disillusioned with academic study. As Frank already has, Rita will come to learn that knowledge of culture and art is worthless if an individual is unfulfilled. Rita has come to his study for interview but Frank is puzzled why anyone would give up their job to gain a degree.

Rita: Aren't you supposed to be interviewing me?

Frank: (*Looking at the drink*) Do I need to?

Rita: I talk too much, don't I? I know I talk a lot. I don't at home. I hardly ever talk when I'm there. But I don't often get the chance to talk to someone like you; to talk at you. D'you mind?

Frank: Would you be at all bothered if I did?

(*She shakes her head and then turns it into a nod.*)

I don't mind. (*He takes a sip of his drink.*)

Rita: What does assonance mean?

Frank: (*Half-spluttering*) What? (*He gives a short laugh.*)

Rita: Don't laugh at me.

Frank: No. Erm – assonance. Well, it's a form of rhyme. What's a – what's an example – erm –? Do you know Yeats?

Rita: The wine lodge?

Frank: Yeats the poet.

Rita: No.

Frank: Oh. Well – there's a Yeats poem called *The Wild Swans at Coole*. In it he rhymes the word 'swan' with the word 'stone'. There, you see, an example of assonance.

Rita: Oh. It means getting the rhyme wrong.

Frank: (*Looking at her and laughing*) I've never really looked at it like that. But yes, yes you could say it means getting the rhyme wrong, but purposefully, in order to achieve a certain effect.

Rita: Oh. (*There is a pause and she wanders round.*) There's loads I don't know.

Frank: And you want to know everything?

Rita: Yeh.

(*Frank nods and then takes her admission paper from his desk and looks at it.*)

Frank: What's your name?

Rita: (*Moving towards the bookcase*) Rita.

Commentary

General points

Text E is not a spontaneous discussion of a story, but a contrived situation for GCSE practice, with an audience of teacher and classmates. Text F is entirely different, an extract from a play designed to entertain and also to begin to establish the main characters for the audience.

Context and purpose

In Text E, the teacher and the whole class is present, but as the purpose of the talk is to provide practice in oral work all initiation has to come from the participants rather than from the teacher, so we do not find the normal 'question, answer, feedback' form encountered in most classrooms. The two participants are on friendly terms, the classroom is familiar and though they are being informally tested they are confident enough to move the furniture to suit their purposes.

In Text F, the setting is a familiar one for Frank: it is his place of work, a study in a university setting. It appears to be a first meeting between Rita and Frank and the purpose seems to be an interview. Our expectations, therefore, might be of some more formal encounter. But this is a play, designed to entertain, and our expectations are subverted. Rita appears confident and assertive and the encounter is amusing and, of course, begins to give the audience an idea of the characteristics of these main protagonists.

A more detailed look at the relationship between speakers, context and purpose

In Text E, A seems to be much more capable in her evaluations. For example, she is more elaborate in her explanations when, for example, she describes the birds as 'a place to retreat to' and that they 'depend' upon him. Her lexis is slightly more sophisticated than B who uses phrases like 'really nice' and 'pretty'. B, however, does use 'coveting' and repeats this when A has responded minimally to her question 'as if he's coveting her sort of thing isn't it?' Both participants use typical spoken discourse features such as tag questions ('yeh'), back-channel features

('Mmm'), and ellipses ('Way he says'). The register is a blend of informal lexis and typical talk features together with some striving after exactness, bearing in mind the purpose of the discussion.

A seems to take the lead and refer to the questions on the sheet and also to bring the discussion back to the text itself. However, the situation asks them to cooperate and this they do.

A's echoing of B:

> B. I think the old man loves his birds.
>
> A. Umm I think he loves …

is one of many attempts to support her friend, who often flounders.

A's acknowledgement of B's few points also serve a supportive role with simultaneous overlapping on eight occasions to indicate cooperative discourse.

> B. trying making it sound pretty and beautiful and ⌈ er
>
> A.   ⌊ Yes

In fact A signals approval with 'yes' or 'yeah' or 'mm' five times to B's once:

> A. Well it's just the language he uses really
>
> B. [Yeh

This may be because A is aware that B, less secure in her knowledge, needs more support.

In Text F, presumably the speakers have just met and this should be some kind of interview, so we might expect Frank to ask all the questions. There are a large number of these: nine in a short sequence, but what is unexpected is that more than half of these are from Rita and the usual question/answer sequence is ignored. This disruption of normal speech act 'rules' provides dramatic interest, foregrounding that Rita is so hungry for knowledge she is not at all disconcerted by Frank's superior academic status or by the interview context. Where most people would be nervous, Rita's desire to be taught is uppermost in her mind.

Frank's questions are all designed to find out what is puzzling him; why should an adult give up a job to pursue what he regards as a discredited endeavour? The first series of questions are unexpected for an interview schema, but this shows the audience how little Frank cares about formal interview procedures:

> *Rita*: Aren't you supposed to be interviewing me?
>
> *Frank*: *(Looking at the drink)* Do I need to?

The second refusal to engage reinforces this, but it also highlights that he is baffled by Rita's motivation and wants to find out something about her attitudes.

> *Rita*: … D'you mind?
>
> *Frank*: Would you be at all bothered if I did?

Her third direct question establishes at least two things: she is a persistent character and she is eager to get learning about poetry straight away since Frank is not interested in interviewing her. Rita has 'thrown' him and he laughs at this sudden topic change. Her eagerness to learn and her desire not to have her cherished hopes mocked are revealed in the bold imperative:

■   *Rita:* Don't laugh at me.

So, the purpose of the extract – to amuse, and to establish character – is well fulfilled here. Russell mimics many of the talk features seen in Text E: the use of a tag question ('I talk too much don't I?'), the **filled pauses** ('erm'), the use of exclamations ('Oh'), and the use of comment clauses ('you see'). However, there are no overlaps or muddled syntax which we see in the real talk. In Text E, for example, when B is trying to recall the word 'symbol' she says: '… what's it called represent Alice because – I dunno why – …' The dialogue in Text F is tidied up dialogue but it does effectively replicate some real speech features. However, as the dramatist needs to arouse an audience's curiosity, the creation of tension and intrigue is important. Even in this short extract our interest is engaged. This is initially achieved through the deliberate flouting of adjacency pairs for dramatic effect, creating a sense of conflict.

Attitudes and values

In Text E, both girls are focused on the task even though, as we have suggested, A seems more confident and possibly more knowledgeable than B. However, their attitude to each other is supportive and cooperative. A does not try to denigrate B's efforts, and B is allowed much of the floor. Their relationship is friendly and easygoing. A allows B to elaborate and express herself, but at one point this ends with B's admission that she is not very good at this kind of discourse when she says jokingly: 'Talk to me Trace' *(both girls laugh)*. Pragmatically, B knows she has made a mess of the explanation and she wants Trace to interrupt and 'dig her out of this hole'.

At other times B also reveals her lack of confidence and her uncertainty in assessing the story, indicated by the tag question here:

■   B. They – represent his granddaughters, yeh?

However, the girls are clearly helping each other: sharing, cooperating and supporting, and responding to the task as well as possible without the usual guiding intervention of a teacher.

In comparison, in Text F, there is more sense of sparring in the crafted text and on Rita's part an assertive, quite aggressive, tone revealed in declaratives like: 'Don't laugh at me.' Rita's attitude is one of a character who is eager to learn and she is fearless in her direct questioning: 'What does assonance mean?' and her initial, cheekily accusing 'Aren't you supposed to be interviewing me?'

Frank's response to Rita's question about assonance moves more closely to natural speech in its use of the filled pause 'erm' to give pause for thought, and the false start: 'What's a – what's an example …' in order to show his equilibrium has been upset. His attitude to Rita is one of bemused amazement. His role as an interviewer has been discarded and Rita leads the questioning.

Comedy derives from Rita mistaking the Irish poet W. B. Yeats for Yates' Wine Lodge, a pub: a sensible error given the **homophone**, but the joke does not hide Rita's lack of knowledge of a major poet. Frank's response in the following simple exchange is non-judgemental; though he has the knowledge she seeks, he does not denigrate her and this suggests he is, actually, a nice person:

Frank: … Do you know Yeats?

Rita: The wine lodge?

Frank: Yeats the poet.

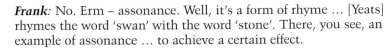

There might be proleptic irony here since Frank is a drunkard and disillusioned with the academic study of literature.

Frank explains assonance in the teaching form of: define the term, illustrate it, suggest what effects it has.

> **Frank**: No. Erm – assonance. Well, it's a form of rhyme … [Yeats] rhymes the word 'swan' with the word 'stone'. There, you see, an example of assonance … to achieve a certain effect.

Though Frank fails to give any suggestion as to what effect it actually has. Her insight 'getting the rhyme wrong' is naively perceptive. Rita's thought processes are quick and clear. Her hunger for knowledge and her value for education are revealed in this short extract.

Frank's penultimate question reveals his understanding of what drives her.

> **Frank**: And you want to know everything?

Rita is clearly ambitious whereas Frank is portrayed here through his gestures and **body language** as well as through his faltering words, as someone who is a little jaded ('Do I need to?', i.e. interview Rita) but someone who has not abandoned his teacherly ways. He realises he must take this potential student seriously and so the scene ends by moving back to the formalities of the interview.

So, the attitudes and values of the characters are revealed by the nature of the topics discussed and by the tone and lexis used. Russell's attitudes would seem to be favouring Rita and her desire for an education. In the final stage direction she is clearly and confidently looking at the bookcase and not behaving in a subservient way with Frank. She is a force to be reckoned with!

> ### Key terms
>
> **Body language:** gestures such as nodding or waving, or facial expressions. Body language can be used to indicate turn-taking in discourse: an inclination of the head or movement of the hand, or a direct gaze.

Summary

The context for each text is a place of study: in one case a classroom and in the crafted text an academic's study. The purpose of the real talk is to rehearse techniques of discussion: very different from the play's purpose. The play scene is a more intimate one, and has the purpose of providing the audience with humour and introducing the main characters. However, features of real talk are mimicked in the play to create realism, but they are tidied up and polished. The play also makes the audience think about the value of education, and presents us with two apparently different attitudes to acquiring knowledge: one jaded and one hungry. The attitudes and values in the transcript are simpler, there is no authorial control and through the lexis and the register used we appreciate the focus and concerns of the speakers and their supportive behaviour.

Pairing 4

Critical response activity

Text G is an exchange from a transcript of a door-to-door canvasser (C) for a company called Damp Detectors and a householder (H).

Text H is an extract from the play *The Dream of Peter Mann* (1960) by Bernard Cops.

- Compare the two texts, showing how they reflect differences and similarities between talk in life and literature, including the relationship between context and purpose, and the ways in which speakers' attitudes and values are conveyed.

There are some hints and questions at the end of the extracts to focus your thinking.

Text G

Key
(.) Pause

C. hello there (.) sorry to disturb you (.) don't worry I'm not trying to sell you any more windows (.) it's from the *Damp Detectors*

H. oh

C. probably seen our adverts in the local papers

H. yes I have

C. yeah (.) just in the area offering a free survey (.) a little electronic device (.) run it across your wall (.) and if we find any damp we advise you the best ways to get rid of it (.)

H. ah

C. takes five (.) ten minutes at the most

H. ah

C. we give ya a knock about this time tomorrow (.) are you usually around (.)

H. oh no (.) I'm not (.) er (.)

C. you're not

H. I'm not interested cos I've had most of it (.)

C. you've had it (.)

H. done

C. oh right

H. yeah

C. how long ago was that roughly (.)

H. about er (.) fifteen months (.) something like that (.) yeah

C. yeah (.) I mean (.) surveyors do recommend that (.) they have the survey done every year to eighteen months

H. yeah

C. I mean (.) we are in the area (.) it's free

H. no

C. I mean (.)

H. yeah (.)

C. we're already seeing twenty to thirty people

H. yeah

C. I mean is it better for you earlier on or later on

H. no (.) no it's (.)

C. no (.) not bothered

H. no

C. I'll leave you with that then (.) if any problems should occur just give us a ring

H. yes

C. and we'll pop round and see ya

H. yeah (.) yes okay sir

C. all right then

H. yes

C. thanks a lot then

H. yes (.) thank you

C. see ya

Text H

A MAN enters carring an umbrella and wearing glasses.

Man: *(To MR BUTCHER who is pulling[1] a chicken.)* Please can I have a tasty, ready for the plate, oven fresh, delicious chicken pie?

Mr Butcher: What did you say?

Man: Can I have an oven fresh, chilled, ready cooked chicken pie?

Mr Butcher: *(Brandishing knife.)* Get out of my shop before I mince you.

Man: *(Going to MR FISH.)* Don't they want customers?

Mr Fish: Can I help you? Lovely haddock? Beautiful flaky cod? Whiting? Fresh water trout? Beautiful Scotch salmon? Just been landed out of the sea.

Man: Fish? Yes! I would like, let me see – *(Consults note.)* Ah yes, a packet of frozen, ready prepared, and absolutely succulent, hygienically-sealed fish fingers, please.

Mr Fish: Did I hear you right?

Man: You should move with the times.

Mr Fish: I'll move you, you little eel.

Man: *(Rushing to MR GREEN.)* What's the matter with everyone here? They are all mad.

Mr Green: Lettuces are crisp today and radishes are juicy. Aubergines are lovely, mauve and sweet. Green peppers are hot and artichokes are cheap and fresh. What do you want? Some bananas? Oranges? Apples? Lemons? Nuts? Cabbages? Sprouts? Lovely fresh peas?

Man: Peas? Yes please. A packet of frozen peas please.

Mr Green: Would you mind repeating that?

Man: Packed foods save time.

Mr Green: Time for what?

Man: Why, time for – time for – what? Time for time of course. Now you're driving me as mad as yourself. Don't you see we haven't got time, that's why we live out of tins. You're all living in the past, everyone buys at the Superstores, that's why this market's dead.

Peter: That's what I told them. Join together, make more money.

Mr Green: *(Simultaneously with MRS BUTCHER and MRS FISH.)* All you make is trouble.

[1] preparing a fresh chicken for sale.

Hints

Here are some notes and questions that might help your thinking.

Context and purpose

Text G

C's purpose is to sell a service and this transaction takes place on the doorstep. Examine the ploys which C uses and look at how he adjusts his 'script' as he encounters difficulties. How does he finish the exchange?

How does the context affect the householder's reactions? Look at H's responses and the kinds of expressions used.

Text H

The context is also a selling situation, but the Man is subverting the attempts of the stallholders to sell him fresh produce. Are our expectations of a market scene being deliberately disrupted? What is the author's purpose here?

Look closely at the interaction and find similarities and differences between crafted and real speech.

Attitudes and values

Text G

What kind of language does C use? (Standard English, colloquialisms?) Does C vary his style, and if so, what is revealed about his attitudes to selling and to the customer? How persistent is he?

What do the householder's monosyllabic replies reveal?

Text H

What are the shopkeepers' reactions to Man's requests? (Look at the expressions and the actions.)

How is the audience meant to react to this scene?

What do you understand by Man's point about time?

Even from this short extract can you detect any authorial attitudes?

■ Pairing 5

■ Critical response activity

Text I is part of a conversation between two male university students, Liam and Jake. Louise was Jake's girlfriend.

Text J is a poem called *No, thank you, John* by Christina Rossetti (1830–94) in which a woman turns down a romance.

■ Compare the two texts, showing how they reflect differences and similarities between talk in life and literature, including the relationship between context and purpose, and the ways in which speakers' attitudes and values are conveyed.

Text I

Key
(.)   Micropause
(…)   Longer pause
[Overlapping speech

JAKE. I'd say girls are twenty-five per cent more arbitrary in their (.) in their role-choosing mechanisms than men (.) I'd say

LIAM. (*laughs*)

JAKE. erm (.)

LIAM. why do you think that (.) what do you think Louise felt about you

JAKE. I think she (.) no (.) I think she really liked me obviously (.) cos I'm great (.) but (.) no (.) I don't think she liked me for that long

LIAM. I think she did (.) like (.) like you (.) that's why I was quite surprised when she went out with you (.) and I was (.) like (.) hey (.) she must like you a lot (.)

JAKE. quite surprised were you

LIAM. yeah no (.) cos everyone was saying (.) everyone was saying behind your back (.) everyone was saying oh (.) she probably likes him but I doubt she'll go out with someone who lives in Reading

JAKE. he (.) he better want her loads (.)

LIAM. well precisely

JAKE. he better treat her well

LIAM. it's gotta mean something (.) then she went out with you and everyone was completely surprised (.) including Lynn (.) Lynn was very surprised (.) and she doesn't know you (.) ⌈ so

JAKE.   ⎹ erm

LIAM.   ⌊ and a bit
weird (.) as well (.) very weird

JAKE. but (.) erm (…) I think she liked me ⌈ and

LIAM.   ⌊ probably why she was so
distraught by you like (.) harshly dumping her

JAKE. thing is (.) when I was thinking whether we were a good couple etc

LIAM. yeah

JAKE. for the last few days the best things I (…) the best things (.) I thought the best the best things I thought (.) erm (.) of of of the last (…) in Butlins I realised (.) weren't things where I thought god she's impressive she's great fantastic (.) I wanna be with her (.) they were more things like (.) I like the way I can be a kind of boyfriend (.)

LIAM. well that's good ⌈too

JAKE.   ⌊which is good (.) no it's good (.) but
I don't mean it in a selfish way like oh I'm so great look at me

LIAM. no no relationships should always make you feel better about yourself (.) that's really the primary role (…) otherwise there's no point (.) apart from like (.)

JAKE. no no but no no (…) no it made me feel (.) procreation or whatever (.) good in like the actual role and like I felt like I could be comfortable (.) but I felt that (.)

LIAM. yeah

JAKE. it was more me than us (.)

LIAM. aah

Text J

No, thank you, John

I never said I loved you, John;
    Why will you tease me day by day,
And wax a weariness to think upon
    With always 'do' and 'pray'?

You know I never loved you, John;
    No fault of mine made me your toast:
Why will you haunt me with a face as wan
    As an hour-old ghost?

I dare say Meg or Moll would take
    Pity upon you if you'd ask:
And pray don't remain single for my sake
    Who can't perform that task.

I have no heart? – Perhaps I have not;
    But then you're mad to take offence
That I don't give you what I have not got:
    Use your own common sense.

Let bygones be bygones:
    Don't call me false, who owed not to be true:
I'd rather answer 'No' to fifty Johns
    Than answer 'Yes' to you.

Let's mar our pleasant days no more,
    Song-birds of passage, days of youth:
Catch at to-day, forget the days before;
    I'll wink at your untruth.

Let us strike hands as hearty friends;
    No more, no less; and friendship's good:
Only don't keep in view ulterior ends,
    And points not understood

In open treaty. Rise above
    Quibbles and shuffling off and on.
Here's friendship for you if you like; but love, –
    No, thank you, John.

Hints

The two genres are obviously very different, but the same comparative approach is needed whatever the literary format is. There is a speaking voice in the poem and distinctive attitudes and values are conveyed. So there is much to analyse and compare here.

Here are some notes and questions which might help your thinking.

Context and purpose

Text I

How well do these students know each other? (Look at the shared knowledge, the informal register, the humour.)

Is this an expressive interaction? Is it informational too? And phatic?

What role does Liam play?

Look at the kinds of lexis, the colloquialisms, the overlaps, the tone: all appropriate for the informal context.

Text J

This seems to be a clear message to John and the listener (us): both informative and expressive. There is no 'setting' as such, but the context is a situation where the female speaker is determined to let John know about her negative views.

What exactly does she point out to John?

Look at the language used and the structure of the poem, rhyming quatrains which have a jaunty rhythm. What effect do the rhyme and rhythm have on the tone? She sounds completely self-possessed and the organised structure with teasing rhythms serves her purpose well.

Of course, it is fictional. We cannot know if John existed and we can only speculate about the personae in the poem. But, part of its purpose is to engage our interest, to draw the listener in and face them with these declarations. The strong views make us reflect on the ending of relationships.

Attitudes and values

Text I

What does a phrase like 'arbitrary in their choosing mechanisms' tell us about Jake's attitudes?

By the end of the interaction (look at Jake's hesitancy and then his final simple declaration: 'it was more me than us'), do you have a clearer view of his approach to relationships? And a clearer assessment of his sensitivities?

Does Liam and Jake's use of colloquial lexis ('bit weird', 'fantastic', 'that long') reveal anything about their attitudes to the topic?

What view does Liam have about relationships? (Look at his lexis, for example 'harshly dumping her'.)

What kind of relationship and attitudes to each other do these two students have? (Look at the balance of turns, the back-channel features and the supportive comments.)

Text J

Look at the lexis and the many negatives which reinforce this very definite 'No'. The speaker's attitude is clearly conveyed by lexical choice. And in particular, look at the hurtful hyperbole: she would rather refuse 50 other Johns than say 'Yes' to him. She even admits she probably has no heart.

How does she describe John? There is a mixture of more elevated, although always simple and often monosyllabic language, for example 'wan', 'hour-old ghost', together with the more down-to-earth 'Meg or Moll would take pity on you'.

What is her attitude to friendship, love and honesty?

Look at how some of the phrasing mimics the real speaking voice: the clichéd 'Let bygones be bygones' and the possibly performative 'Here's friendship for you' in the final verse. Also, a comment clause like 'I dare say' is telling: it creates a speaking voice but also denotes a somewhat patronising tone.

Where do your sympathies lie at the end of the poem?

What values does it make you reflect on?

Approaching the examination

◩◩ Pairing 6

Sample question

Text A is an extract from a transcribed exchange between a pharmacist (P) and a female customer (C) who is asking advice about her cough.

Text B is an extract from the television script of a surreal comedy sketch (*Monty Python*) in which a customer is complaining to the shopkeeper that his recently purchased parrot is dead.

Compare the two texts, showing how they reflect differences and similarities between talk in life and talk in literature, including the relationship between context and purpose, and the ways in which speakers' attitudes and values are conveyed.

AQA specimen paper

Text A

Key

| (.) | Short pause | = Latched talk |
| (…) | Longer pause | [Overlapping speech |

P. good morning (.) can I help you

C. er (…) yes I a(..) was wondering if (…) you could give me some advice I've I've actually got quite a bad cough (.)

P. erm (.) how long have you had this cough

C. 'bout two days

P. 'bout two days (.) have you had a cold before or not

C. no =

P. = no =

C. = no =

P. = well what kind of cough is it a hard dry cough (.) or (…) d (…) are you getting (.) a lot of phlegm (.) or wha (.)t

C.   [no… it's a sort of hard dry cough with a sore throat

P. have you got a temperature (.)

C. I don't think so =

P. = you don't think so

C. no

P. but you've got a sore throat

C. yeah (.) yeah

P. erm (.) well what I would take (.) would be something like this erm (.) mentholated bronchial balsam (.) which

C.   [yes

P. is a cough suppressant (.) which stops the cough so

C.   [yes

P. that you don't have this irritation (.) but at the

C.   [yes

P.   same time it's also got in what we call guaithenesin (.)

C.   [yes

P.   which will liquefy any mucus which might be

C.   yeah

P.   (.) stuck (.) in the (.) bronchials (.) so that

C.   [yeah   [yeah   [yeah

P.   it's doing two jobs at once (.) if you want to take it in

C.   [yeah

P.   hot water it's also mentholated and it'll release some

C.   [yeah

P.   (.) y'know menthol (.) so that you'll clear your

C.   [yeah

P.   nasal passage..es (.) I would have thought that that

C.   [yeah

P.   sounded the right thing for you

Text B

Mr Praline walks into the shop carrying a dead parrot in a cage. He walks to the counter where the shopkeeper tries to hide below the cash register.

Praline: (JOHN)* Hello, I wish to register a complaint … Hello? Miss?

Shopkeeper: (MICHAEL)* What do you mean, miss?

Praline: Oh, I'm sorry, I have a cold. I wish to make a complaint.

Shopkeeper: Sorry we're closing for lunch.

Praline: Never mind that my lad, I wish to complain about this parrot what I purchased not half an hour ago from this very boutique.

Shopkeeper: Oh yes, the Norwegian blue. What's wrong with it?

Praline: I'll tell you what's wrong with it. It's dead, that's what's wrong with it.

Shopkeeper: No, no it's resting, look!

Praline: Look my lad, I know a dead parrot when I see one and I'm looking at one right now.

Shopkeeper: No, no sir, it's not dead. It's resting.

Praline: Resting?

Shopkeeper: Yeah, remarkable bird the Norwegian Blue, beautiful plumage, innit?

Praline: The plumage don't enter into it – it's stone dead.

Shopkeeper: No, no – it's just resting.

Praline: All right then, if it's resting I'll wake it up. (*shouts into cage*) Hello Polly! I've got a nice cuttlefish for you when you wake up, Polly Parrot!

Shopkeeper: (*jogging cage*) There it moved.

Praline: No he didn't. That was you pushing the cage.

Shopkeeper: I did not.

Praline: Yes, you did. (*takes parrot out of cage, shouts*) Hello Polly, Polly (*bangs it against counter*) Polly Parrot, wake up. Polly (*throw it into the air and lets it fall to the floor*) Now that's what I call a dead parrot.

Shopkeeper: No, no it's stunned.

> *Praline*: Look my lad, I've had just about enough of this. That parrot is definitely deceased. And when I bought it not half an hour ago, you assured me that its lack of movement was due to it being tired and shagged out after a long squawk.
>
> *Shopkeeper*: It's probably pining for the fiords.
>
> *Praline*: Pining for the fiords, what kind of talk is that? Look, why did it fall flat on its back the moment I got it home?
>
> *Shopkeeper*: The Norwegian Blue prefers kipping on its back. Beautiful bird, lovely plumage.
>
> *Praline*: Look, I took the liberty of examining that parrot, and I discovered that the only reason that it had been sitting on its perch in the first place was that it had been nailed there.
>
> * The names 'John' and 'Michael' refer to actors John Cleese and Michael Palin, who play the characters of Mr Praline and the shopkeeper.

Sample answer

The examiner's comments are shown alongside the essay, with a summary of the strengths and weaknesses at the end.

A clear start with some summary of purpose and context.	Text A is a transactional exchange between a pharmacist and a female customer presumably in a chemist's shop. The main purpose of the conversation is to sort out the customer's medical problem. In contrast, Text B may have the same shop setting, but its purpose is to entertain the audience. This is a comical sketch with a particular audience in mind.
Some sensible comments on the schema for A and our expectation, together with some evidence from the texts.	In Text A the pharmacist will obviously be the commanding figure, asking questions before coming to a conclusion. That is why at the start of the interaction the pharmacist asks 'how long have you had this cough' and 'have you had a cold before'. In this context the customer is the reactive figure, often answering with simple one-word answers like 'yes' or 'no'. The schema of a customer seeking help from a professional is what we might expect and this is, on the whole, a cooperative exchange with agreeable results.
A comparative approach: good! An awareness of the comic purpose shown. Mentions Grice usefully. Very clear about the difference in purpose. A useful comparative point.	In Text B, by contrast, our normal expectations of a transaction are subverted for comedic effect. The situation is absurd: a dead parrot is returned to the shop and Praline wants an explanation. This is not a cooperative exchange as the shopkeeper denies that the bird is dead and asserts it is only 'resting', he also veers away from the subject with ludicrous comments on its Norwegian blue plumage and says that it could be 'pining for the fjords'. The normal rules of successful conversation – Grice's maxim of relevance – are flouted hilariously. The purpose here is to entertain and so the shopkeeper is made to be very unhelpful and this is reflected in his speech. Immediately he is confrontational asking 'What do you mean, miss?' This contrasts with the pharmacist's 'How can I help you?'
Some simple talk features outlined, but not just feature-spotting: points are made. Rather a forced point about female talk: less convincing.	In Text A we see many non-fluency features which we would expect in such an interaction: repetition of I, I've; voiced and unvoiced pauses – erm. Also, there are phrases of encouragement such as 'yes', 'yeah'. The pharmacist often repeats back what the customer has said just to confirm the details and it shows also that they have been listening carefully – as we would expect. Such encouragement is often a feature of female talk and, of course, would be enhanced with paralinguistic features such as nodding. In contrast Text B has none of the non-fluency features or repetition. It is very focused on its purpose of providing

comedy and it moves swiftly to the final punch-line about the parrot being nailed to its perch.

The turn-taking and use of adjacency pairs also reveals differences between these texts. In Text B the turn-taking is equal between the two characters, although it is the customer who leads the exchanges, becoming more frustrated and annoyed by the replies. The adjacency pairs of question and answer are effective in creating the humour. For example, when Praline says 'Hello? Miss?' this allows the shopkeeper, who has been hiding, to respond with 'What do you mean, miss?' This series of interrogative sentences in response to each other makes the opening of the scene very dynamic. In opposition to this, the speech in everyday life is full of hesitations, repetitions and because of the nature of the transaction, mostly the pharmacist explaining about the medicine and the customer listening. Apart from the opening the balance of turns is uneven, whereas in the comic sketch we focus equally on both participants.

In Text B Praline's attitude is clearly one of rage and annoyance that he has been tricked into buying a dead parrot. This is shown when he says: 'It's dead, that's what's wrong with it.' The shopkeeper thinks he can trick Praline into thinking the parrot is 'resting'. This portrays that the shopkeeper believes Praline is quite ignorant and stupid. He does try to distract Praline with declarative sentences such as: 'remarkable bird, the Norwegian blue ... innit.' And the writer here mimics real speech with the tag question 'innit'. This attempted agenda-setting by the shopkeeper fails as Praline responds – again mimicking real, grammatically inaccurate speech: 'The plumage don't enter into it – it's stone dead.'

In contrast, in Text A the professional, questioning attitudes of the pharmacist are revealed by the slow explanation and the use of field specific lexis such as 'mentholated' and 'liquefy'. But the pharmacist does want to help and this is shown by the detailed explanation, but also with some convergence where she simplifies her lexis at times: 'stuck in the bronchials'. Compared with Text B we learn little about the speakers as individuals. The topic of conversation between the two speakers is purely to achieve the task of finding the right medicine for the customer. With the exception of the phatic utterance: 'good morning' the rest of the conversation is said in order to achieve the end result and the pharmacist acts professionally. It could, however, be said that maybe the customer becomes impatient with the long explanation because the back-channel noises change from yes to yeah and become more frequent, perhaps suggesting irritation.

Both of these texts highlight attitudes and values from the 1990s to today. Text A reflects the service we expect from people doing their job. The pharmacist is efficient, taking the woman's symptoms into account before recommending treatment. Text B highlights the service we wouldn't expect in order to add humour. The shopkeeper is very unhelpful and avoids the complaint, much to the anger of the customer. In this situation people would react angrily, which is demonstrated when the customer takes the parrot out of the cage and throws it into the air. All very surreal and crafted for comic effect.

In conclusion, Text A and Text B show great contrast in the ways that Text A is non-standard and the flow of conversation is disjointed, and in Text B the conversation is dynamic and humorous to appeal to the audience.

More on interactional features and a useful comparative approach.

A little laboured and less clear about the flouting of adjacency pairs. And 'dynamic' is not really explained.

Straightforward but apt points of comparison. More could have been said about, e.g. modes of address in B and the interesting mixture of the colloquial – 'kipped' – and the crafted, alliterative – 'definitely deceased.' Also, the actions, indicated by the stage directions: all part of the genre.

A detailed and clear account of attitudes, simply supported by textual references. Some good points about crafted talk

Some detailed explanations of attitudes in both texts.

A summing up of attitudes and values: fair points.

A better summing up for B than A, although the sense of 'dynamic' is unclear.

■ Examiner's summary

This is a very competent answer which sustains a comparative approach throughout. Fluency of expression varies and it is sometimes a little repetitive; nevertheless, it does look closely at the texts and explores the context and purpose well for each extract. There is more that could have been said about the humour and the crafted language in Text B but there is a very sound section on attitudes and values and an appreciation of how these are conveyed for both texts. The candidate is beginning to explore the texts confidently and this essay would deserve to be placed in the second-top band.

■ What kinds of extracts are likely to be in the examination?

Talk in life

Be prepared for anything from monologues and speeches to transcripts of formal interviews and informal discussions. As long as you have the 'tools' for analysis, you can handle any kind of extract.

Example 1

Here is an example of a sports report which is a transcribed commentary on a football match between Newcastle United and Derby County (BBC Radio Derby: Commentators GR and IH).

> **Key**
> (.)   Brief pause
> (..)   Pause
> (…)   Long pause

> GR. Here's Burton (.) on the ball for the first time (.) good pass up into the box. Darryl Powell there (.) goes to the by-line forces it back (*voice rises*) but cover is good (.) it is Charret and he knocks it away for Derby County's fourth corner (..) fifth corner (..) fifth corner of the game (.) all in the second half actually (..) Schoor is going to take the corner (.) Derby trail two-nil (..) here it comes (.) from the left hand side not good enough (.) it's headed out by Rob Lee (.) big chase back for Darryl Powell (.) nearly back to half way line (.) he gets it, played it to Prior (..) Prior is tackled very late (*voice rises*) that's free-kick and it might be a booking actually as well (..) Yes (.) Spencer Prior left on deck and that is Charrett (..) he's been booked for a late tackle on Spencer Prior Derby with the free-kick (.) twenty yards into the Newcastle half in the wide left channel (.) we must start counting down the time (.) there's just about eighteen minutes of regular time to go at St James's Park (..) the two goals (..) thirteen minutes Dabizas header (.) seventeen minutes Stephen Glass (.) a shot after a lovely move that started when Newcastle cleared a Derby free-kick in their own goalmouth (.) right down the field and Glass scored from it (..) tough few weeks for Derby County (.) let's see who's in town next Saturday (.) Manchester United (..) on the following Wednesday Arsenal and then Leeds United (.) Derby take the free-kick (.) it's up into the box it's headed down (*voice rises uncontrollably*) it's in the net (.) and I think Burton's turned it home (..) the header back was by Darryl Pov (…) by er (…) Paulo Wanchope back into the middle and bustling forward Dean Burton got a piece of it and sent it up into the roof of the net (..) it's Newcastle two (.) Derby County one

IH. Well it was a good free-kick er (…) nicely placed wasn't it (.) to the far post and Darryl er (…) Paulo Wanchope (.) who I think's improved in the air this season (.) just got up in classic style for goal scorer goal poacher it was a goal goal poacher's sort of goal just er (…) bustled the ball in off his chest or shoulder or certainly his body and just went into the (..) into (.) Newcastle (.) into the top of the net and er (…) Newcastle (.) I said a minute or two ago (.) I should like to see this defence under a bit of pressure (.) Newcastle's and er (…) well of its type a good goal although Newcastle defensively will be asking questions about it (.) particularly why Wanchope wasn't under greater challenge but did the job er (…) and Derby County right back in this game (..) I've been saying all along I think that if Derby can get a goal with this wind (.) it's a big influence this wind (..) they've started getting corners now and they've started getting parity in this game

GR. Newcastle two (.) Derby one (.) Dean Burton's first goal of the season and Newcastle kick it off again (.) we've had a bit of a delay while the referee was seeing something about the goal net over on that far side (..) flag up for offside here on er (…) Alan Shearer and that'll be a free-kick to Derby some fifteen to twenty yards inside their own half

IH. I'm pleased for Burton (.) he's played well at times in his corner at Derby (.) he hasn't got the goals he really ought to have done and it's drained his confidence a bit (..) it'll be interesting to see how he plays after he's scored now wasn't it and he er (…) certainly is a mobile sort of player and he's given Derby a bit since he came on

Critical response activity

- How does the context – a radio commentary, unscripted – affect what is said?
- What different roles do the commentators take?
- Look closely at the language used and highlight the main features.
- Reflect on how this choice of language reveals their attitudes and values.

Commentary

As this is a radio report, the commentators must describe everything in detail so that the listener can imagine the scene. The purpose is to give information, which is mostly done by GR, and to evaluate what is happening, which is the role of IH. The excitement of the match has also to be conveyed and we can imagine the rising pitch of GR's voice; we are told it 'rises uncontrollably'. The commentary is mostly in the present tense with active verbs, 'he knocks it away', but with some passive verbs to give variety, 'is tackled'. The typical field-specific lexis of a sports reporter is seen in phrases like 'goal poacher,' 'turned it home', 'into the box', 'got a piece of it'. The lexis is informal with IH more hesitant and using more hedges, but also IH uses more abstract lexis in his evaluations, for example 'parity' and 'influence'.

GR seems knowledgeable and he gives the audience some background information, but his approach is friendly with the use of first person plural ('we must start counting down the time'). IH has more pauses and hedges, but his attitude appears to be more critical of Newcastle than Derby, and he openly emphasises that he believes in Derby: 'I've been saying all along I think that if Derby can get a goal'.

There is obviously much more that could be said about this extract, including about the use of tag questions, the ellipses, the interesting mixture of colourful language (bustling) and down-to-earth simple phrases like 'a bit'.

Practical activity

Producing your own transcripts is really enjoyable and provides you with material to analyse. You could:

- interview a relative or friend – asking them, for example, about childhood memories, or views on a contemporary topic
- set up a discussion/debating group and allow everyone time to prepare thoughts on a chosen topic: anything from canned music to air travel to euthanasia. Remember always to get everyone's agreement to record the talk
- record an extract from a television programme: reality TV programmes can be very useful in providing you with ready-made fairly spontaneous talk. Or you could record a sports commentary, a political speech (from the daily transmissions from the House of Commons) or an extract from a discussion from breakfast television or any news magazine programme. *Question Time* is a useful source too.

The radio is rich in resources for transcripts, from discussions on Radio 2 to interviews and informal chats about music on Radio 1 and other digital channels. Get listening, recording and analysing.

Example 2

This has been chosen because it is a monologue and rather different from some of the earlier examples used. This is a transcribed account of a visit made by the speaker (Anna) and her aunt (Aunty Sheila) to the house where the aunt had spent her childhood. During the visit, Aunty Sheila was recognised by Anna's great uncle whom she had not seen since childhood. Anna is telling her women friends about the visit.

Key

[...]   Material has been omitted

-     Hyphen indicates incomplete word or utterance (e.g. was - I took my aunt)
.   Full stop indicates short pause
–   Dash indicates long pause

Ooh I didn't tell you about my trip to Derby did I?

Last weekend with Aunty Sheila and Jessie.

It was so funny.

This was - I took my aunt, my father's sister, really our only surviving relative that we know about, to Derby, because that's where she and my father grew up. [...]

And then just on the off-chance she took me to this little village called Fairfield.

Now my father always used to talk about Fairfield Hall where my great-grandfather lived when my dad was a child. [...] So we went to Fairfield, and we went to look for Fairfield Hall. [...]

And I'd pictured this great big house on top of a hill with a big gravel drive and it wasn't like that at all.

It was just a very very nice Georgian - very big Georgian country house with a relatively short gravel drive, and nothing - particularly like I'd imagined.

And we had a look, and thought it was very interesting,

and we were all getting back into the car, [...]

and Aunty Sheila said, 'Are you not going to knock on the door then?', and I said 'No. No, I don't think so'.

And then I thought - but then I thought, 'Hang on a minute – why not?', you know.

The worst that can happen is they could be really rude and slam the door shut and yell, 'Go away'.

So I said, 'OK let's go and see'. [...] So we walked up to the front door and I – I rang the bell,

and this man answered the door who was about my aunt's age,

and I said, 'I'm sorry to bother you but are there any members of the Lamb family still living here?',

and that was the family surname then, and he looked at me, and he said, 'Why do you ask?' and then he looked at my aunt and he said, 'Are you Tezhy?',

and Tezhy was her nickname as a little girl. It was short for Treasure, really obnoxious. You can imagine.

She – she was a little girl in the thirties with those silly dresses and a big bow on the side of them.

And this happens to be Bruno who's like a great uncle of mine. Bruno Skinner his name was.

And he recognised Aunty Sheila, and he said, 'Come in, come in', and he took us into the house. [...]

I just thought it was really strange to sit in this room in this house that had been in the family for like a hundred years, and to think that my dad had played there as a child,

and my grandfather and all these people - all these people who I've got photographs of,

and I've only heard about their lives through snatches of stories [...] and it was really really strange.

N.B. There is **no need** to comment on the transcriber's other uses of punctuation.

Critical response activity

- What is Anna's purpose in telling this story and what is the context (i.e. setting and audience)?
- Make a copy of the text, look closely at her expressions and annotate the text accordingly.
- Does Labov's narrative theory help us to analyse the text?
- How are Anna's attitudes and values conveyed?

Commentary

We are told that Anna is with a group of women friends, so it would seem that her aim is to amuse and interest them. The register is informal, and she begins with an exclamation and a tag question to arouse their interest. The audience, we assume, is attentive but this is very much a first-person account with much use of 'I thought' and 'I said'. There are the expected hesitations, ellipses and elisions, discourse markers, and all of the features we might expect in real talk. But she is telling a story, and Labov's theory helps us to appreciate the structure. She begins with the *abstract*, 'my trip to Derby' and the *orientation*, 'last weekend with Aunty Sheila; the *evaluation* or point of interest in the story, 'we went to look at Fairfield Hall'; the *narrative*, the details of the visit; and the *result*, the recognition of Bruno and his acknowledgement of Sheila; the *coda*, her reflections on the strangeness of it all.

Anna conveys her attitudes through excited exclamations together with many expressive and evaluative utterances such as 'very interesting', 'silly dresses', 'really strange'. Her sense of the contrast between her childhood memories and the reality of the house facing her are shown. Her nerve at knocking on the door suggests an attitude of confidence and a genuine curiosity and interest in the past and her own family history.

Talk in literature

Be prepared for extracts from any era and a range of genres.

The prose fiction extract could be from a pre 20th-century author such as Charles Dickens, Jane Austen, Thomas Hardy, etc. Or it might be from a more modern text such as a novel by Ian McEwan, Yann Martel or Khaled Hosseini. It could be any sub-genre from detective novel and thriller to a more epic tale. What the extracts will have in common is some 'talk' or 'dialogue' as part of the text.

Practical activity

- Make up your own opening to a short story which contains mostly dialogue, or find an extract from a short story which contains some dialogue. It needs to be at least 300 words long.
- Exchange extracts with another student who is not familiar with the piece you have written or chosen.
- Write a commentary about the extract you have been given, analysing how the situation affects the way the characters talk; how their talk differs from real talk, and what attitudes and values are revealed.
- Retrieve the commentary which has been produced about your chosen extract. Mark this and then feed back to the writer.

Writing your own extracts is enjoyable but also extremely useful at making you aware of how a writer crafts dialogue. You could also do this exercise with a play extract.

Similarly, a play extract could be from an 18th-century play like Goldsmith's *She Stoops to Conquer* or from a later dramatist like Ibsen or Shaw. More recent 20th-century writers could be anyone from Miller to Stoppard to Alan Bennett, Caryl Churchill or David Hare.

Poetry, too, could be from any era: the 19th-century dramatic monologues of Browning, the 20th-century verse of Sylvia Plath, or the more recent poetry of Derek Walcott or Carol Ann Duffy. Poetry is often written in the first person, as if the poet is speaking to the listener, but the poem chosen is likely to have a distinctive speaking voice and/or include dialogue.

Practical activity

Start to make your own collection of extracts which contain some dialogue. When you come across a poem or a section in a novel or play which contains dialogue that interests you, photocopy or copy out a short section. You will then have a selection of different pieces which you can use for analysis.

The more you read, the more you reflect, and the more you write about texts the easier such analysis becomes.

■ How will the examination be assessed?

There will be a mark scheme and examiners are given guidance about how to apply it, but there is no single right answer. Examiners have open minds and they are looking for well-argued, clearly-expressed essays, which use evidence to support their points; they do not have a prescriptive checklist. A Level examinations encourage individual, thinking responses.

■ Further reading

A good introduction to talk with plenty of examples to work through:

■ Cockcroft, S., *Living Language: Investigating Talk*, Hodder & Stoughton, 1999

An accessible text geared for A Level:

■ Pridham, F., *The Language of Conversation*, Routledge, 2001

A text from a series which emphasises practical exercises. Titles range from *Dialects* to *Sentence Structure*. This interesting one is on pragmatics. The intended audience is undergraduate level: a more challenging text:

■ Peccei, J. S., *Pragmatics*, Routledge, 1999

Another text geared more to the undergraduate market, but a useful reference source:

■ Brown, G. and Yule, G., *Discourse Analysis*, Cambridge University Press, 1983

A very readable and accessible general introduction to linguistics:

■ Hudson, R., *Invitation to Linguistics*, Blackwell, 2000

A very useful reference book:

■ Matthews, P. H., *Oxford Concise Dictionary of Linguistics*, Oxford University Press, 1997

An enjoyable text to dabble in:

■ Flavell, L. and R., *Dictionary of Idioms and their Origins*, Kyle Cathie Ltd, 2006

This unit covers:

- the study of literary texts by two of the writers included in the lists below, covering two of the three genres of prose, poetry and drama

- the creative transformation of two texts by these writers into different genres or sub-genres

- how to write a commentary that provides an insight into the process of writing and the table below the creative interplay between the base texts and the new texts.

■ Introduction

The coursework folder may contain *either* two free-standing transformations, each with its own commentary, *or* one combined transformation of two texts, together with a single commentary on the process of creating a transformation based on two linked texts.

- The total length of the transformation(s) must be between 1,500 and 2,500 words.

- The total length of the commentary(s) must be between 1,000 and 2,000 words.

It is important to note that if you decide to write two free-standing transformations, they do not need to be of equal length as long as the total length of the two pieces falls between 1,500 and 2,500 words. It does not follow that a relatively short transformation will provide less scope for a detailed and closely written commentary.

The writers whose works are studied must be drawn from the list in the table below.

Prose	Poetry	Drama
Jonathan Swift	Geoffrey Chaucer	William Shakespeare
Jane Austen	John Donne	Ben Jonson
The Brontës	Robert Browning	Aphra Behn
Thomas Hardy	Christina Rossetti	Henrik Ibsen
R. L. Stevenson	Emily Dickinson	Tennessee Williams
Kate Chopin	Edward Lear	Alan Bennett
P. G. Wodehouse	Wilfred Owen	Caryl Churchill
F. Scott Fitzgerald	John Betjeman	David Mamet
William Trevor	Grace Nicholls	Harold Pinter
Margaret Atwood	Seamus Heaney	Brian Friel
Angela Carter	U. A. Fanthorpe	Alan Ayckbourn
Hanif Kureishi	Benjamin Zephaniah	Tom Stoppard

In the case of poetry, a substantial body of work by the chosen poet must be selected, and this also applies to short stories by writers in the prose list. Texts written by the specified writers should be selected on the basis of their literary merit and their suitability for transformation into new texts, in accordance with the requirements for this unit.

How the unit will be assessed

This unit carries 40 per cent of the A2 marks and the breakdown of the individual Assessment Objectives is shown in the table below.

Assessment Objective	Descriptor	Percentage of A2 mark
AO2	Demonstrate detailed critical understanding in analysing the ways in which structure, form and language shape meanings in a range of spoken and written texts	10%
AO3	Use integrated approaches to explore relationships between texts, analysing and evaluating the significance of contextual factors in their production and reception	10%
AO4	Demonstrate expertise and creativity in using language appropriately for a variety of purposes and audiences, drawing on insights from linguistic and literary studies	20%

AO4 is assessed in the transformation(s) and AO2 and AO3 are assessed in the commentary(s). Although it might be tempting to focus your thinking on the transformation part of the task, you also need to think about the commentary element from the outset, as this carries the same assessment weighting as the transformation(s). You must avoid making the mistake of assuming that the commentary task is a bolt-on component that can be left until all the important work is done. In fact, good commentaries depend upon careful planning and note-making during the process of writing the transformation.

The coursework context gives you the opportunity to draft and redraft your work, just as the writer of the base texts that you work on was able to do. You will seriously undermine the effectiveness of your work if you do not show thoroughness in your drafting and proofreading skills.

14 Overview

This chapter covers:

- what a transformation is
- what a commentary is
- the role of the teacher.

▪ What is a transformation?

In one sense, any piece of writing in any form is a transformation of the ideas, memories, emotions, thoughts and activities that a writer has assimilated, created or experienced. The starting point may be a confused amalgam of incompatible or contradictory ingredients, and the task is to create written texts that select some of the raw material in the writer's mind and reject other material as unsuitable for, or irrelevant to, the task. Planning how to transform your material into a coherent narrative, description, reflection, plea, or whatever other purpose the writing needs to serve is clearly essential, and leads on to the next stage – getting the words onto paper, or a computer screen. This part of the process may well entail adjusting the original plan, and in this way improvements and refinements to the original conceptions will be a continuous part of the process from the initial idea to the submission of the final draft.

For the purposes of this unit, a transformation is more precisely defined in the AQA specification as a reworking of the original text(s) 'into a different genre or sub-genre'. For example, part of a novel written in the third person could be transformed into a series of linked poems in which two or three characters give their own distinctive first-person accounts of events and their reflections upon those events. A play might be transformed into a short story in which an omniscient narrator filters, edits and interprets the dialogue, and adds a texture of description and comment that guides the reader to particular evaluations of characters' words, actions and motives.

Successful transformations are based on thorough preparation. You need to study the texts you have chosen for your transformations, not merely skim read them to get the gist of what they are about. AQA's specification refers to the need to 'apply the knowledge, understanding and insights gained from literary and linguistic studies'. These words are as relevant to your study of texts for this unit as they are for those studied for the examination Units 1 and 3.

Examples of how to approach transformations of particular texts are given in Chapters 5–8 in Section B. In each case, suggestions are made about how you might approach your study of the original texts, and many of these suggestions can also be applied directly to other texts that you might choose to work with. However, it is important to understand that part of the point of this coursework unit is to give you the scope to be creative and imaginative and to apply what you have learnt about studying language and literature. The coursework unit provides a framework which is designed to set out a clear context within which you can write and reflect on the writing process but also to give you the freedom to be creative as a writer. For this reason, it is important to avoid giving you the idea that there are particular 'correct' ways of writing transformations and simple directions that you must follow. Instead, some examples covering a range of different approaches are offered in the hope that you will be inspired to adapt and apply them to the particular ideas that you will want to discuss with your teacher or lecturer as you embark on your own transformation writing.

Individual writers have their own preferred methods of working, and it would be unwise to try to impose one person's preferences on another.

Nevertheless, however they arrange the details of how, when and where they write, all successful writers think carefully about the process of planning and crafting their work, whether it is prose, poetry or drama, or any sub-genre within these broad categories.

In a radio interview with John Tusa, William Trevor, the Irish novelist and short-story writer, gives a useful insight into one writer's creative processes. The following is an unedited extract from this interview:

> ... when I use the expression 'raw material' it's really I'm talking about life itself. There it is, lots of things happening and lots of people. I have to gather up the stuff of that that I want. It's far too much, so that when I write the draft of a, a short story I think I'm going to write in this way. I think the point of the story is that. I think the characters are going to be five, six, seven and coming down to finish it, to actually complete that, everything changes, but you have to have something to change and that's all I mean by raw material. It's what I tell all the young writers who write to me and ask me how to, how they should do it, I do remind them that you, you need to have something as a kind of a jungle to make your way through and to find out what you want and what you don't want.

BBC Radio 3, *The John Tusa Interviews, www.bbc.co.uk*

In the case of your transformations for this unit, the raw material, as Trevor puts it, is given: it is there as the original work that you are going to transform. Your judgements about what to use from this raw material, and how to use it, are just as important to the success of the transformations as Trevor's judgements about the raw materials of 'life itself' are to the success of his short stories and novels.

As you write, you need to think about writing as a craft. It is not enough simply to have exciting ideas; those ideas need to be expressed by words that convey your intended meanings clearly, engagingly, effectively. Writing is a transaction between you and your audience – you have intentions and your readers have expectations. Where these two sides of the transaction are in harmony, effective communication can take place. As you write you make a series of choices that are intended to make the reader–writer transaction successful. In other words, you need to have a strategy – a method of selecting and arranging details that will convey your intended meanings.

Your strategy for writing transformations should include:

- being clear in your own mind about precisely what you are trying to achieve, and maintaining a sure focus on your central purpose
- creating a structure that will ensure a clear sense of direction or unity in your writing and coherence to ensure that the relationships between parts or sections serve that unity of purpose
- exercising judgement in the language choices you make: your choices of lexis and grammatical structures, and your awareness of their likely impact on readers
- drafting your writing, so that the process of composing and improving is recognised from beginning to end.

▪ What is a commentary?

In addition to your transformation, you have to provide a commentary which 'reflects upon [your] work, demonstrating greater understanding of the creative process,' according to the specification.

Your commentary should focus on explaining and evaluating some of the most significant decisions and choices you made as a writer in your transformation work. Weak commentaries tend to become bogged down in description and generalisation of the sort we see in the following sentence: 'I used mainly simple sentences so that the reader would be drawn into the action.'

Comments of this sort say almost nothing of value and are often inaccurate. Did the writer actually use 'mainly simple sentences', or were there short compound and complex sentences that the writer failed to describe accurately? (That is often so when candidates make this claim in their coursework commentaries.) Even if it is true that the candidate used 'mainly simple sentences', it seems very unlikely that they were the most important factor in 'drawing the reader into the action'. What other aspects of the writing helped to engage and sustain the reader's interest?

Instead of offering vague, generalised remarks, the commentary needs to explain the precise link between:

- the writer's intentions and language choices
- the effects which have (or have not) been achieved.

A good commentary needs to be precise and demonstrate the following qualities:

- a perceptive awareness of how structure, form and language shape meaning in the transformations
- systematic and informed comments on a range of salient features, including lexical choice and the use of grammatical structures and particular stylistic features
- clear and assured awareness of the creative interplay between the source text and the transformations
- an understanding of how the transformation achieves its own identity as a text that moves beyond the base text(s).

You should print out an early draft of your writing so that you have a record of the differences between your first attempts and the final submitted version. Using the 'track changes' function in your word-processing software will also create a record of your choices and improvements during the various stages of planning and writing. You will then be able to make specific points about the drafting process, including a discussion of changes made and the reasons for making them as you progressed from first to final draft. In many writing tasks, there is little need to keep early drafts (and word processing makes it easy to lose sight of anything but the final version), but keeping a record of the writing process for this transformation task will be invaluable as you plan and write your commentary.

Because you have a total of only 1,000–2,000 words available for your commentaries, you must be selective and concise in what you write. The following guidelines should be used not as a checklist to be applied slavishly but as a menu from which you select the items that are most appropriate to your transformations and the key decisions you made as a writer. In other words, an effective commentary must be tailored to the particular characteristics of your individual transformations and your judgements about what were the most significant aspects of the creative process. Your focus must be on the words of your transformation, and not on the planning process that went on inside your head before you put pen to paper, or finger to keyboard.

Your commentary will need a brief introduction so that you can establish the context of your transformation, including:

- the genre and sub-genre conventions, and the implications of your transformation choices (for example transforming an Elizabethan revenge tragedy into a 20th-century crime novel)
- the context of the transformation within the structure of the base text as a whole (for example the opening chapter of a novel, or the final scene of the third act of a play)
- the target audience, if the transformation is aimed at a group or sub-group that differs from that of the base text
- the purpose or rationale for transforming the base text in the way you have decided, which is inevitably closely related to your choice of genre/sub-genre forms.

It is worth stressing again that this introduction must be brief. The most valuable work will be done in the sections that follow, in which you will make specific points about the process of writing and the significance of the choices you made as a writer.

The role of the teacher

The partnership between you and your teacher or lecturer is important to your success in this unit. Remember that because this is coursework, your teachers will assess your work and the examination board, AQA, will moderate the marks awarded. This means that your teacher will apply AQA's assessment criteria carefully in order to ensure that you and your fellow students are awarded appropriate marks, but that those marks are subject to the approval of AQA's moderators, whose role is to ensure that the correct standards are applied to all students, irrespective of which school or college they attend.

Your teachers will have been trained to carry out assessments and it is important to listen carefully to the guidance they offer. They will, of course, want to give sound advice that will help you achieve the highest possible marks and it would be very unwise to reject that advice. You must also realise that there are limits to how much help your teacher is permitted to give. General guidance about how to approach the transformation tasks is entirely appropriate, as is more specific advice about how you might plan a task on particular texts that you are keen to work on. For example, your teacher is not able to take a draft of your work and make detailed and specific corrections, or to rewrite sentences for you. If your teacher reads your draft and makes comments such as the following, this is completely acceptable within the regulations for supervising coursework:

- 'There seem to be some inconsistencies of style in the dialogue between the main characters.'
- 'The narrative is developed clearly and effectively, although careful editing is needed to correct the frequent technical errors, especially in sentence punctuation.'
- 'The characterisation seems unconvincing in the concluding section. What might explain such a sudden about-turn in the protagonist's reaction to events?'

The actual writing must be your own unaided work and it is for you to apply recommendations and advice that your teachers offer. To sum up: the distinction in this unit between teachers as *advisers/assessors* and students as *writers* is essential to fair play to all.

Preparing to write the transformation and commentary

This chapter covers:

Using a style model

It is particularly important to have a clear sense of the genre characteristics both of your base text and your transformed text. For example, you could transform part of *Hamlet* into the genre of a 20th-century crime novel but you might (very sensibly) decide to use a particular author, such as Raymond Chandler or Peter Robinson, as a more specific style model within that broad genre of crime fiction. This more specific task provides you with a repertoire of stylistic techniques, including grammatical, lexical and structural characteristics. Far from being a restriction on your creative potential, the use of a specific style model provides an opportunity for creative adaptation and, successfully carried out, this is a route to the very highest marks. The use of a specific style model also gives you excellent opportunities in your commentary to show how and why particular linguistic adaptations from base text to transformed text have been carried out, and to discuss the likely impact of these adaptations on readers.

For transformations into non-fiction genres, style models are also an essential part of the planning and writing process. If you decide to create a transformation as a newspaper report or a magazine article, it is essential that you tailor your writing to the demands of a particular newspaper or magazine if your work is to appear authentic. A travel article for the *Guardian* or the *Telegraph*, for example, is likely to have been commissioned to a standard length of 1,250 or 2,500 words (the former being conveniently suitable for a single transformation for this unit) and there are also issues of house style which you should try to become familiar with. The *Guardian*'s current style guide is available online at www.guardian.co.uk/styleguide (click on the alphabet to see the various subjects that it covers). The 1928 edition, which provides interesting insights into changes of convention and taste over an 80-year period, can be found by performing a search on the internet.

It is a great mistake to think that it is easier to write in the style of a tabloid such as the *Sun* or the *Mirror* than for a paper like *The Times* or the *Independent*. Whichever paper you take as your style model, careful analysis of published pieces similar to the one you have in mind is essential preparation if your transformation is to succeed as a convincing and authentic piece of writing.

Preparing to write the commentary

In your commentary you will need to discuss selected, specific examples of the stylistic and structural decisions you make, together with some evaluation of the drafting process whereby you amended earlier choices in order to improve the clarity or the authenticity of what you adopted as your final draft.

Your comments might include a discussion of some of the following:

- your specific language choices, at the levels of lexis, grammar and phonology
- the creation of distinctive narrative voices, including through the use of dialogue

- the structure and organisation, such as differences between the base text and the transformed text, and between successive drafts of the transformed text
- how your sense of the target audience influenced decisions about the structure of your writing and specific judgements about lexical and grammatical choices
- an evaluation of your transformation, taking advantage of the opportunity to reappraise earlier decisions made as you were writing your final draft.

Do:

- make notes from the beginning of the transformation process so that you have a record of decisions, changes and your reasons for them
- write a selective linguistic analysis, using key concepts to illuminate your writing process
- select the most significant aspects of your transformation and comment on them succinctly
- focus on the text itself
- respond thoughtfully to the transformed text, focusing on the linguistic issues that you think are the most interesting and significant.

Do not:

- regard the commentary as something to be thought about after you have completed your transformation
- simply describe your transformed text
- write an account of your transformation which becomes a running commentary, sentence by sentence
- make anecdotal comments
- follow a checklist so that you write superficially about a large number of aspects of your transformation.

■ Plagiarism

Plagiarism is the attempt to pass off work that has been done by another person as your own. If you look up the word 'plagiarism' in a thesaurus you will find it in the company of these words: theft, forgery, falsification and counterfeit. Where plagiarism is detected in coursework or examination scripts it can lead to the disqualification of the candidate, not only from the examination in which the breach of regulations occurs, but also all other examinations taken at or around the same time.

The reason it is mentioned here is that a transformation must consist of a creative interplay between the base text and the newly crafted text. In the transformed text there may well be some direct quotation from the base text, but this would not constitute plagiarism as long as it is incorporated within a substantially new piece of writing which complies with the requirements for this unit as set out in the specification. Specifically, the transformation must be 'a different genre or sub-genre from the original work' and there must be a 'creative process' which is explored in the commentary that you have to write to accompany the transformation. As long as there is no attempt to misrepresent elements of the original as your own created text, there is no reason to avoid selective use of, for example, a piece of dialogue from the base text.

How much direct quotation in your transformation is allowed? It is impossible to give a short answer which applies to all possible

■ Key terms

Plagiarism: the uncredited or unauthorised copying or close imitation of another writer's words or ideas and passing them off as your own.

transformations that might be produced. The best general advice is to err on the side of caution and avoid any possibility that you might be thought to have used too much of the base text in an untransformed way. The other essential guidance is that you should discuss with your teacher the specific task you are working on and take advice on whether you are in danger of using too much of the untransformed language of the original. For example, it would not be acceptable to take from a novel a chapter consisting mainly of dialogue and submit that same dialogue – set out in the form of a play script – as your own creative transformation for this unit. Apart from not being within the spirit of the unit, such an approach would show only very low-level evidence of your own creativity.

The question of how far the boundary between plagiarism and creativity can become blurred is explored in a radio play by Jerome Vincent, *This Cold August Light*. In one scene, Vincent recreates a conversation between the author of *Frankenstein*, Mary Shelley, and Byron's doctor, John Polidori, who accompanied Byron and the Shelleys to Switzerland in the summer of 1817. Polidori has ambitions to be a writer but is frustrated and demoralised by his lack of progress. Mary Shelley tries to persuade him to rework one of Byron's abandoned stories, but after he retorts, 'I will not be a plagiarist Mary' she tries to encourage him:

> Aren't we all plagiarists in some form or another? Don't we take our stories from the world, steal from what's around us? Don't the stories already exist? Perhaps they are elements to be found in the air, in the cold air especially, in the grey summer of 1816, John. There are so many stories. Reach out and take one and if it happens to have passed through Byron's being first, then all the better! Don't we see with second-hand light anyway? Isn't light hiding all its colours waiting for a prism to refract it?

Jerome Vincent, This Cold August Light, *2008*

The point of this is to emphasise that plagiarism is essentially an act of dishonesty, but that transformation, while building on what another person has written, is an act of true creativity. In practice, most of us know the difference between the dishonest appropriation of what someone else has written and valid, creative transformation. Moderators and teachers are adept at placing work in one category or the other and, where necessary, using the internet to check the validity of a piece of work.

■ Published transformations

Who wrote the story of Troilus and his wooing of Cressida during the Trojan War? One answer to this question is Shakespeare. If we ask the same question but change the spelling of 'Cressida' to 'Criseyde', the answer is Chaucer. Shakespeare borrowed his plot from Chaucer, as well as other sources, but where did Chaucer get it from? He in turn had borrowed it from Boccaccio, the 14th-century Italian poet, who knew versions of the story from Greek mythology. It was referred to in different versions in many works of Greek literature, including the *Iliad* and the *Odyssey* by Homer. It can also be found in the works of the Roman poets, Virgil and Ovid. Many other English writers of Shakespeare's period also published versions of the story. The point is that in various ways, all surviving versions of the story of Troilus and Cressida are transformations from earlier sources. And the process continues.

There are prose and verse retellings and translations of Chaucer by David Wright, Neville Coghill and Peter Ackroyd, and there are innumerable adaptations of Shakespeare, ranging from the prose versions written for children by Charles and Mary Lamb to film versions that vary hugely in their faithfulness to the plays. *Macbeth*, for example, has been a favourite for adaptation and transformation.

For the plot, Shakespeare drew loosely on the historical account of King Macbeth of Scotland by the chronicler Raphael Holinshed. Shakespeare's play, in turn, has been transformed into an 1847 opera by Verdi, as well as numerous other musical versions. The first film version appeared in 1904 and at least 14 more film adaptations were released between then and 2006. Of these, some of the most adventurous are *Scotland, PA* (2001) which relocates the setting to Scotland, Pennsylvania and retells the story as a black comedy set with the unlikely backdrop of a hamburger stand.

Some film adaptations of Shakespeare's *Macbeth* include the following:

- *Maqbool* is the Indian film-maker Vishal Bhardwaji's *Macbeth*, a 2003 Hindi version set in the criminal underworld of Mumbai. It includes two corrupt cops who predict Maqbool's rise and fall, echoing the role of Shakespeare's three witches.
- *Macbeth 3000: This Time, It's Personal* is a Canadian film released in 2005 that transforms the story into a cross between the Shakespearian play and a James Bond 007 movie.
- *Macbeth*, directed by the Australian film-maker Geoffrey Wright, is a 2006 version which places the action against the backdrop of gang warfare in Melbourne.

Some literary transformations of *Macbeth* are as follows:

- *Light Thickens* is a 1982 Inspector Alleyn mystery novel by Ngaio Marsh, which concerns the five weeks of rehearsal for a London production of the play.
- *Wyrd Sisters* is a 1988 novel by Terry Pratchett, whose plot combines those of Macbeth and Hamlet. It is one of many novels set in the Discworld fantasy world.
- *MacBeth* is a 1999 Finnish comic book, adapted by Petri Hannini with artwork by Petri Hiltunen.
- *The Third Witch* is a 2001 novel by Rebecca Reisert, told from the point of view of one of the witches in the play.

■ Producing a successful transformation

Successful transformations are built on the foundations of thorough knowledge of the stimulus texts. You need to study the texts and respond in a range of ways, both with your head and your heart, because your transformation needs to show a creative interplay between the text that you read and the text that you write. In studying the base texts, it is well worth recording your responses and reactions in a notebook. You will find these notes a rich source of ideas when you come to review what you thought at previous stages of the planning and writing process and in writing the commentary.

Before you commit yourself to detailed preparatory work on your transformation texts there is one vital preliminary question you need to answer: do you have a genuine enthusiasm for each text that you have chosen to work with?

If the answer to that question is yes, these following questions will also be worth asking:

- What ideas does the base text convey to you?
- To what extent do you accept the writer's ideas; or do you challenge and reject them?
- What ideas of your own are stimulated or suggested by the text?
- What are your emotional responses to different episodes or situations in the stimulus text, and to the characters, and to the writer's language?
- What experiences of your own does the base text reawaken in you – perhaps parallel situations or memories of a person similar to those encountered in the base text?
- What ideas for transformations of the text do you find most engaging, and can you make these ideas engaging for your readers?

Remember that for this unit, a transformation is defined as a newly created written text that is based on an existing text or texts. It is not acceptable to use your base texts as the starting point for a journey into the creative unknown, in which the base text and the transformation have only the slightest connection with each other. The creative interplay that has been mentioned before entails a two-way relationship: the base text is a stimulus for the transformation text and the transformation text in some sense illuminates your understanding and appreciation of the base text.

Your literary base text may be adapted into any of a large number of non-literary forms, such as newspaper or magazine articles of various sorts. For example, you might decide to adapt part of a novel into a piece of travel writing. However, that decision is only the beginning of your planning. You need to know the travel-writing genre well enough to have a clear sense of how you are going to approach the writing. You may have read something by Bill Bryson, Tony Hawkes, Dervla Murphy or Paul Theroux, for example, and decided that you would like to base your transformation on the style and approach of one of them, or another travel writer whose work you enjoy.

- What are the characteristics of your chosen writer's style and approach?
- How could you use aspects of that style and approach in your transformation?

One possibility here would be to take an incident from a novel you have chosen as a base text and to ask the questions: What would Bryson, Hawkes, Murphy or Theroux make of this situation if they had happened to wander into the world of the novel on one of their travels? How would their characteristic views of the world and their characteristic writing styles have come into play if they had written about that situation in their next travel books?

■ Transformation in the form of a parody or a pastiche

Each of these approaches to writing transformations offers excellent opportunities for creativity within a clear framework. A parody is a work created to mock or poke fun at another work or at its subject and ideas by the use of humorous and satirical imitation. The real target of a parody is not necessarily a particular writer or book: the target may be the social context or the attitudes and values which are embodied by particular characters. In popular culture, parodies are often referred to as spoofs or lampoons.

A pastiche is an imitation of another writer's style and approach, usually light-hearted, but there can also be a harder edge of ridicule, mockery or satire. Pastiches can also reveal an underlying respect for the original writer's work, as is the case with Charlie Higson's *Young Bond* books and the *Star Wars* films that are based on traditional science-fiction stories. Even from the first appearance of Sir Arthur Conan Doyle's Sherlock Holmes stories, pastiches based on his detective have been popular. Tom Stoppard's *Rosencrantz and Guildenstern are Dead* is a pastiche of Shakespeare's *Hamlet*, and Robert Nye's *Falstaff* is a novel which takes Shakespeare's fictional character from *The Merry Wives of Windsor* and both parts of *Henry IV* and gives him the space and licence to tell his own life story:

> Everything the way I tell it, in the order I give it to you, none of your literature. When a man has scaled as many ramparts and breached as many maidenheads as I have, he doesn't need to make a sentence bob and curtsey.

Robert Nye, Falstaff, *1976*

An excellent way to sample pastiches is to read some of John Crace's pieces from the *Guardian*'s 'Digested Read' column. Each pastiche is about 500 words long and lampoons the style of authors, and often their attitudes and values too, by summarising their books. Crace deals with non-fiction as well as fiction and the pieces are available on the *Guardian* website and are also published by Guardian Books.

Each issue of *The Spectator* magazine has a competition in which readers are given a task that frequently involves writing a pastiche, typically of up to 150 words or 12 lines. For example, one competition invited readers to describe a visit to the opera at Glyndebourne or the music festival at Glastonbury in the style of an author of their choice. The winning entries for this competition were published on 6 September 2008 (your public library should have back copies) and the flavour of these is given in the following:

> Whanne that the summer shoures, lyke Noye's fludde,
> Turneth fayr fields of tentes to seas of mudde,
> And whanne the raine still bucket-wise downfalls
> Thanne longen folke to goon to festivalles,
> That they may wel disport themselves withal,
> At sexe and drugges, and eke with rockenrol.
> So with the yonge squires hied I me.
> As whilom Arthur did, to Glastonbury,
> To heare and see the famed minstrels playe
> Upon a stage two thousand yerd awaye.
> A wylde wyf ther was, Winehouse yclept,
> The whiche did singe, and as she sange she lept,
> Just when I came nye her playing-place,
> And so she struck her ellebowe to my face,
> That I did falle, and laye ther al forlorn.
> Methinks anon I shall try Glyndebourne.

Brian Murdoch in the style of Geoffrey Chaucer, The Spectator, *2008*

On attaining a low eminence, I beheld a sight that filled me with wonder. A veritable city of tents lay before me, and a multitude of voices was raised in songs of praise and gladness. I heard the words of a nativity hymn 'We will rock you' and divined that I was witnessing a Lovefeast of our brethren. A passing native of that place confirmed that these people spoke much of Love as the conqueror of War, adding that they were 'at it all the time'. The name of the place, he said, was Glastonbury, and I marvelled that that very centre of witchery and superstition was now become a citadel of goodness and truth. I would have fain joined them, but reminded myself that my task lay not with those already ardent for truth, but with those who remained in darkness; and so I rode on my way rejoicing.

Noel Petty in the style of John Wesley, The Spectator, *2008*

These are skilful pastiches, as will become apparent if you compare them with the original texts on which they are based:

■ Geoffrey Chaucer: the opening lines of the *General Prologue*.
■ John Wesley: *Journals*.

The word counts of the Geoffrey Chaucer and John Wesley transformations are 123 and 150 words respectively, which is about one-tenth of the length of each of the transformations that you will need to produce.

16   Advice and ideas

■ Writers on writing

The following comments reveal a range of opinions and attitudes about the process of writing. Writers are as individual and distinctive in their views as any other group of people and you will probably find that you are drawn more to some of these comments than to others. Think about each comment in turn and judge which of them seem to be most helpful to you as you prepare to write your own transformations.

■ To what extent are the different comments complementary?

■ To what extent are they contradictory?

■ Which comments seem to reflect your own attitudes to writing?

Laurence Sterne:

> Writing, when properly managed (as you may be sure I think mine is), is but a different name for conversation.

Sylvia Plath:

> And by the way, everything in life is writable about if you have the outgoing guts to do it, and the imagination to improvise. The worst enemy to creativity is self-doubt.

James Michener:

> I'm not a very good writer, but I'm an excellent rewriter.

Mark Twain:

> The time to begin writing an article is when you have finished it to your satisfaction. By that time you begin to clearly and logically perceive what it is you really want to say.

Anton Chekhov:

> Don't tell me the moon is shining; show me the glint of light on broken glass.

William Safire:

> If you reread your work, you will find on rereading that a great deal of repetition can be avoided by rereading and editing.

Jill Paton Walsh:

> A fiction is always, however obliquely, about the time and place in which it is written.

W. Somerset Maugham:

> A good style should show no signs of effort. What is written should seem a happy accident.

Robert Louis Stevenson:

> The difficulty of literature is not to write but to write what you mean.

Bill Bryson:

> Shakespeare didn't scruple to steal plots, dialogue, names and titles – whatever suited his purpose … [His] particular genius was to take an engaging notion and make it better yet.

■ **Practical activity**

Choose between three and five of the above quotations and apply them to a text you know well – perhaps one studied for GCSE or for the AS units on this course. Note down specific examples of how you think the writer has or has not applied or exemplified the advice given in your chosen quotations.

■ **Practical activity**

Select a piece of creative writing that you produced during your GCSE course and apply the same quotations that you selected for the previous activity to your own writing. If you were going to rewrite your work, what changes would you make and why?

Robert Peake:

> Emulation – as defined by a desire to imitate and transcend the spirit and tactical successes of works one admires – can actually enhance originality. So many poets are concerned about losing their voice, and so many poets and non-poets hold the misbelief that art can exist in a vacuum – or that inspiration strikes best in a sealed cave, cut off from tradition.

George Orwell:

> A scrupulous writer, in every sentence that he writes, will ask himself at least four questions, thus: 1. What am I trying to say? 2. What words will express it? 3. What image or idiom will make it clearer? 4. Is this image fresh enough to have an effect?

■ Other reading to help you to prepare

An extremely useful source of advice on particular literary and non-literary forms is the series of seven 24-page *How to write …* booklets published by the *Guardian* in 2008. The *Guardian* website gives you access to some of these materials if you are unable to get hold of the booklets themselves (see www.guardian.co.uk/books/series/howtowrite).

The seven booklets cover:

- plays and screenplays
- memoir and biographies
- books for children
- journalism
- fiction
- poetry
- comedy.

If you are likely to choose any of these genres or forms for your transformations (and it would be difficult not to be thinking about at least one of them), you are strongly recommended to read the relevant booklet. The booklets are brief enough to be read quickly and their sharp focus enables key points to be made clearly and directly. For example, the booklet *How to write fiction* discusses:

- where ideas come from
- genre
- research
- creating and developing characters
- place and atmosphere
- point of view, or narrative perspective
- advice on style.

Below is a list of other books that you might find helpful. All have useful advice to offer, but whichever books you read to prepare for the transformation work, make sure you build in reading time well before you start to write the transformations. Of course, internet research is useful as well: Wikipedia can be a helpful starting point, as long as you bear in mind that its editorial policy means that it is essential to verify via other sources any information you get from it. Also worth remembering is that Amazon's 'product description' sections on each book often provide a useful brief synopsis that may help you to decide if an unfamiliar text is one you may wish to investigate further.

- *What If?* by Anne Bernhays and Pamela Painter. Subtitled 'Writing Exercises for Fiction Writers', this book is highly recommended as a practical guide to developing writing skills and becoming a constructive critic of your own writing, and not just within the field of fiction. Even if you have time for nothing else, at least read the 30 pages of the chapter entitled 'Invention and Transformation'.

- *How to Read a Play* by Ronald Hayman. A director, actor and dramatist show how to use the play script to recreate a performance in your mind's eye.

- *The Art of Fiction* by David Lodge. Each of 50 short chapters uses an extract from a novel to focus on a particular aspect of the novelist's craft.

- *How Not to Write a Novel* by Sandra Newman and Howard Mittelmark. Subtitled '200 mistakes to avoid at all costs if you ever want to get published', this book is an entertaining survey of what can go wrong when aspiring writers do not think carefully enough about structure, characterisation, plot, dialogue and many other aspects of writing fiction.

- *1001 Books You Must Read Before You Die* edited by Peter Boxall. A reference book that gives a 300-word introduction to 1,001 novels that between them chart the development of the form from *Aesop's Fables* to the present day.

- *Exercises in Style* by Raymond Queneau. A simple story is retold 99 times in different forms and styles, ranging from Cockney speech to philosophical reflection: 99 transformations in 178 pages.

- *The Poem and the Journey* by Ruth Padel. Padel guides us through the reading of 60 poems, approaching each as a journey.

- *On Writing Well* by William Zinsser. An informal, friendly and humane exploration of how to write clearly and effectively.

- *The Ode Less Travelled* by Stephen Fry. In the words of the blurb, 'an idiot's guide to the writing of poetry', but there is much more to it than that.

17 Overview

■ One transformation or two?

In this section you are going to look at a range of examples of how you might use specific texts as your starting points for single transformations. There are also three examples of how you could produce a single transformation based on two texts. Although this is a more demanding task because you need to make sure that each of your base texts is fully represented in the transformation you create, it also allows you to develop your idea in a lengthier and more fully developed piece of writing, so there is a potential advantage in approaching your transformation writing in this way.

The decision about whether you write two freestanding transformations, which are between 1,500 and 2,500 words long in total, or a single combined transformation of that length, is a vital one. This decision will depend on your choice of texts, the transformation ideas you devise, and your assessment of which of the two approaches will show your writing and transformation skills at their best. You should probably keep your options open until you have discussed your own ideas and preferences with your supervising teacher(s). Many candidates are likely to opt for two freestanding transformations as the safer choice during the first year or two of this new specification, but there are pros and cons to each option and you will need to consider carefully which is the right choice for you. If you do attempt a combined transformation and it proves more difficult to create a successful new text, all of the marks awarded will reflect the quality of your combined transformation, and there will be no second chance. On the other hand, if you decide to write two freestanding transformations and the first turns out to be less successful than you had hoped, you will be able to learn lessons from that and produce a second transformation that avoids the pitfalls of the first.

■ The examples in this book

The examples of text transformations provided in this section deliberately avoid using an identical template for each one. This is to underline the fact that there is no single 'correct' way of approaching the transformation. One of the reasons for including coursework as part of AS and A2 English Language and Literature is to provide more opportunities for students to develop their own enthusiasms. You are able to do this by exercising individual choice of the texts you study, and coursework provides greater scope for creative and sustained writing responses. Neither of these benefits is available in traditional examinations. So, as you look at the examples of ways of working with different texts, you will see that the writers of this book have approached the task of introducing the texts and suggesting ways of planning and writing the transformations in different ways.

As well as offering a wide choice of texts and a broad range of valid approaches to transformation writing, this section of the final A2 unit provides a clear structure and guidelines that you must never lose sight of. Perhaps the most obvious constraints are the word limits for the transformation itself and the commentary. Although there will be no penalty in the form of a specific number of marks that will be deducted if your work falls short of, or exceeds, the upper and lower word counts, those word counts are important in setting the context for the tasks you undertake. Within the range of 1,500–2,500 words for the transformation(s) your teacher and AQA's moderator will be interested in how well you can fulfil your own intentions and AQA's requirements for the unit. If you write transformations totalling, say, 1,000 words, the lack of development will be self-penalising, and if you write a commentary of 3,000 words, the extra 1,000 words by which you exceed the upper guideline will not benefit you. It would clearly be unfair to candidates who comply with the guidelines if those who exceed it are given extra credit for failing to work within the structure that is set out clearly for all candidates to abide by.

It may be that you decide to work on one of the texts covered in the examples that follow, and the ideas within will help you to develop plans and approaches that will result in successful transformations. Or perhaps the ideas in the book will help you to come up with alternative or modified transformation approaches to the texts covered; that is also part of the book's aim. The most important thing to remember is that with some minor or major adaptations all of the ideas presented here could be applied to other texts.

■ The scope of your transformation

How much scope do you have for embarking on your transformations? In the list of prescribed authors there are 12 poets, 12 dramatists and 12 writers of prose. This equates to hundreds of novels, short stories and plays, and thousands of poems. Depending on your own wider reading, you will almost certainly know something about some of the writers on the list, and you may already have a shortlist of texts you are considering to use as base texts. Some of the texts discussed in the following sections will probably be new to you, but do not let that put you off. Some background information is provided that will enable you to start thinking about the ideas for transformations even if you have not yet read the books, and perhaps you will be encouraged to work on a text that is new to you. Whatever your choice(s), it is extremely important to read your chosen base texts closely and research their context so that you are well prepared when it comes to writing the transformation(s). Your teacher(s) will no doubt give you support and guidance as you come to make your decisions.

■ How your transformation will be assessed

Whichever texts you work on and whichever transformation ideas you settle on, make certain that you keep the Assessment Objectives for this unit firmly in sight (see the table below).

Assessment Objective	Descriptor	Percentage of A2 mark
AO2	Demonstrate detailed critical understanding in analysing the ways in which structure, form and language shape meanings in a range of spoken and written texts	Commentary
AO3	Use integrated approaches to explore relationships between texts, analysing and evaluating the significance of contextual factors in their production and reception	Commentary
AO4	Demonstrate expertise and creativity in using language appropriately for a variety of purposes and audiences, drawing on insights from linguistic and literary studies	Transformation

Remember too that you should think about the commentary at every stage of the planning and writing of the transformation, keeping notes to help you when you write the commentary after the transformation itself is complete.

As you are considering which base texts to use for your transformations, use the AO2, AO3 and AO4 criteria to focus on how other writers have embarked on the task of creating narrative, plot, character, mood, etc. The following activity illustrates the kind of approach you will be able to apply to your chosen base texts as you think about transformation opportunities.

Practical activity

Look at the following opening sentences which are all taken from texts that fall into the genre of crime writing:

- 'The boy's body sat propped against the graffiti-scarred wall in a ginnel off Market Street, head lolling forward, chin on chest, hands clutching his stomach.'
- 'On the morning Vera died I woke up very early.'
- 'It was a Thursday in December, the night that Debbie saw the killer.'
- 'I sat in the courtroom and watched Richard Moody get the bad news from the judge.'
- 'Long as had been my acquaintance with Sherlock Holmes, I had seldom heard him refer to his early life; and the only knowledge I ever gleaned of his family history sprang from the rare visits of his famous brother, Mycroft.'

1 Think about what each writer was trying to do in these opening sentences, and ask yourself whether they encourage you to read on. Why, or why not?

2 Think about the point in the narrative to which each of these openings takes us. What predictions can you make about how the story is likely to unfold?

3 Think about each writer's choice of lexis in these opening sentences. What expectations do these choices evoke in you? How do these choices place the story in a particular time and place?

4 Think about each writer's choice of syntax. What expectations do these choices evoke in you? How do these choices put the story in a particular time and place?

18 Prose transformations

This chapter covers:

- ideas for approaching transformations based on novels by Thomas Hardy

- ideas for approaching transformations based on novels by Margaret Atwood

- ideas for approaching transformations based on novels and short stories by Kate Chopin.

You can apply the approaches and critical response exercises in the transformations in this chapter to a wide variety of base texts.

1 Thomas Hardy

Thomas Hardy (1840–1928) was a poet, short-story writer and novelist writing from the last third of the 19th century through the first quarter of the 20th century. He grew up in Dorchester, Dorset, and trained as a church architect, but he gave up that profession to become a full-time writer. His novels are largely set in and around the area he loved – the countryside of Dorset, Devon, Somerset and Wiltshire – which he calls 'Wessex' in his novels.

Although his earlier novels were lighter in tone, they grew increasingly dark. His later novels show the changes which were affecting rural life in his time, such as the advent of more agricultural machinery, and his plots also show his belief in the impact of fate – often as a malicious force – on his characters.

Before you begin

Before you decide on how to do your transformation, you really need to think about the key features of the text you are transforming: your base text. Then you can decide how to use or adapt some of these in a different genre and format.

Remember that it is often helpful to think of the key features of a literary work under six headings:

- Plot
- Characterisation
- Themes
- Settings
- Mood/atmosphere
- Style

Plot

- In a Hardy novel the outcome is often tragic: in *The Return of the Native* and *The Mayor of Casterbridge*, for example, there are clear echoes of Shakespeare's tragedy *King Lear*.

- In novels by Hardy, the plot usually involves a sense of fate.

- The protagonist's downfall is also due to the character's own faults or mistakes.

- There is often an impact on the local community of the arrival of an outsider (for example Farfrae in *The Mayor of Casterbridge*) or of a returning local (for example Clym Yeobright in *The Return of the Native*).

Characterisation

- Those who compromise, or expect little, survive (for example Tamsin Yeobright in *The Return of the Native*, Elizabeth-Jane in *The Mayor of Casterbridge*).

Tragic heroes: the main characters in a tragedy, who have great qualities but also flaws which lead them to fall from prosperity to adversity and (usually) death.

Complex sentences: sentences which contain more than one clause, linked by subordinating conjunctions (words which join clauses in such a way that some clauses are dependent on others for meaning).

Intrusive commentary: the author interrupts the story to comment on, for example, the social background or related philosophical ideas.

Imagery: this refers to figurative language. An image or picture can be created by imagery, but it can also be created by plainer speaking: 'The grass is green.'

Accent: a form of pronunciation associated with a particular district.

AQA Examiner's tip

Remember to keep the required Assessment Objectives in mind all of the time you are planning and writing your transformation(s).

You need to show critical understanding in analysis of structure, form and meaning (AO2); to explore relationships between texts, evaluating the significance of context (AO3); and to demonstrate expertise and creativity in your use of language (AO4).

■ **Tragic heroes** or heroines (such as Eustacia Vye in *The Return of the Native*) have qualities greater than others but also flaws and failings which contribute to their destruction.

Themes

These include:

■ the malevolence of fate
■ social injustice
■ the problems of marital ties
■ the destructive power of money and of poverty
■ the impossibility of escaping one's past
■ the destructive power of organised religion
■ the impassivity of nature in the face of human suffering.

Setting

Hardy's settings are specific and usually based around the Wessex countryside. They often reflect the themes or mood, for example:

■ Egdon Heath: a stretch of wild natural landscape implacable to humankind
■ Casterbridge: a former Roman town which reminds us of the fall of past empires.

Mood/atmosphere

■ In Hardy's novels the mood is often gloomy, with a sense of impending disaster.
■ However, some of his earlier novels, such as *Under the Greenwood Tree* and *Far From the Madding Crowd*, have a lighter side.

Style

■ There are many **complex sentences** and Latinate words.
■ Hardy uses himself as an omniscient third-person narrator; he often gives an **intrusive commentary**, remarking on social attitudes or on the motives of his characters.
■ There is a strong use of **imagery** and of symbolism.
■ His creation of dialogue often includes representations of local dialect and **accent** features.

Choosing your genre

Remember that you are going to write in a different genre or sub-genre. Hardy's novels are prose fiction, so you need to decide on another genre, such as:

■ a speech given at a political meeting
■ a dramatic monologue
■ a sonnet or series of sonnets
■ a sermon
■ a descriptive poem
■ a radio documentary
■ a television soap-opera script.

You can choose almost anything, in fact, which is not prose fiction, and which does not simply act as an extension of the existing novel.

Transformation of part of *The Mayor of Casterbridge* into drama

The comments below should help you to think about any transformation of any text, but to make them more precise here is an example using a specific text: Hardy's novel *The Mayor of Casterbridge*.

Imagine that you decide to write a transformation which will show new insights into the clash between Farfrae and Henchard as businessmen. Farfrae and Henchard have very different views. When Henchard loses his business Farfrae becomes mayor because Farfrae is steadier and also because he, unlike Henchard, willingly uses new methods.

You could imagine Henchard and Farfrae in some comparable modern situation, where you reflect Farfrae's attitudes but use a style of English that suits the contemporary setting. For example, you could see a 21st-century Farfrae as keen to introduce new technology or new business methods, and you could write an extract from a play where the younger man confronts the older, warning of the consequences for his business if changes are not made.

Critical response activity

List all of the modern equivalents you can think of where a businessman (such as Henchard) needs to be more forward-thinking and might be overtaken by a more innovative competitor (such as Farfrae). For example:

- in introducing technology
- in introducing energy-saving ideas
- in redesigning the work premises
- in advertising techniques
- in keeping up with contemporary fashions.

Another idea could be to write a scene where a modern-day Farfrae confronts Henchard about his affair with Lucetta. Or you could imagine a confrontation between Susan and Lucetta about their different relationships with Henchard. You would then need to think about the style of your drama: it would be useful to look at works by a range of 20th- and 21st-century dramatists, especially those such as Tennessee Williams, Harold Pinter and David Mamet, who often depict confrontational exchanges. For example, how would Harold Pinter embark on a dialogue between Farfrae and Henchard?

In drama – especially (given your word count) what would inevitably be an extract from a play – you would need to convey the necessary context and background for your audience without spelling it out too obviously. This scene-setting technique is called exposition, and to see a deliberately comic example of how *not* to do it, you have only to read the opening scene of Tom Stoppard's play *The Real Inspector Hound*.

Transformation of part of *The Mayor of Casterbridge* into a political speech

Instead of transformation into drama, you could write a speech. For example, the speech which a modern-day Farfrae might give at a political party conference after being selected as a candidate for Casterbridge. To do this you would need to consider contemporary speech-making styles.

AQA Examiner's tip

Remember that you should look carefully at the novel, analysing the distinctive features of lexical and grammatical choices that are characteristic of individual speakers' 'voices', as well the attitudes and values that those speakers convey.

AQA Examiner's tip

Remember that you will write a much more successful transformation if you not only know your 'base text' very well but also research possible styles of the new genre that you want to use.

Practical activity

If you enter 'speech-making' into an internet search engine, you will find numerous sites to help you with technique.

You can also look up politicians' speeches on the internet, including speeches at party conferences.

Key terms

Rhetorical: to do with the art of persuasion and effect, especially in speech-making.

Alliteration: the use of the same consonant at the beginning of words close together, for emphasis.

AQA Examiner's tip

Your transformation needs to show knowledge of the base text, but you could well use your new genre to give your reader fresh insights into its ideas, themes and characters.

Let us apply the six key features to the idea of a formal political speech by Farfrae.

Plot

The term 'plot' is not really applicable here. Think instead about content:

■ What ideas or messages would Farfrae want to get across?

■ What promises would he be prepared to make to his electorate?

Characterisation

■ You would not have to introduce and describe a range of characters; but you would have to ensure that your speech reflected Farfrae's character as you have interpreted it from the novel.

Themes

■ Which of the novel's themes would it be appropriate for Farfrae to mention? For example, is he likely to suggest that fate affects the lives of himself and his constituents – or rather to feel that failure is due to foolish human error? How would he propose to improve the local economy?

Settings

■ This would not really need to be described, though Farfrae might want to make some reference to the importance of the occasion – and perhaps to the media.

Mood/atmosphere

■ Would Farfrae be jubilant or thoughtful? How would he want to present himself to the electorate?

■ Would this be likely to be a conciliatory speech or would he attack those with opposing views?

Style

■ How would Farfrae appeal both to his audience and to the television audience who might well see extracts from a party conference? What 'sound bites' might Farfrae introduce?

■ Any political speech delivered to a large and potentially national audience would need to take account of **rhetorical** techniques and devices such as:

  – triplets
  – **alliteration**
  – rhetorical questions
  – deliberate repetition
  – antithesis.

Starting to write

Any good orator knows the importance of gaining the attention of the audience straight away. How is your Farfrae going to do this? Remember to keep in character even though you may want a surprising or startling opening comment.

2 | Margaret Atwood

Margaret Atwood is a contemporary Canadian writer of poetry, novels and short stories. She also writes about the process of writing. She is an active feminist, and her writings reflect this, as well as her strong awareness of environmental issues. Because she has views (that are often controversial) about many aspects of modern life, her work presents readers with a variety of topics to consider.

Some themes of Atwood's novels are:

- consumerism
- nationalism/national identity
- power: its use and misuse
- gender stereotyping
- genetic engineering
- sexual abuse of children.

Before you begin

Whichever Atwood novel or short-story collection you are using as your base text, you will need to decide which issues she is most keen to present, and consider the means she uses to present them, including the fact that in works such as *The Handmaid's Tale* and *The Blind Assassin* she deliberately plays on the idea of fiction as a **construct**, and presents the reader with possible tantalising alternatives.

Her vision of the world is not always comfortable, and both *The Handmaid's Tale* and *Oryx and Crake* present **dystopias**.

Atwood herself – as well as literary critics reviewing her work – has commented upon her interest in **Gothic literature**, for example such aspects as the 'doppelganger' or double. This is also associated with her examination of identity. In *The Blind Assassin*, for example, one sister's apparent identity as author is taken over by the other. In *The Handmaid's Tale* the use of a double is more physically obvious: when Offred says, 'Doubled, I walk the street', we at first may think she means 'doubled over', but then find that she is walking alongside someone who is dressed to look exactly like her.

She is also inventive in the use of narrative voice, sometimes (as in *The Blind Assassin*) having more than one narrator, or (as in *The Handmaid's Tale*) a narrator whose identity we never discover.

Having a good grasp of Atwood's methods and style will help you to create a transformation which shows that you have the 'critical understanding in analysing the ways in which structure, form and language shape meaning' required by AO2, and will also enable you to write a much more focused commentary.

Choosing your genre

Let us look at *The Handmaid's Tale* as the base text for a possible transformation. To begin with, you need to identify the aspects of Atwood's writing which you think are most significant. You might consider the following:

- the creation of an 'inner voice' which tells Offred's story, especially in the chapter called 'Night'
- the imagery, especially of the garden

> ### Key terms
>
> **Construct:** something carefully shaped and created rather than naturally occurring.
>
> **Dystopias:** pictures of an unpleasant, harsh world (the opposite of a utopia, which envisages an earthly paradise).
>
> **Gothic literature:** a genre (particularly popular in the early 19th century) which combines aspects of horror, mystery and romance.

■ the use of colours

■ the juxtaposition of domestic scenes with scenes of violence

■ the juxtaposition of past and present

■ the use of Biblical references and quotations

■ links with real historical events, such as Nazism

■ the use of puns and other language play

■ the ending which subverts our view of the whole story.

Because *The Handmaid's Tale* is prose fiction, you cannot easily use prose fiction for your transformation. It is permissible to use a different sub-genre, but in practice that is likely to be a very demanding and risky way of creating a transformation and you might be better advised to think in terms of poetry or drama.

If you are studying poetry for your other base text, you may already have thought of some ways in which *The Handmaid's Tale* could be transformed. For example, Moira's story (Moira is a rebellious character in *The Handmaid's Tale*) could be written in a modern English version of a Chaucerian Canterbury Tale, or in a prologue such as that in 'The Wife of Bath's Tale'.

Transformation of part of *The Handmaid's Tale* into a monologue

If you are studying a drama text as your other base text, you may have thought about ways in which dramatic techniques could be used.

One dramatist whose work might lend itself as a model for a transformation could be Alan Bennett, whose *Talking Heads* and *Talking Heads 2* monologues offer a possible way of looking at some of the characters and events in *The Handmaid's Tale* in a new light.

Bennett wrote two series of six plays in his *Talking Heads* series for television, though they have since been performed on the radio and in the theatre. You can see these on DVD, which is a very good way of ensuring that you respond to them as drama and not just as words on a page.

Let us suppose that we decided to write a *Talking Heads*-style monologue with Serena Joy as the character.

What are the characteristics of a Bennett monologue?

■ One character gradually reveals himself or herself to us; there may well be a twist at the end.

■ The character may have a guilty secret.

■ The character is often self-deluding, seeing himself or herself in a light which the audience gradually comes to realise is different from the reality.

■ There is often a wry humour, though the character may not be conscious of it.

■ The character's comments and situation are often **ironic**.

■ The character speaks about his or her relationships with others; often these are failed relationships, though the character may not be fully aware of this.

■ Bennett often creates a very particular 'voice' for his character, with **idiosyncratic** ways of speaking.

Different dystopias

In order to ensure that your monologue for Serena Joy is a really creative transformation, and not simply an extension of the original novel, it would be a good idea to think of aspects of a different dystopia in which you could place her. Since Atwood has said that there is nothing in *The Handmaid's Tale* which has not, in essence, happened in real life, can you think of other regimes which exercise, or have exercised, strict control, especially over women?

Another way into a transformation would be to think of aspects of Serena Joy's situation which lend themselves to adaptation:

■ Her husband wants a child, and is prepared to use a woman other than his wife. An equivalent (though in a different political setting) could be a man who tells his infertile wife that the live-in au pair is prepared to have his child.

■ She is a former television star who knows that she is now crippled and getting old, and is no longer popular. An equivalent could be a former star, or media celebrity, who is embittered and does all she can to hurt a younger woman over whom she has control.

■ She relishes control, but knows that she has lost it over her husband; she controls her garden instead. An equivalent could be a modern TV gardening expert who finds consolation in her television career for the failure of her marriage and for her own infertility.

Characteristics

Although you want to transform the base text, you might find it useful to keep the physical characteristics of Serena Joy and some of her activities and preferences, as they are shown in *The Handmaid's Tale*. You could begin by skimming through the novel again (you will need to have studied it in some depth already before starting on your transformation) looking for details about Serena Joy. We know, for example, from the first part of the novel, that she:

■ walks with a limp, using a cane
■ smokes cigarettes (which are supposedly unavailable)
■ likes her garden
■ is blonde with hard blue eyes
■ wears lily-of-the-valley perfume.

Try to build up for yourself a complete picture – as far as Atwood allows it – of Serena Joy. Then decide which aspects you want to present in your character.

Structure

Now you have to think how to structure your monologue. To help you plan, it is useful to ask yourself some questions:

■ What do I want to have revealed about Serena Joy and her life by the end of the piece? Am I going to suggest something surprising about the character? Will Serena Joy be aware of how much she has revealed?

■ Where am I going to begin? How am I going to deal with the exposition – that is, the need to let the audience know who Serena Joy is, where and how she lives, etc. without being obvious and dull?

■ **Link**

For further help about avoiding an exposition that is too obvious, look back at p113 on transforming works by Thomas Hardy.

■ **Key terms**

Connotations: associated ideas suggested or implied by the words.

Secular: not to do with religion.

You will not want to start:

> My name's Serena Joy. Well, it isn't really, but that was my name when I appeared on television. I am now married to a powerful man and we live in a house with a garden which has red tulips in it and red is a significant colour in our country …

However, you may want to let your audience know all of these facts, or similar other background details, and you need to think of a natural way for them to come into her monologue.

Content and style

Then you need to decide what exactly it is that Serena Joy wants to talk about in the main section of the monologue. It is essential to plan the content of your work.

You will also need to consider which aspects of Atwood's style you are going to introduce:

■ You might want to try to emulate her word-play: for example, when Offred says 'I must compose myself' it is clear that she means both 'I must remain calm' and 'I must create the character they expect'.

■ You might want to introduce some Biblical references such as Atwood uses. Even the names of the cars she describes – Whirlwind, Chariot – have Biblical **connotations**.

If you have no Biblical knowledge yourself, you could introduce your own pattern of words and ideas with **secular** connotations. For example, you could include names to do with flowers, or television programmes, or authors – whatever would fit with the new context in which you place your transformation. Remember that you would then want to write about this in your commentary.

Atwood frequently writes using the present tense even when describing incidents which have been completed. You could use this technique to reflect her style.

■ Critical response activity

Read several pages of *The Handmaid's Tale* (at any point in the novel) and make a list of any stylistic features which particularly strike you.

Keep the list so that (a) when you write your transformation you can bear these points in mind; and (b) you can refer to them in your commentary.

Context

You also need to think about the context of your piece. Atwood places her Handmaid in a repressive regime which has developed after nuclear experiments have left many women infertile.

Although Atwood is considering contemporary problems, she is in fact setting her novel in the future – or in a kind of 'parallel society'. Will you transformation be set in a society where infertility is the result of human activity? What might be a contemporary situation? For example, many women nowadays have to undergo fertility treatment because they have delayed having children until their careers are established. Could this be an appropriate equivalent context?

Starting to write

So, once you have considered structure, content (or plot), style and context, you may well be ready to begin writing your script.

Now you must consider your opening and closing lines with particular care. You really want to engage your audience from the beginning and to enthral them at the end. Imagine the curtain going up, or the TV show starting: what are your character's opening words going to be?

3 Kate Chopin

Kate Chopin was an American novelist and short-story writer whose fiction explored what was, at the time, startling and dangerous territory: the need for women to assert their rights to emotional and intellectual independence in a society dominated by unquestioned notions of male superiority. By offending the conventional tastes and assumptions of polite society, Kate Chopin triggered the moral outrage of the social and literary establishment. Within five years of the publication of *The Awakening*, the book which killed her career, yet ironically the book for which she is best remembered, she was dead, aged 54.

Born Kate O'Flaherty in St Louis in 1851, of French and Irish ancestry, Chopin was mother to five sons and one daughter by the time she was 28. When her husband died in 1882 she ran the family cotton plantations, but in 1884, after an affair with a married man, she returned to St Louis to live with her mother. The following year her mother died too. Partly as a therapy to help her emerge from depression, but also to provide an income, her doctor encouraged her to write. Her reputation today rests mainly on *The Awakening*, published in 1899, and on her short stories. Even if you base your transformation on one of Kate Chopin's short stories, you should be aware of the devastating impact that the publication of *The Awakening* had on her life.

Background information

Opinions of *The Awakening*

These are extracts from reviews when the book was published in 1899:

- '[The novel] leaves one sick of human nature'
- 'it is not a healthy book'
- 'the purport of the story can hardly be described in language fit for publication'
- 'trite and sordid'.

Compare those with this response from an American reader almost 100 years later:

- 'This is my absolute favorite novel. I read it for the first time in high school, and have reread it several times since my initial engagement with Edna and her strength to decide not to be the woman society tells her she should be. Perhaps it is the writing and story that drew me in initially, but it is the message that keeps me going back to this book ... Kate Chopin's thoughts and words are amazing – a message many today need to appreciate, a message about women as strong individuals, not haphazard followers. *The Awakening* is incredible!'

The Awakening

The Awakening opens with Mr and Mrs Pontellier and their two small children on holiday on Grand Isle, a fashionable place for the wealthy.

Edna Pontellier becomes tired of the predictable routine in which her identity is defined by her roles as mother and wife. She feels that she has not yet really lived and that she must break out of these cloying constraints before it is too late. The following two short extracts from the opening chapter give the reader an insight into the relationship between Edna and her husband.

Extract 1

'What folly to bathe at such an hour in such heat!' exclaimed Mr. Pontellier. He himself had taken a plunge at daylight. That was why the morning seemed long to him.

'You are burnt beyond recognition,' he added, looking at his wife as one looks at a valuable piece of personal property, which had suffered some damage.

He yawned and stretched himself. Then he got up, saying he had half a mind to go over to Klein's hotel and play a game of billiards …

'Coming back to dinner?' his wife called after him. He halted a moment and shrugged his shoulders. He felt in his vest pocket; there was a ten-dollar bill there. He did not know; perhaps he would return for the early dinner and perhaps he would not. It all depended upon the company which he found over at Klein's and the size of 'the game'. He did not say this but she understood it, and laughed, nodding good-by to him.

Kate Chopin, The Awakening, *1899*

■ Critical response activity

The following questions may be used as discussion points if you are working with other students. If you are working on your own, you could use them either as triggers for making notes about the extract, or simply as raising issues that you think about as you study the extracts.

■ What is your impression of Mr Pontellier and his relationship with his wife?

■ What does Kate Chopin suggest about Mr Pontellier's attitude towards his wife in the following simile?

'[L]ooking at his wife as one looks at a valuable piece of personal property, which had suffered some damage'

■ Look again at Mr Pontellier's response to his wife's question about whether he will be coming to dinner: how is it that Edna is able to interpret his wordless actions as precisely as she does?

■ Does Kate Chopin write as a dispassionate observer or is it clear where her sympathies lie?

■ From what you have read in this section so far about Kate Chopin's personal and professional life, in what senses do you think Edna might experience 'awakenings' as the story unfolds?

■ What might be the dangers to Edna as well as the benefits that liberation might bring?

Compare this opening snapshot of the relationship between Edna and her husband with the following description of Edna with Robert Lebrun, with whom Edna had been bathing. He has joined his mother to stay on Grand Isle during the summer vacation and is a friend of the Pontellier family.

Extract 2

Her eyebrows were a shade darker than her hair. They were thick and almost horizontal, emphasising the depth of her eyes. She was handsome rather than beautiful. Her face was captivating by reason of a certain frankness of expression and a contradictory subtle play of features. Her manner was engaging …

In colouring he was not unlike his companion. A clean-shaven face made the resemblance more pronounced than it would otherwise have been. There rested no shadow of care upon his open countenance. His eyes gathered in and reflected the light and languor of the summer day.

Mrs Pontellier reached over for a palm-leaf fan that lay on the porch and began to fan herself, while Robert sent between his lips light puff from his cigarette. They chatted incessantly about the things around them, their amusing adventure out in the water – it had again assumed its entertaining aspect; about the wind, the trees, the people who had gone to the Cheniere; about the children playing croquet under the oaks, and the Farival twins, who were now performing the overture to 'The Poet and the Peasant'. Robert talked a good deal about himself. He was very young and did not know any better. Mrs Pontellier talked a little about herself for the same reason.

Each was interested in what the other said.

Kate Chopin, The Awakening, *1899*

Critical response activity

- How does the communication between Edna and Robert compare with that between Edna and her husband in the previous extract?
- How does Kate Chopin suggest that the relationship between Edna and Robert might have the potential to develop beyond a platonic friendship?
- What predictions do you think it might be safe to make about the quality of communication between Edna and her husband when he eventually returns from Klein's hotel? Look carefully at the third chapter to see how accurate your predictions are.
- Do the events of the third chapter make it seem more or less likely that Edna and Robert's relationship will develop further?

How might you use *The Awakening* as the basis for a transformation?

Kate Chopin is an omniscient narrator in this novel. She tells the story with full knowledge of the thoughts and feelings of all of her characters, as we see vividly in the final lines of Extract 1, in which she gives us an insight not only into the unspoken thoughts of Edna but also of Edna's interpretation of the unspoken thoughts of her husband as he makes only a non-verbal response to her question: 'Coming home to dinner?'

Later in the novel Edna says, as Robert is about to depart for Mexico: 'Write to me when you get there, won't you, Robert?' and he replies: 'I will, thank you. Good-by.' But no letters come, except for one from Robert to Mr Pontellier, which he refuses to allow Edna to see. A transformation could be built around the alternative scenario that Robert did write to Edna herself and that it was not intercepted by her husband. What might his letters have contained, and how would Edna have replied? How would their exchange of letters have affected the development of their relationship?

This sort of transformation moves us from a third-person omniscient narrator to dual first-person narrators. It is worth reflecting on what effect this will have on the unfolding of the alternative narrative direction:

■ The continuous sense of Kate Chopin's explanation and evaluation of the moral choices that her characters make is lost; they seem more autonomous and independent because they speak for themselves without Chopin's explicit authorial presence.

■ The decision to transform the novel by having Edna and Robert communicating by letter while they are hundreds of miles apart inevitably affects the development of their relationship. Apart, without any kind of direct communication, their feelings for each other may develop on the basis of each character's memories and wishes; separated from each other but communicating through the exchange of letters, their feelings for each other become more interactive, more dynamic, and the potential for each to declare feelings and plan futures becomes empowering for them.

■ The opportunity for creative interplay between the base text and your transformation empowers you. You have to consider a range of questions as you plan the new direction for Edna and Robert's relationship:

  – What does Robert write in his first letter to Edna? Does he maintain a polite distance or does he hint at his true feelings?

  – How does Edna reply? Does she keep him at arm's length or does she encourage him to become closer?

  – Do the letters cause greater emotional turmoil or do they allow Edna and Robert to arrive at a shared conclusion about what to do for the best?

  – Do Edna and Robert make decisions that produce a happy or a tragic outcome?

To sum up, this transformation would need to be based on detailed knowledge of, and reflection on, *The Awakening*. You would need to develop the relationship between Edna and Robert by creating the letters that each writes to the other, a form of narrative that differs markedly from that of an omniscient narrator, as used by Kate Chopin.

The short stories

Instead of working on part of *The Awakening* for your transformation, you might prefer to use one of Kate Chopin's short stories. Some that offer rich possibilities for transformations are suggested below, but the following section looks in more detail at the first two in this list:

■ 'Désirée's Baby'
■ 'The Story of an Hour'
■ 'Elizabeth Stock's One Story'
■ 'Lilacs'
■ 'At Chênière Caminada'
■ 'Athenaise'.

'Désirée's Baby'

Désirée was adopted by the childless Monsieur and Madame Valmondé, wealthy **Louisiana Creoles**, after being discovered abandoned as a baby at the gateway to their estate. Madame Valmondé saw the arrival of Désirée as the gift of 'a beneficent Providence to be the child of her affection'. When Désirée is 18 she is seen at the same gateway by Armand Augbinys, the heir to the estate of another wealthy Creole family. They appear devoted to each other and eventually Désirée gives birth to a baby boy. At first Armand is overjoyed, but by the time his son is three months old, Armand becomes distant and uncommunicative. It becomes apparent that there is something unusual about the baby: his skin colour is the same as that of the quadroon (one-quarter African) nursemaid.

Because Désirée was a foundling and her precise racial background is unknown, Armand immediately assumes that she is part black. **Miscegenation** was by no means uncommon, but racist attitudes in the Deep South meant that for some people it was a matter of shame. Madame Valmondé suggests that Désirée and the baby return to the Valmondé estate. Désirée asks Armand if he wants her and the baby to go. 'Yes, I want you to go,' he replies. Désirée then takes the baby and walks off into the backwater of a river. They are never seen again.

Later, Armand burns all of Désirée's belongings and the baby's cradle, as well as all of the letters that Désirée had sent him during their courtship. He also notices one written from his mother to his father that had slipped to the back of the drawer in which the other letters had been kept. He reads it and discovers these words: 'above all, night and day, I thank the good God for having so arranged our lives that our dear Armand will never know that his mother, who adores him, belongs to the race that is cursed with the brand of slavery.'

> **Key terms**
>
> **Miscegenation:** the mixing of different racial groups, by marriage or extramarital sexual relations; having children with a partner from outside of one's racially or ethnically defined group.

Critical response activity

Imagine that as time passes Armand Augbinys forces himself to confront the enormity of his actions towards his wife, and of the deep-seated racism within his own community that he had never questioned until he found the revelations contained in his mother's letter. Just as Michael Henchard in *The Mayor of Casterbridge* writes a will-cum-declaration of worthlessness, so Armand writes a private memoir which is to be given to members of his family on his death, and your task is to write this memoir-cum-confession. In it you will need to achieve a balance between his account of some of the key events of his life and his reflections on the moral decisions he made.

- What would Armand include in his memoir? Would he be more concerned with explaining his behaviour or apologising for it? Would he want to warn his kin of the poisonous consequences of racist attitudes or would he restrict his comments to his own private guilt?

- Would Armand's memoir be in the form of a letter addressed to named recipients or a personal statement not addressed to any particular individual?

- Is Armand an educated man or not? How would his style of writing reflect his background and his personality?

The Story of an Hour'

This short story describes Mrs Mallard's reaction to the news of her husband's death in a railway accident. The story ends with the discovery that he was not in fact on the train. As he arrives home, the shock of his reappearance causes his wife to utter a 'piercing cry' and she collapses and shortly after dies (of 'heart disease', as the doctors later claim). The story is not so much concerned with this device of a sudden plot reversal as with the psychology of the wife and her private response to the news that her husband is dead. In the story the only words she utters are:

■ 'free, free, free' (to herself in the privacy of her own room), repeated over and over, and 'Free, body and soul free!'

■ 'Go away. I am not making myself ill' (to her sister who is concerned for her safety and tries to persuade her to open the door).

Everything else we discover about Mrs Mallard is mediated through the authorial voice of Kate Chopin.

■ Critical response activity

Imagine that Robert Browning (or Alan Bennett in the style of *Talking Heads*) had known of the events which inspired this story and had given Mrs Mallard a voice in the form of a dramatic monologue. Your task is to transform 'The Story of an Hour' by adopting this form and creating a voice and a sustained and explicit account of her thoughts upon hearing of her husband's death in the train crash. In effect, this will allow Mrs Mallard to express in her own words the thoughts and feelings that Kate Chopin gives us at one remove, by means of such comments as: 'Her fancy was running riot along those days ahead of her' and 'She breathed a quick prayer that life might be long'.

■ What would be Mrs Mallard's thoughts and musings as she is alone in her room? You will need to base her thoughts on the hints about her relationship with her husband that Kate Chopin builds into her story. It seems likely that your characterisation of Mrs Mallard will incorporate reflections on their past and on her expectations about what the future without her husband will be like.

■ Should your transformation be in verse (like Browning) or prose (like Bennett)? A prose transformation would probably allow you to focus more on the voice and the thoughts of Mrs Mallard, and on controlling the structure of her self-revelation.

19 Poetry transformations

This chapter covers:

- ideas for approaching transformations based on poems by Robert Browning

- ideas for approaching transformations based on poems by John Betjeman

- ideas for approaching transformations based on poems by Seamus Heaney.

You can apply the approaches and critical response exercises in the transformations in this chapter to a wide variety of base texts.

1 Robert Browning

Robert Browning was one of Britain's most prominent Victorian poets. His writing still excites critical interest today due not only to his command of poetic form and language, but also because of the depth of psychological insight he offers on the characters in his poems. For the purposes of this A2 unit, you will need to study a number of works by your chosen poet in order to build a comprehensive critical understanding and subsequently create an assured and controlled transformation. Fortunately, Browning wrote a series of poems which share a generic link and in analysing the style and **characterisation** techniques he employs in all of these cases you can apply your informed understanding to one text for the eventual transformation.

Robert Browning was a leading exponent of the dramatic monologue form. This is a useful genre of poetry to study for this unit because of its clear conventions.

Background information

Dramatic monologues

- These poems are narrated by one character to an unseen audience. The readers themselves are treated almost as a jury who are invited to pass judgement on the speaker.

- Very often Browning's narrators are real people from history (or are involved in specific historical events), and they offer their thoughts at crucial moments in their lives.

- The monologue itself, while coming from only one moment in time, contains enough evidence (or as much as Browning decides is necessary) to explain the whole of the event it is a part of.

- The character is an eloquent speaker with an elevated command of language; this makes any infelicities or mis-steps in expression notable.

- Dramatic monologues are often written in blank verse form, using iambic pentameter due to its closeness to normal speech in its rhythmic patterns. However, some of Browning's monologues feature rhyme schemes as well.

- One of the key aspects of the form is the narrator's apparently unwitting revelation of character. There are two different voices at work in the poems: the speakers who relate events and feelings (which they think are completely reasonable and explicable) to the audience, and the poet who is revealing and commenting on other aspects of the character by implying that what the narrator claims to be true about their behaviour is probably otherwise.

Within the dramatic monologue form there is scope for a poet to exploit a range of these conventions; Browning certainly employs a variety of different devices. Some of his key poems you could choose to study are:

- ■ *My Last Duchess*
- ■ *Porphyria's Lover*
- ■ *Soliloquy Of The Spanish Cloister*
- ■ *Johannes Agricola In Meditation*
- ■ *Fra Lippo Lippi*
- ■ *Andrea Del Sarto*
- ■ *The Bishop Orders His Tomb*
- ■ *The Laboratory*.

■ Critical response activity

While studying each poem, create a character study of each narrator. For each point, provide a few quotations in support:

- ■ How would they like their characters to appear to observers?
- ■ How do they actually present their characters?
- ■ What things in life do they value?
- ■ For what things in their lives do they have disdain?
- ■ Who is it that they disapprove of? Why?
- ■ What do they do in order to achieve their goals?
- ■ What kind of language do they use? Is there any noticeable shift in lexis or register as the poem progresses? If so, what effect does it have on your attitude towards them?

Focusing on Browning's style, also note:

- ■ Which words does Browning highlight? What techniques does he use to do so?
- ■ Are there any other obvious poetic or figurative methods used (**enjambement**, alliteration, **assonance**, simile or metaphor)? What is their effect on your approach to the character?
- ■ How does Browning arrange his verse? Is the metre regular throughout? Does the superficial appearance of the poem confirm or contradict the narrator's character?

■ Key terms

Enjambement: the continuation of a phrase or unit of meaning from one line to the next without a break in a poem.

Assonance: the repetition of similar vowel sounds, especially within words on stressed syllables.

When you come to contemplate the specifics of your transformation, you will need to pick one poem in particular to use as a primary base text. However, you must bear in mind that you will be using your understanding and appreciation of Browning's work as a larger body and therefore should reflect this in your commentary.

For the purposes of this section, we will focus on the specifics of one poem in particular in order to flesh out a method for analysis.

■ Background information

My Last Duchess

- ■ Written in 1842, this poem's narrator is most likely a real character called the Duke of Ferrara who was a prominent member of the European court in the 16th century, but more importantly a renowned patron of the arts and collector of paintings and sculpture.

- The Duke is showing an emissary (who is representing a Count) round his art collection.

- The poem focuses mainly on a commentary from the Duke on his favourite painting: a portrait of his last wife.

- He outlines the circumstances surrounding the painting's creation and the aspects of the Duchess that it captures best.

- After alluding to the passing of this woman, he goes on to begin negotiations for the terms of the forthcoming marriage.

- Before letting him leave, the Duke shows his guest one more piece of art: a spectacular classical sculpture.

When investigating one of Browning's monologues, you should ask yourself what message he is conveying to his contemporary audience through his choice of character and events. 'My Last Duchess' shows his concern with materialism: he uses the example of the Duke to warn that an obsession with an object over the love of the natural thing it is based on is unhealthy. Browning seems to be worried by the **Renaissance** idea that human achievement in the realm of the arts puts us on a par with God as supreme creators.

Browning's monologues are like mysteries. By piecing together clues which are carefully placed throughout the poem, an attentive reader can gain a gradual appreciation of the narrator and his grotesque behaviour.

What does Browning suggest implicitly in *My Last Duchess*?

- The reason for this visit and consequent guided tour is initially unclear, although it soon becomes apparent that the Duke is planning to marry the Count's daughter and wants the emissary to go back to his master with a clear understanding of what Ferrara expects from a wife, as well as a greedy expectation of a big dowry ('The Count your master's known munificence / Is ample warrant').

- The Duke praises the painting ('I call / That piece a wonder now') but suggests that the reason for its beauty is the care that the painter took in creating it ('Fra Pandolf's hands / Worked busily a day'). He seems to believe that the artist flirted too much with his former wife, which resulted in the beautiful 'spot of joy' captured in her expression ('perhaps / Fra Pandolf chanced to say … "Paint / May never hope to reproduce the / Faint half-flush that dies along her throat"').

- His jealousy towards the attentions other men paid his wife (the viciously harsh **fricative** spit in 'The bough of cherries some officious fool / Broke in the orchard for her is clear') is only matched by his disdain for her apparent simplicity in not noticing them ('She had / A heart – how shall I say? – too soon made glad').

- He is a vain man who is keen to make sure the emissary notices the exclusivity of his art collection and his wealth ('I said / "Fra Pandolf" by design … Notice Neptune … thought a rarity, / Which Claus of Innsbruck struck in bronze for me!'). He is also used to having command and being obeyed ('Will't please you to sit and look at her? … I choose / Never to stoop … Will't please you to rise?').

- His self-centred nature is evident: note the number of times the personal pronoun crops up. Similarly, he likes to appear to be a modest and self-effacing man ('Even had you skill / in speech – (which I have not) – to make your will / Quite clear') at the same time as producing a highly polished sequence of elegant rhyming couplets.

■ Key terms

Renaissance: (literally 'rebirth') between the 14th and 17th centuries, Europe was swept by a cultural movement which saw a revival in intellectual, artistic and political innovation and experimentation, placing a renewed emphasis on the supremacy of man's artistic achievements.

Fricative: a severe sound created by breath forcing out the consonant 'f', in this example.

■ **Key terms**

Litotes: understatements for rhetorical effect, often based on a denial of a statement, e.g. 'He is not the most generous person I know'.

■ Compare the well organised and superficially ordered nature of the regular iambic pentameter and rhyming couplets with the increasing rage contained within the lines. At times, the sequence of enjambment shows his irritation physically spilling over the lines (every line between 31 and 40 runs on). The structure of the poem cannot contain his emotions. This echoes the Duke's personality: polite and cultured on the outside, bitter and angry on the inside.

■ His anger with his wife's apparent flirtatiousness is equalled by his disappointment that she does not recognise the magnitude of his generosity and personality ('Sir, 'twas all one! My favour at her breast / The dropping of the daylight in the west'). Similarly, the **litotes** in his euphemism for the natural wonder of a beautiful sunset shows his disregard for the wonder of nature as compared to his art collection. He is a man who craves control of beauty ('none puts by / The curtain I have drawn for you but I').

■ The ultimate puzzle we need to put together is what happened to the last Duchess? The Duke never explicitly states that she is dead, instead referring to her non-presence euphemistically. She is his 'last Duchess', he twice comments that the accuracy of the painting makes it seem 'as if she were alive', and eventually all of her irritating habits, such as indiscriminate smiling, suddenly 'stopped together'. But the sinister nature of lines 45 to 46 is apparent in the brusque and brutal caesuras of the punctuation, plainness of the statements and menacing sibilance: 'This grew; I gave commands; / Then all smiles stopped together'.

What would be the best form for the transformation?

Your analysis of the poem should have made it clear by now that this base text lends itself to a mystery or detective story. This genre would complement the nature of the Browning's piecemeal revelation of clues and suggestions that lead to an opaque conclusion inviting closer investigation.

In such a transformation, in order to shed fresh light on the source text, you could offer a switch in narrative perspective from the biased protagonist (the Duke in the case of *My Last Duchess*) to a detached observation by a detective trying to work out the whys and wherefores of the crime (the disappearance of the Duchess). In this way, you would transform the inferences made by the audience into the conclusions reached by the detective in response to the biased evidence presented by the 'criminal'.

A number of detective and mystery writers could provide a clear style model for your transformed text. From Arthur Conan Doyle's seminal Sherlock Holmes stories to Dashiell Hammett and Raymond Chandler's legendary American hard-boiled detectives, and Sara Paretsky and Harlan Coben's 21st century cynical and ironic protagonists, there are plenty of styles to explore.

You need to decide whether you want to write a section from a longer novel or an entire short story. The short story could be a more rewarding form: it can be taken in at a single sitting, you can complete the journey of events from the poem, you can build towards a genuine climax, constructing a complete and coherent narrative structure. However, remember the word limit for your transformation: do not attempt a text type that cannot be sensibly achieved within those parameters.

When you have decided on a suitable style model, complete the following activity, which is about analysing the genre conventions.

AQA Examiner's tip

The unit Assessment Objectives call for you to show a control over the new genre, an awareness of the conventions and structures and an effective concern for the audience. You will need just as close a familiarity with the genre characteristics of the transformed text as you do with the source texts.

Practical activity

- How is the story narrated? In the first person from the point of view of the detective, or by an omniscient third person?
- Does the narrator intrude at all in the story, making comments directly to the reader?
- How is the story framed? Is it part of a flashback (as many of the Sherlock Holmes stories are, with Watson looking back on notable cases from their past) or are we learning about events along with the narrator?
- What is the tone of the story? Is the narrator embittered and cynical, or enthused and excited?
- Does the case serve as the primary focus of the detective, or is it something else to be dealt with alongside other events (for example the Easy Rawlins stories by Walter Mosley are set against the investigator's personal struggle with the racism of post-war America)?
- What is the setting? Does the author employ the **pathetic fallacy** to create atmosphere and mood?
- What kind of figurative techniques are used? Chandler is fond of unusual and vivid similes and metaphors; Conan Doyle's Sherlock Holmes shuns embellishment for clinical and precise forensic explanations.
- What distinguishes the sentence types? Are they clipped and brief, or florid and complex? How does the author employ them to build up to climaxes?
- Does the story follow one gradual arc of intrigue, or is it full of frequent cliffhangers?

Key terms

Pathetic fallacy: a literary technique where the author applies human emotions to inanimate objects or nature, and uses the description of surroundings to reflect a character's mood. For example, if a protagonist is miserable then the weather will be grey, drab and raining in sympathy.

2 John Betjeman

John Betjeman (1906–84), one of the most popular and widely read of 20th-century English poets, was Poet Laureate from 1972 to 1984. He was also a popular broadcaster, which gave his varied output a large audience. Betjeman covered an enormous range of subjects, giving a distinctive and often eccentric series of snapshots of English life and society. He may not have been an innovator but he achieved clarity and directness within traditional poetic forms. He had a particular gift for comic writing, exploiting rhythm and rhyme with great technical skill.

Good starting points for those who do not know Betjeman's work are The Poetry Society (www.poetrysoc.com) and The Poetry Archive (www.poetryarchive.org), which has excellent audio files of Betjeman's own reading of two of his poems:

- *Youth and Age on Beaulieu River* shows Betjeman's ability to describe humans in a landscape and deals with mortality, one of his abiding concerns.
- In *A Subaltern's Love Song* Betjeman the light-hearted satirist pokes fun at himself and the upper middle-class world of tennis clubs, courtship and summer balls.

Betjeman's poetic voice and style

The following section introduces four of Betjeman's poems to show something of his characteristic voice and poetic style. All of the poems referred to here, along with many others, may be found in various anthologies and on this website: http://famouspoetsandpoems.com/poets/john_betjeman/poems.

It will be helpful if you print out copies, make annotations and record your comments as you think about the points raised in the activity sections that follow.

Inexpensive progress

This poem questions the dubious benefits that come from the transition from traditional, rural ways of life to lifestyles that demand rapid transport and the despoiling of the environment by a relentless process of construction: more roads, more buildings, more high streets in the image of other high streets in other towns and cities.

■ Critical response activity

Read the poem carefully and then analyse the techniques Betjeman employs, focusing on how the various features relate to meaning and the appeal to readers' thoughts and feelings:

■ *Form*: including his use of rhyme schemes and the structure of stanzas.

■ *Lexical choice*: including the choice and placing of nouns and noun phrases, verbs and adjectives.

■ *Syntax*: including the use of imperative and declarative sentences.

■ *Text structure*: including the relationship between adjacent stanzas and the development of the poet's argument.

■ *Phonological features*: including rhyme, rhythms, alliteration, assonance.

Slough

In *Slough* Betjeman describes the town of that name, which he sees as an example of the worst excesses of heartless development, with its ugly and dehumanising factories and, for the people who worked in them, inadequate and cramped houses and flats. Betjeman urges the bombs to destroy the vulgar profiteers but to spare the bald young clerks who were innocent victims of their bosses' greed. The poem was published just two years before the outbreak of the Second World War.

Critical response activity

The following phrases are used in other stanzas to describe the businessman Betjeman seems to regard as a representative of the greed-driven classes responsible for the ruination of Slough:

■ 'that man with double chin'

■ 'his repulsive skin'

■ 'his boring dirty joke'

■ 'the stinking cad'.

1 Read the whole poem to see how these phrases are used by Betjeman within the stanzas in which they occur.

2 Print out a copy of the poem and use highlighters to mark in one colour references that are critical or condemnatory, and in another colour references that are neutral or sympathetic.

3 Look at the text structure of the poem to see how Betjeman makes his case. Does Betjeman present an argument or does he assert a particular view?

In Westminster Abbey

In this poem Betjeman is visiting the abbey when he becomes aware of another visitor. He overhears (or imagines he overhears) her saying a prayer, which reveals an uncomfortable clash between her conventional, but hardly heartfelt, concerns for her fellow human beings and the prejudice and self-interest which lurk beneath her façade of respectability.

Critical response activity

The following lines are used to show how Betjeman regards the woman's moral code during a time of war, giving evidence of her narrow self-interest and her elevated sense of personal importance:

- 'And, even more, protect the whites.'
- 'Lord, put beneath Thy special care
  One-eighty-nine Cadogan Square.'
- 'So, Lord, reserve for me a crown.
  And do not let my shares go down.'
- 'And now, dear Lord, I cannot wait
  Because I have a luncheon date.'

1 Read the whole poem to see how Betjeman uses these lines in the stanzas in which they occur.

2 Print out a copy of the poem and use highlighters to mark in one colour references that are critical or condemnatory, and in another colour references that are neutral or sympathetic.

3 Look at the ways in which Betjeman uses juxtaposition to make his points. Does Betjeman present an argument or does he assert a particular view?

How to Get on in Society

In *How to Get on in Society* Betjeman mocks those members of the nouveau riche class who try to acquire the outward signs of gentility and good taste that they associate with the upper classes. The narrator is shockingly pretentious and by trying to use what she mistakenly believes to be socially superior language and manners, she places herself firmly outside the social circles she wishes to gatecrash.

Critical response activity

Language has always been a means of discriminating between members of different social groups. Your accent, your grammar, your choice of vocabulary will be used by some as a basis for thinking that you are 'one of us' or an 'outsider'. How often do parents (and teachers) say, 'Don't talk like that' or 'Don't use that word'? Betjeman uses this aspect of language to satirise particular habits of expression and behaviour.

- Read the whole poem and try to identify words and phrases that seem to give the game away about the pretensions of language and behaviour of the would-be social climber whose voice we hear in the poem.
- What does Betjeman intend the italicised words and phrases to reveal about the speaker?

Transformation ideas

How might you use these poems or others by Betjeman for your transformation? In *How to Get on in Society* and *In Westminster Abbey* Betjeman creates a simple context in which each speaker's attitudes and opinions are expressed, but he does not create dialogue – he had no need to, because the monologue serves his satirical purpose by allowing the speakers to reveal themselves. How might a short-story writer or novelist incorporate either of Betjeman's characters into the medium of prose fiction?

The starting point is the character as created by Betjeman. The prose writer's imagination comes into play by deciding on:

■ *a situation or context in which the character's story is played out*: for example, two or three of Norman's wife's friends come to afternoon tea, or the Westminster Abbey woman's luncheon date

■ *the other characters*: are they like-minded, or are they going to challenge the opinions and prejudices of Betjeman's characters that you are going to adopt in your transformation?

■ *the sub-genre of prose fiction that you are going to adopt*: will you write, for example, a comedy of manners, or will you write a dark and merciless satire, or a gentle and affectionate story which stresses the humanity of your characters?

In the case of *Inexpensive Progress* and *Slough*, there are opportunities for writing a non-fiction transformation. Imagine that Bill Bryson or another travel writer whose work you know had visited the places that Betjeman described in either of these poems. Taking Betjeman's observations as your starting point, your task is to write a section from a travel book that describes the place and the people you encounter there, as well as giving a sense of their way of life, and your own opinions of the town, the people and their way of life.

If you decide to use the genre of travel writing it is essential that you familiarise yourself with books by some writers in the field. It is a hugely diverse genre and your choice is enormous: as well as Bryson you might look at works by Paul Theroux, Dervla Murphy, Nicholas Crane, or an anthology edited by Jane Robinson entitled *Unsuitable for Ladies*. There are hundreds – thousands – of suitable alternative books that you could select from. Do not neglect the travel articles of the weekend editions of newspapers such as the *Times*, the *Telegraph*, the *Independent* and the *Guardian/Observer*. Study them carefully and check how long they are in relation to the guidelines for length that you need to apply (you might be surprised):

■ Look at the techniques these writers use for controlling the text structure of their pieces – particularly how they begin and end. How do they develop ideas in the main body of the articles? What can you learn from their example?

■ Remember, you need to show a creative interplay between the base text and your transformation, and your commentary needs to pay close analytical attention to this aspect of your work. Do avoid the danger of embarking on a piece of writing and losing any genuine sense of contact with the base text.

Away from travel writing, some further transformation ideas for 'Slough' might include:

■ In the play *Under Milk Wood*, Dylan Thomas inserts an invented extract from a guide book to introduce a different and incongruous style of description of the small town of Llareggub (try reading that name backwards). You could do something similar for Slough by taking Betjeman's poem and using it as the basis for a radio documentary which puts a positive spin on the very things that Betjeman objected to. You could create first-person contributions to the documentary from characters Betjeman refers to as well as others living in the houses and flats he talks about.

■ Another approach is to take Betjeman's poem as the basis for a short story which is essentially true to the vision of Slough presented in the poem.

3 Seamus Heaney

Seamus Heaney's poetry reflects his local surroundings of Northern Ireland, where he was born. Although there are occasional references to the political and religious divisions that were a backdrop for much of his life, he is not primarily a political poet. The presence of Ireland and its people is pervasive in Heaney's poetry, yet he deals with universal themes and this, in part, explains his worldwide readership and reputation. He reaches out from the here-and-now of his subjects, which are often domestic and personal, to explore the links between past and present within his family and his community and the wider world. He is an acute observer of the small details that can take on great significance in the thoughts and feelings of the people he writes about, including himself. Heaney's view of poetry is well represented in the following quotation from his essay, 'The Government of the Tongue':

> In one sense the efficacy of poetry is nil – no lyric ever stopped a tank. In another sense, it is unlimited. It is like the writing in the sand in the face of which accusers and accused are left speechless and renewed…

and in these words from *Personal Helicon*:

> I rhyme
> To see myself, to set the darkness echoing.

Death of a Naturalist was Heaney's first published collection (1966) and contains some of his best-known work. There are 34 poems in the collection; they are concerned with childhood experiences, family relationships, personal identity and life in an agricultural community.

Heaney's poetry

The following section introduces three of Heaney's poems. All of the poems referred to here, along with many others, may be found in various anthologies and on this website: www.poemhunter.com/seamus-heaney/poems.

If you decide to base a transformation on one or more of Heaney's poems, you will need to read far more widely than this so that you develop a richer sense of his poetic voice and techniques, as well as his subject matter, but the three poems below provide an excellent starting point for the purposes of this section. Print out copies of the poems, read them carefully and then re-read them. Annotate them with any or all of the following:

- your first thoughts as you read particular lines or phrases
- questions that spring to mind as you read
- highlighting of particular words or phrases and comments about the technical devices they exemplify and the effects they achieve
- comments on the structure of the poem
- comments that reflect the ways in which your first thoughts are modified by further reading of the poem
- ideas that come to mind about transformation possibilities.

Critical response activity

As you study each of the three poems, note Heaney's descriptions of specific details and think about the effect each of these has on you.

- Think carefully about Heaney's specific choices of language, such as his use of alliteration, similes, metaphors and symbols.
- How does Heaney structure each of these poems, and how does the structure reflect the changing thoughts and feelings that he writes about?
- Are there any individual words that surprise or even shock you? Which are they? Try to explain to yourself why you react to them as you do.
- How is Heaney's choice of form related to his choice of subject and his treatment of that subject.
- How does Heaney use the rhythms and sound of everyday speech and what effects does he achieve?
- How does Heaney use the final line, or the final thought, to conclude each poem and leave an echo in the reader's mind?

Death of a Naturalist

This poem describes the experience of young boy collecting frog-spawn. He feels threatened and repulsed by the flies and the 'gross-bellied frogs'. The boy runs away from the flax-dam, his career as naturalist over before it has properly begun.

- Is the boy Heaney himself, or is Heaney describing the reaction of one of his friends?
- Was the boy/Heaney alone or were there two or more boys at the flax-dam? If there were two or more, what possibilities for dialogue are there? (You might find it helpful to look at Dennis Potter's play *Blue Remembered Hills* to see what can be achieved through the dialogue of young children playing together.)
- What possibilities are there for exploring more fully scenes or incidents that Heaney mentions in passing (such as the schoolroom exchanges with Miss Walls)?
- What scope is there for making the boy(s) more prominent as characters in their own right rather than as observers/describers, as in the poem?

Digging

Digging explores the generational links between father and son – and grandfather. Whereas they used the spade to dig potatoes and peat, the poet's tool is the 'squat pen', resting between finger and thumb, 'snug as a gun', but Heaney rejects writing as aggression and uses his pen as an instrument of excavation and exploration.

■ Is the poet suffering from writers' block when he looks out of the window to see his father digging? Could a short-story transformation focus more on the internal thoughts of the poet himself rather than the reflections on his father and grandfather?

■ Does the image of the squat pen resting 'snug as a gun' open up other possibilities about the poet's thoughts, bearing in mind the political and criminal context of Northern Ireland during 'the troubles'?

■ The tables could be turned: the poet's father takes a break from his digging, turns round and through the window sees his son, pen in hand, apparently lost in thought. The short story becomes his, reflecting on the earlier and later generations of his family from his perspective.

■ Where is the mother? What is her story as she sees her son writing, or trying to write, and her husband doing the physical work in the garden? Are there comic possibilities in this new scenario? Could the short story become a **parody** of Heaney's poem?

Mid-term break

This poem records Heaney's recollections of the death of his four-year-old brother, Christopher. He describes waiting in the college sickbay until his neighbours take him home, and then meeting his grieving father in the porch and the visitors paying their respects, before he sees his brother's body in its coffin the following morning

■ Heaney's poem focuses on some details of the family tragedy but other aspects are mentioned in passing or not at all. What scope is there for expanding on the poet's experiences conveyed in the first three lines, for example? How might the mother become a more prominent figure in a short story based on the poem?

■ How might the situation and account be transformed by relating events from the perspective of one of the other characters – perhaps the father, the mother or even Big Jim Evans?

■ How do the events described in the poem relate to earlier and later times which are merely implied, and how might these be incorporated more directly in the short story?

■ Could the priest's funeral homily be incorporated in the story? What would he (or could he) say to comfort the family?

Transformation ideas

All three of the poems you have looked at present incidents and episodes that lend themselves to transformation into short stories. The short story is a condensed and economical form (let us not worry too much about definitions here, other than to say that there are long short stories and short short stories), but the word guidelines for this unit will give you scope to expand on Heaney's highly condensed poems. Do remember that your transformation will benefit from a wide understanding and appreciation of a range of Heaney's work and you will be able to draw on this in your commentary. Use the bullet-point questions for each poem as a basis for thinking through what Heaney writes and how he writes it and, if you find it helpful at this stage, make notes to record your ideas as you consider each question in turn. Alternatively, if you read the poems with other students, the questions may be used as the basis for your discussions about each poem.

Key terms

Parody: imitation of the style or approach of another writer, usually for comic or satirical effect.

Practical activity

Writing a genre transformation from a poetry base text to a short story is one of many possibilities. All of these poems could also be the stimulus for a transformation into a playscript. Discuss or note down your own ideas about ways in which a short story transformation and play script transformation would differ in terms of the opportunities and the constraints of each form.

You could use the SWOT analysis model to help you in this activity. Think about:

■ S: the strengths of each form for producing transformations

■ W: the weaknesses of each form for producing transformations

■ O: the opportunities associated with each form

■ T: the threats associated with each form.

This way of considering the pros and cons of transformation ideas is a useful way of focusing your planning and preparation and avoiding the frustration of starting a transformation task and finding that you have to abandon it because unforeseen problems emerge after you have done a good deal of writing.

Drama transformations

This chapter covers:

- ideas for approaching transformations based on plays by William Shakespeare

- ideas for approaching transformations based on plays by Aphra Behn

- ideas for approaching transformations based on plays by Harold Pinter.

Key terms

Tragedies: plays which show the fall of a previously great character, often at least partly through their own fault, and usually ending in their death.

Comedies: plays which may include scenes of sadness and loss, but are predominantly cheerful, ending in harmony, often symbolised by a marriage.

Romance plays: plays which move away from realism to include scenes of magic and mystery, often also introducing elements of music and dance.

You can apply the approaches and critical response exercises in the transformations in this chapter to a wide variety of base texts.

1 William Shakespeare

Shakespeare wrote well over 30 plays, so you have plenty to choose from. He wrote various types of plays, including **tragedies**, such as *Othello* and *King Lear*; **comedies** such as *As You Like It* and *The Taming of the Shrew*; and **romance plays** such as *The Tempest* and *The Winter's Tale*.

Although he was writing around the end of the 16th century, the themes and issues he was dealing with are still relevant today, and his examination of characters' motives and psychology is full of insight and subtlety.

Because there is such a variety within his drama, you can consider using Shakespearean drama for many different kinds of transformations.

Before you begin

Before you decide on how to do your transformation, you really need to think about the key features of the text you are transforming: your 'base text'. Then you can decide how to use or adapt some of these in a different genre and format.

It is often helpful to think of the key features of a literary work under six headings:

- Plot
- Characterisation
- Themes
- Settings
- Mood/atmosphere
- Style

For *King Lear*, you might come up with ideas such as the following:

Plot

- Parallel plots (or example, both Lear and Gloucester having deceitful children/being blind, mentally or physically).
- Madness.
- Desire for power.
- Betrayal.
- Faithful devotion (Cordelia, Edgar, Kent, the Fool).
- Villainous plans, deception, greed and violence (Edmund, Cornwall, Goneril, Regan).

Characterisation

- Aged but powerful men (Lear, Gloucester).
- Young people keen for power, and ruthless (Edmund, Goneril, Regan, Cornwall).

- Young and loyal children (Cordelia, Edgar).
- Servants, both faithful and untrustworthy.
- Apparently mad or blind but perceptive characters (Lear (later), Gloucester, the Fool).

Themes

- Nature of humanity.
- Love: parent/child; marital love/lust.
- Service and loyalty.
- Kingship.
- Seeing/expressing the truth.

Settings

- Palaces.
- The heath in a storm.
- Cliffs at Dover.

Remember that in a play you do not see the settings unless the stage designer has created a version; but you may hear them described by characters.

Remember also that directors can decide in which historical period to set their plays – so *King Lear* may be set in ancient Britain (when the 'real' King Lear was supposed to have existed), or in Shakespearean times, or in modern or even future times. In your transformation, if for example you want to produce part of a novel, you too will have to think about the setting – and to describe it.

Mood/atmosphere

- Largely gloomy and bleak, but with moments of humour and tenderness.

Style

- Frequent use of **blank verse**.
- No narrator.
- Much **imagery**.
- Some use of song.

Choosing your genre

You cannot really begin until you have decided on the genre you are going to work in.

Poetry

You could, for example, write a poem dealing with the events of the play, or one character's perception of them (in the form, say, of a dramatic monologue by Edmund, or Cordelia, or even the Fool).

You may know Browning's poems *My Last Duchess* or *Porphyria's Lover*, which work like this – or you may have come across U. A. Fanthorpe's poem *Not My Best Side*, which tells the story of St George and the dragon in three verses, each of which is in the voice, and expressing the opinions, of one of the characters: the dragon, the maiden and the knight.

AQA Examiner's tip

You need to produce a transformation which is in a different genre or subgenre. *King Lear* is a drama and a tragedy, so you could produce a different kind of play, but it would probably be advisable to consider a totally different genre, i.e. either prose or poetry.

Link

Do not forget that there is further information on Browning's work in Chapter 6, Poetry transformations.

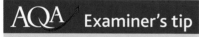
Prose

If you wanted to write prose, you might present a short story, or part of a novel, giving a new angle on the plot.

You may have already come across Jane Smiley's novel *A Thousand Acres*, which is based on the *King Lear* story but set on a 20th-century farm in Iowa. You could attempt a similar treatment, but you would need to bring your own ideas to the transformation so that the setting and situation are different even though similar themes and moral dilemmas are explored.

Transformation of *King Lear* into part of a detective novel

Suppose you decide to write the opening chapter of a detective novel, where Edgar sets out to find out who has 'framed' him. You would then need to think about the six key features of your new *King Lear*, including a new title.

Plot

- ■ You will need to show a good knowledge of the original plot, but of course you are going to retell it from a different perspective and perhaps with different emphases.
- ■ You will not be able to write at great length (because of the word count restriction).
- ■ Which parts of the play are you going to deal with?

Characterisation

- ■ You will need to show knowledge of, and insight into, the characters of your 'base text', so you should not move too far away from the originals, but you could well rename them. (In *A Thousand Acres* Jane Smiley had Larry, Ginny and Caroline instead of Lear, Goneril and Cordelia; but you could move further away from the originals as long as their roles were clear.)
- ■ You might also want to show them in a different light; do you approve of Cordelia's refusal to placate her father in the opening scene? Does Goneril have grounds for being so angry with Lear? What about Edmund: is Gloucester's treatment of him fair?

Themes

- ■ Which theme(s) are you going to concentrate on? You will not have scope to deal with many; in fact, probably choosing just one would be sensible. You could focus, for example, on loyalty; or use the symbolism of eyesight, as in Shakespeare's play, to suggest the importance of seeing the truth. Either of these could lend themselves quite neatly to a detective novel.

Setting

- ■ Where and when are you going to set these events? Is it Britain? Or in a foreign country? Perhaps, if you still want royalty, they are set in a foreign principality.

Mood/atmosphere

- ■ There is no need for you to keep to the same mood as your base text.
- ■ However, the atmosphere you recreate must be appropriate to other aspects of your new piece.

If you decided to make your transformation of *King Lear* humorous (and remember that writing humorous material is one of the most difficult things to do!) then you would have to think very carefully about such matters as who your narrator is (see Style below).

Style

- The style you choose for your novel will depend largely on the narrative voice that you choose. Is there an omniscient third-person narrator? Or a first-person narrator? Is this Edgar? Or a detective he calls in? Or even Edmund, as an **unreliable narrator**?

- Although you are creating your own narrative voice, you will want to include some aspects which show that you are familiar with the Shakespearean text, such as imagery. For example:
  - there are many references to savage animals in the imagery of *King Lear*
  - blindness and eyesight are used both literally and metaphorically
  - there are many plays on the words 'nature' and 'natural'.

- Then you will want to think about structure. Where are you going to begin your novel?

- Your novel does not have to progress chronologically as the play does. It could begin at the end – looking back over events – or in the middle, after Edgar has had to run away and disguise himself

> **Key terms**
>
> **Unreliable narrator:** a first-person narrator who, the reader gradually finds out, has been concealing material facts or being deceptive about events.

▉ Critical response activity

Think about the modern equivalent of some of the characters in *King Lear*. For example, what kind of disguise might Edgar take nowadays?

Starting to write

Getting started on writing a transformation is always easier if you are familiar with the kind of new material you want to produce. For example, writing the opening of a detective novel would be much easier if you felt familiar with the genre and with the very wide range of styles you might use. Even a brief look at the range might suggest:

- The Sherlock Holmes stories of Sir Arthur Conan Doyle
- The Inspector Poirot stories by Agatha Christie
- The Lord Peter Wimsey detective novels by Dorothy L. Sayers
- The Philip Marlowe novels by Raymond Chandler
- The detective fiction of P. D. James
- Colin Dexter's Inspector Morse series
- The Inspector Banks series by Peter Robinson
- Crime investigations set in other times: for example, in the Middle Ages in the Brother Cadfael stories by Ellis Peters (Edith Pargeter) or the Falco stories set in ancient Rome by Lindsey Davis.

Try to read a range of at least some of the genre that you think you want to use. You will notice that each writer has a different style and each detective has a different and distinctive voice.

Imagine that you decide to set your novel in a contemporary city, where Edgar, having run away, decides he must try to find out the truth about his supposed crime. Here he is, as a first-person narrator, in a contemporary setting, beginning his story:

It was raining. It was always raining that summer. Even under the subway there were drips and puddles, and anyway, I couldn't keep out of sight all the time. I needed to see the papers, find out how close they were on my tail, what else I was supposed to have done. And sometimes I needed to phone Edmund.

It surprised me how helpful he'd been, right from the start. I'd always thought he held it against me, that I was the one who was going to inherit Dad's business. OK, so I was the elder brother, but I know Edmund wanted a share. Yet when it came to the point, when someone set me up, made Dad think I'd planned something awful – even to kill him – it was Edmund who had helped me, Edmund who suggested how to get away, keep out of the hands of the police. I wouldn't be here now if it weren't for him.

Some novels – for example *In a Dry Season* by Peter Robinson – use both first- and third-person narrators. You could try this too, and even include another genre, such as a newspaper article. The paragraph below is a third-person view of Edmund, though it is told using **free indirect speech**, enabling the author to get inside Edmund's head:

'You're bad,' they'd told him, 'born bad.' Well, he didn't disagree. It wasn't just because he was the result of a 'fling', as his father called it. It was just the way he was. His nature, he supposed.

He was enjoying it all now – the way his father trusted him, the way Edgar was relying on him, not knowing, not realising. Edmund strolled across the busy High Street to Costa Coffee, ordered a cappuccino and took a paper off the rack. The headline made him smile.

HE'S EVIL
Deceived dad denounces son on the run.

> ### Practical activity
>
> Practise writing paragraphs depicting the same event but using different narrators and viewpoints.

Key terms

Free indirect speech: a narrative method in which the actual words of a character are not reproduced, but the reported words reflect the tone of voice of the speaker.

Commonwealth: the system of government between 1649 and 1660 after Oliver Cromwell and his Roundhead army defeated Charles I in the English Civil War. It is traditionally seen as being a time of severe, stark Puritanism, e.g. theatres were closed and mince pies were banned.

2 Aphra Behn

Aphra Behn is one of the most renowned playwrights from the Restoration era, penning 15 plays between 1670 and 1686. She was a controversial woman who worked as a spy for Charles II and spent time in debtors' jail. Today, she is still regarded as a pioneer: one of the first women to earn a living as a writer, bringing bawdiness back to the English stage after the austere period of the **Commonwealth**. More significantly, she was responsible for foregrounding strong-willed and powerful female characters on the stage. Virginia Woolf regarded Behn as a heroine, writing in her 1928 book *A Room Of One's Own* that:

> All women … ought to let flowers fall upon the grave of Aphra Behn … for it was she who earned them the right to speak their minds.

Behn's plays were the big-budget blockbusters of their time. Celebrity actors such as Nell Gwyn wore lavish costumes on extravagant sets in front of large and socially diverse audiences.

It is fitting to study how to use Behn's *The Rover* as a base text for a transformation, given that the play itself was an updated and reinvigorated version of Thomas Killigrew's *Thomaso*. Behn seems to deny this in a postscript to the play:

> A report about town (made by some either very malicious or very ignorant) that 'twas Thomaso altered … That I have stolen some hints from it, may be a proof that I value it more than to pretend to alter it … I will only say that the plot and business (not to boast on't) is my own.

Aphra Behn, The Rover, 1677, Postscript

However, *The Rover* was controversial simply because Behn was accused of barely concealed plagiarism: a reminder to all English Language and Literature Unit 4 candidates that they should not just copy the characters, events and genre of their chosen base text wholesale. *The Rover* also became infamous for its frank sexual content; as society became more reserved, Behn's most famous work was considered unstageable.

Restoration comedy has many notable conventions, and Behn adapted and then integrated them into *The Rover*. You will need to bear these in mind when fashioning your transformation: how can you use them, mould them, cast new light on them in your piece and for a new audience?

Background information

Restoration comedy

■ Stock character types were used uniformly:
  – a rake, or libertine (a party-loving rogue with a taste for women and debauchery) as the sympathetic but rascally hero
  – a fop, or booby (the bumbling but endearing fool who ends up as the butt of everyone's jokes) with rakish aspirations
  – a spirited heroine keen to break free from the shackles of society
  – domineering parents or other family members, keen to rein in the heroine, but ultimately thwarted
  – the fallen woman (a prostitute in need of salvation)
  – a woman scorned, seeking revenge on the powerful man who has left her behind.
■ Plots revolved around love matches, rival suitors and mistaken identity.
■ Disguises, costumes and masks; all the better to provide opportunities for mistaken identity.
■ Farcical action, with chases and hiding and liberal use of trap doors.
■ Bawdy songs and music and dancing.
■ Duels, fights, swordplay and perhaps the opportunity for some inadvertent comedy debagging.

All of these must serve the purpose of comedy: there will be a happy ending. Behn takes these ingredients and flavours them with some dangerous spice in *The Rover*.

■ Critical response activity

List the characters in *The Rover*, then note how they both fulfil and subvert the roles of the stock character types. For example, Angellica Bianca and Lucetta represent either end of the spectrum of prostitutes. Angellica, however, casts aside the traditional role by searching for true love and becoming a more complex version of the scorned woman. Lucetta is depicted as more cunning than a simple whore, becoming a business woman in her own right, and this is the impetus for some anti-English, booby-baiting humour.

The play is set in Naples, during carnival time. This helps Behn frame her themes potently, as the carnival represented the world turned upside down in revelry and celebration.

■ Background information

Themes in *The Rover*

- ■ Outsiders: Willmore, Belville and Frederick are banished Cavaliers, rootless and wandering.
- ■ Men versus women: who are the real heroes?
- ■ What is love: is it something merely to be bought and sold? How trustworthy is it? How do the different genders view it?
- ■ Sexual respectability and notoriety: is it better to preserve your dignity or celebrate your sexuality?
- ■ Escaping control: whether it is a patriarchal social structure or your own reputation.

■ Critical response activity

- ■ Take each one of the themes and explain what Behn is telling her 17th-century audience about it. Find five quotations per theme to support your argument.
- ■ Are any of these messages relevant to a modern audience? Could you take Behn's attitude and alter it in order to present a different point of view as a modern author?
- ■ Can you spot any other themes that Behn is addressing – some that may suit your transformed text better?

What should the focus of the transformation be?

One way of shedding new light on a play text is by basing it on a more minor character. The more objective nature of the play's narrative means that an immediate transformation is available by focusing on the first-person perspective of a particular character. Ned Blunt is one of the most interesting minor characters in *The Rover*; he is an outsider, the butt of the Cavalier heroes' jokes, a stereotypical Restoration comedy booby.

Blunt is a japer and buffoon, but he wants to join the 'in-crowd' and gain acceptance from his peers. Superficially, Blunt is full of harmless jollity, but events in the play lead to the audience inferring a **misogynistic** malcontent side to his character.

This is a particularly interesting theme to choose and enables a perceptive transformation of Behn's play. The playwright, while celebrating different aspects of female sexuality and freedom through the

Key terms

Misogynistic: relating to someone who hates women.

characters of Hellena and Angellica and providing the opportunity for some superficially exhilarating and titillating content, was also looking to challenge the prevailing attitude towards libertinism. Libertines had a flagrant disregard for authority and convention, especially in matters concerning sex; but while Behn supported this popular liberal trend, she was afraid that it resulted in the subjugation of women. There is a fine line between fun-loving libertines and male predators using women for their own ends. Behn's **proto-feminist** beliefs show through in *The Rover*, with Willmore's excesses becoming dangerous and hurtful, while Hellena and Angellica's desire for his companionship is always to be negotiated on their terms.

As Blunt moves from a benign to an embittered character, his attitude towards women is worthy of investigation in a new text.

■ Critical response activity

You could also do the following exercise with a character from any other text, particularly novels or drama.

Listed below is a chronological quotation bank for Blunt. Some are Blunt's words which reveal aspects of his character, others are observations about him made by other characters. In each instance, note what we learn about him and chart how his personality develops during the course of the play. Watch out for Behn's use of irony and **prolepsis** too.

- ■ Act 1 Scene 1 line 50: 'When did you ever hear of an honest woman that took a man's money?'
- ■ Act 1 Scene 2 line 224: 'I have beauties which my false glass at home did not discover.'
- ■ Act 1 Scene 2 line 299: 'the rogue's sturdy and would work well in a mine.' (Frederick)
- ■ Act 1 Scene 2 line 305: 'one that knows no pleasure beyond riding to the next fair.' (Belville)
- ■ Act 1 Scene 2 line 312: 'he's our banker ... and if he fail we are all broke.' (Belville)
- ■ Act 2 Scene 1 line 62: 'gentlemen, you are wits; I am a dull country rogue.'
- ■ Act 2 Scene 1 line 88: 'there are things about this Essex calf that shall take with the ladies, beyond all your wit and parts.'
- ■ Act 3 Scene 1 line 140: 'Fortune is pleased to smile on us, gentlemen.'
- ■ Act 3 Scene 2 line 9: 'I'm an honest gentleman.'
- ■ Act 3 Scene 4 line 4: 'What a dog was I to believe in Woman? Oh, coxcomb!'
- ■ Act 3 Scene 4 line 14: 'confirms it I am a dull, believing, English country fop. But by my comrades! Death and the devil, there's the worst of all!'
- ■ Act 4 Scene 4 line 1: 'my mind's a little at peace since I have resolved revenge.'
- ■ Act 4 Scene 4 line 10: 'I shall never be reconciled to the sex more; she has made me as faithless as a physician.'
- ■ Act 4 Scene 4 line 14: 'Oh, how I'll use all womankind hereafter!'
- ■ Act 4 Scene 4 line 36: 'Dost thou know, miserable woman, into what den of mischiefs thou art fallen?'
- ■ Act 4 Scene 4 line 63: 'I will strip thee stark naked; then hang thee ... with a paper of scurvy verses fastened to thy breast in praise of damnable women.'
- ■ Act 4 Scene 4 line 74: 'Dissembling witches!'
- ■ Act 5 Scene 1 line 56: 'Ned Blunt is not ... an ass to be laughed at, sir.'
- ■ Act 5 Scene 1 line 577: 'I look altogether like a bag of bays stuffed full of fool's flesh.'

■ Key terms

Proto-feminist: an early version of the doctrine advocating equal social, political and sexual rights for women.

Prolepsis: in literature, this is a technique where an author anticipates events either through a character's unwitting comment, by direct narrative intrusion, or with symbolism; for example, a young Cinderella wistfully wishing she could find a pair of comfortable shoes that really fit her properly.

What would be the best genre for the transformation?

In order to shed new light on Blunt's character, some kind of first-person diary or recount genre would suit well. There is a genre of autobiographical, confessional books (for example Dave Peltzer's *A Child Called 'It'* or Frank McCourt's *Angela's Ashes*) which could serve as a style model for a new text. In the transformation, the personality of Blunt could produce a typically multi-layered character; the new light shed in the new text could be the presence of honesty and self-realisation as compared to the deception presented in the original character. Suitable incidents from Blunt's story in *The Rover* could contribute to the events chronicled in the new text.

Another similar genre model could be Samuel Pepys's diary. Pepys was alive during the same period as Behn, and writes in his diary about going to see her plays. He presents his thoughts and feelings directly in his writing without any thought for how polished and elegant they might appear on the page, and reading extracts from his work would provide you with the added advantage of an accurate and authentic **contemporary** voice for Blunt.

Whichever genre of autobiography you choose, you will need to pick out a number of incidents from the play to form the basis of your new writing. With the Pepys option, you could use the character of Blunt himself and the actual events from *The Rover*. If you follow a more modern path, then both Blunt and the selected occurrences from the play will need to be transformed into relevant equivalents.

Whichever genre you choose, you will need to work out how it has been put together (in terms of lexis and structure) so that you can ultimately produce an effective and controlled transformation. Building a close understanding of the author's craft will also provide material for your commentary.

■ Critical response activity

■ What is the predominant tense in the style models suggested above? Pepys's diary is in the present tense and seems to have been written contemporaneously. Pelzer's work is often in the present tense, but written from the perspective of an adult looking back on events. Frank McCourt writes uses the past tense and is able to comment in the present on how the experiences have shaped him. What effect is achieved by these differing approaches?

■ What is the typical sentence style: complex and descriptive? Simple and conversational? For example, Pepys's true diary format ignores conventional grammar.

■ Is the language figurative and florid, or sparse and undecorated? Is the author in control of their emotions as they write, or giving full vent to their feelings?

■ Does the writer take time to reflect on events and assimilate their effect, or do they appear to act and react without contemplation?

■ What kind of relationship do they attempt to build with the reader? Is there any true discourse between author and audience, or does the writer appear to be oblivious and focused on themselves?

Another good way to create tangible links between the base text and your transformation is to use motifs from the source text in your new version. Perhaps Willmore's drunken encounter with Florinda's shoelaces could make an appearance, or the trapdoor down which Moretta sends Blunt.

After all, Behn admits to having done the same thing, 'stealing' one of Killigrew's visual trademarks from Tomaso (the courtesan's alluring picture) and placing it in *The Rover* as a tribute to her source text:

> I, vainly proud of my judgement, hang out the sign of Angellica (the only stolen object) to give notice where a great part of the wit dwelt.

Aphra Behn, The Rover, 1677, Postscript

3 Harold Pinter

Harold Pinter won the Nobel Prize for Literature in 2005. The academy said that his work 'uncovers the precipice under everyday prattle and forces entry into oppression's closed rooms'. Pinter's plays bear a distinctive stylistic stamp, address stark themes and feature vividly drawn characters, making them a good choice for text transformation. Pinter followed in the footsteps of the **Theatre of the Absurd** playwrights, and when his plays were first performed on stage they shocked and surprised the audience, making them feel uncomfortable and challenging their preconceptions of what theatre should be like.

One of Pinter's most celebrated plays is *The Caretaker* from 1960. It is a drama in which there is very little action, the events all taking place in one room claustrophobically crowded with junk, and featuring three characters who engage in some bizarre turns of conversation. The three protagonists are Mick (the landlord of the house in which the action occurs), Aston (his brother who lives in the room and is supposedly renovating the property) and Davies (a homeless man whom Aston met on the street and then offered a temporary place to stay). As the play progresses Pinter develops the men's characters through how they talk to each other and what they say about themselves. He addresses themes relevant to 1960s British society. By the end the audience may be uncertain about their attitude towards what they have just seen, but they are normally clear in their dislike of Davies.

Davies is singularly unpleasant and unsympathetic and as he becomes more and more demanding in asserting his authority over Aston, the audience turn more against him. When it seems that Davies is finally about to be sent back out onto the streets, we applaud the solidarity between Mick and Aston and are glad that Aston has finally done something.

How can you base a transformation on one of these characters?

When you are working out your idea for a transformation, your primary motivation should be to offer a new audience a new perspective on the base text. In transforming *The Caretaker*, you could portray Davies's plight from his own point of view: he has been taken in by an apparently friendly and charitable man only to be subjected to bizarre mental torture and forced to accomplish menial tasks. The new text would be full of pathos, focusing on the story of the homeless man and his opinions about Mick and Aston. Another feature of his character in the play, where he appears to make up bizarre stories about his past exploits and has a mysterious identity, could also be transformed to truth, offering the new audience a different perspective: Davies is not a thieving, lying 'filthy old skate', but a military veteran cast aside by a cruel society and then tormented and mocked by a pair of sadistic middle-class layabouts.

> **Key terms**
>
> **Theatre of the Absurd:** a European theatrical movement from the mid-20th century. The plays shared a number of characteristics including a jarring juxtaposition of tragedy and comedy, characters behaving repetitively, nihilistic scenarios, cyclical plots, nonsense dialogue and a challenge to realism on the stage.

■ Critical response activity

Build a character study of Davies on a single sheet of paper. Pick out short key quotations from the text (keep them to a few phrases long and, for easy referencing later on, note on which page of your edition of *The Caretaker* they occur). Then annotate them with an adjective to describe his behaviour or personality as demonstrated by the quotation. You can use his own words or observations made about him by Mick or Aston. Try to gather a number of examples to support your observations about his character. For example:

■ 'When he came at me tonight, I told him. Didn't I? You heard me tell him, didn't you?', and 'If anyone starts with me though, they know what they got coming'. Davies is full of empty bravado.

■ 'If only I could get down to Sidcup! I've been waiting for the weather to break', and 'I'll be down there any day, I tell you. I was going down today, but I'm … I'm waiting for the weather to break'. Davies is a chronic **procrastinator**.

■ 'I've had dinner with the best, and I got my rights … nobody's got more rights than I have', and 'I been to plenty of other places. They always let me sleep. It's the same the whole world over. Except here'. Davies is keen to receive respect, whether it is deserved or not.

Now make a list of all the peculiar, odd or plainly **fallacious** things Davies says about himself and his past. For example, note down his incredibly brief marriage which fell foul of comically unreasonable behaviour on his wife's part: 'I took the lid off a saucepan, you know what was in it? A pile of her underclothing, unwashed'.

It is important to analyse how Pinter establishes Davies's character not only by what he says, but by how he says it. Many of the techniques he employs are typical of his plays in general to the extent that some of them have become clichéd trademarks, labelled as Pinteresque when used by other authors.

■ Key terms

Procrastinator: a person who puts off doing something, usually out of laziness or carelessness.

Fallacious: deceptive, misleading, illogical, wrong.

■ Background information

Pinter's style

■ *Pauses*: much of the dialogue in Pinter's plays is punctuated with long pauses. Why? Just as in real life, what is not said by a character is often just as meaningful as what is. Often these pauses create tension or suspense, with the audience and characters waiting to hear and see what is about to happen. They can highlight a character's ignorance or discomfort in that situation. In each circumstance, you need to establish what effect the pause is creating.

■ *Naturalistic dialogue*: using the understanding of language concepts such as conversation theory that you learned during your AS course and for Unit 3, you can see how Pinter employs methods such as adjacency pairs, chaining, non-fluency features (like fillers and hedges), cooperative signals, discourse markers and phatic utterances.

■ *Tragicomedy*: a technique which forces menace and humour together. Is he doing so to make a comment on how these two always go hand in hand during everyday life? Is he deliberately trying to unsettle the audience by making them laugh when they know they should not?

■ *Symbolism through detailed stage directions*: before the play even starts, the script of *The Caretaker* has a page-long precise description of what the room looks like. Such specific attention to detail leads us to assume that each one of the objects must have some significance, either in plot terms ('an electrolux, which is not seen till used') or as a representation of a theme or aspect of a character's personality (the 'statue of Buddha'). Sometimes these stage directions themselves contain jokes: Pinter fulfils the tired cliché by filling the room with everything including the 'kitchen sink'.

Critical response activity

For each one of these techniques, find an example which applies to Davies. How is Pinter using symbolism, a stage direction, a pause, a tragic–comic situation, some naturalistic dialogue to define Davies's character?

In some circumstances, Pinter makes a thematic point by having Davies deliberately confound our expectations and break the pattern and effect of these stylistic traits. For example, Davies is clearly ignorant of the conventions of how to make conversation: he ignores opportunities offered by incomplete adjacency pairs; he talks in repetitive circles, often returning to a comment he was making a number of minutes ago; he is fond of non-sequiturs. Find examples and then analyse what they tell us about Davies's personality.

Now that Davies's character, and the techniques that Pinter uses to create it, have been analysed, it is worth establishing which of the play's themes will provide another focus in the transformed text. In this way your transformation will be firmly anchored in the base text instead of becoming a vaguely associated vessel floating aimlessly on the sea of creative writing.

Background information

Themes in *The Caretaker*

The Caretaker contains many messages for its contemporary audience. Some of the themes that Pinter addresses are:

- *Isolation*: how people become separated from their family, friends and 'normal' society, what happens to them when they do, and what the causes and remedies are.
- *Alienation*: which is tied to the first theme but is more outward looking than **solipsistic**. Davies's xenophobia, Aston's self-imposed exile, Mick's guilty disgust at his brother's inefficacy: how do these character traits alienate the men from each other and from the morals and practices of 'normal' society?
- *Status*: all three characters are involved in a struggle to assert authority over the others. Pinter shows this through the language they use, topics they talk about, the style of conversation they engage in, their body language and physical behaviour.
- *Identity*: who are these people? What defines them? Do we truly know them or merely the façades they present? Davies is a clear example of a man searching for identity; he does not seem to know where he came from, where he belongs, what he does, even what his name is. Pinter underscores the characters' uncertain geographical identity by employing the **motif** of a confusion of place names peppered throughout the play: from streets to towns and cities. In his 1964 screenplay for the film version he even inserted a new, virtually dialogue-free, scene in which Mick offers Davies a lift in his van, drives him in a big circle around the block and then drops him off again where he started.

Key terms

Solipsism: in philosophy, solipsism is an extreme form of scepticism which holds that the only absolute knowledge is the knowledge of one's own existence.

Motif: a recurring image that gains significance from its repeated use throughout a text.

Critical response activity

For each theme, find a related quotation in the play, and then briefly outline what you think Pinter's ultimate message is. Find three quotations and subsequent explanations per theme. For example:

■ *Status*: (Mick) 'Venetian blinds on the window, cork floor, cork tiles. You could have an off-white pile linen rug, a table in … in aframosia teak veneer.' Mick is using the aspirational language of modern interior design to flaunt the wealth and glamour of his ambitions to a homeless old man who could not possibly understand a word he is saying. Pinter is demonstrating how in modern Britain material objects confer status on individuals and have become shorthand for power.

By doing this, you will not only be collecting material for your commentary, you will also have a clearer sense of what Pinter was saying to his audience in 1960. Are these themes and messages relevant today? How could they be adapted to suit the concerns of a modern audience? Make a list of how issues of isolation, alienation, status and identity manifest themselves in your society.

What would be the best form for the transformation?

In this transformation, it is possible to show how Davies is actually a misunderstood character. The apparent idiosyncratic parts of his personality and life (of which you have already made a list) are actually all true. Objectively viewed, he is an outcast from society who has plenty of virtues but has now suffered the final indignity of victimisation by a pair of men who represent heartless modern Britain. This kind of story appears regularly in the feature articles of supplements in the quality national press, or magazines such as *The Big Issue*. BBC Radio 4 broadcasts a weekly segment called *From Our Own Correspondent* which uses a similar in-depth brand of analysis. An exposé of how a poor individual has been trampled on by society is a calling card for many campaigning journalists and writers: Paul Foot, John Pilger, Robert Fisk, Feargal Keane and David Leigh have all been lauded for their investigations and articles, both broadcast and in print. As writers they have distinctive styles, but more generally this kind of article has a number of clear techniques and conventions.

Practical activity

Go to the library, newsagent or online and access a sample of this week's quality British printed press. Especially look at the supplements, magazines and pull-out sections. Find an in-depth profile piece or extended interview with an individual. Analyse the following:

■ How do the journalists make their presence felt in the articles? On a prosaic level, do they write about where they meet the interviewee, how they got there, the circumstances of the day? On a deeper level, do they express their own feelings – either explicitly or implied? Do they refer to themselves specifically?

■ How do they reveal the subject's past? Does it all come in one big section, or is it revealed as and when necessary during the course of the article? Are some revelations held back for dramatic effect?

■ Are the interviewees' comments woven into the fabric of the paragraphs, embedded in the story, or are parts of the conversations laid out like a transcript?

- Do the writers ask questions that seem to suggest they have a particular agenda? Do they actually tell you what questions they are asking, or do the answers become evidence in a more analytical series of paragraphs?
- Do the writers' contacts with the subjects stretch over a long period – is it the product of spending a few days or a week with them, with observations and comments drawn not solely from a brief interview with one person?
- What is the tone of each of the articles? What is the register of the language? What are the typical types of sentence and paragraphs used?
- Graphologically how are they laid out? Do they have a headline, teaser headline, subheadings throughout, pull-out quotations?

Read a spread of such feature articles. Pop stars, sporting figures, politicians as well as 'real' people who have suffered injustice or done noteworthy things all provide good subjects for this genre of writing.

By using Davies as the focus, you can utilise his distinctive voice as well as the bizarre events he has been involved with. A reporter who has spent a number of days with him after he has left Mick and Aston's house would be able to paint a picture not only of a homeless man's life, but also the story of his rejection by society.

AQA Examiner's tip

Always remember to ensure that the article focuses on events that occur, or are mentioned, in *The Caretaker*. Do not be tempted to spend too much time writing about Davies as he appears in Pinter's play: only write enough to fulfil the stylistic requirements of the new text. Your job is to offer a new perspective on the character from the base text, not to produce a piece of creative writing using that character as a starting point.

Combined transformations

AQA Examiner's tip

If in doubt, always consult your teacher about the viability of your ideas. Your teacher may also wish to contact AQA's coursework adviser before you begin to work on your transformation.

1 Geoffrey Chaucer, Jane Austen and Henrik Ibsen

If you decide to attempt a combined transformation (i.e. one transformation using two base texts rather than two transformations using one base text for each) then you will be embarking on what could be a very tricky piece of coursework: but it could also be extremely lively and interesting. And of course you would not have to divide your word limit between two pieces.

Remember that as your two base texts will cover two genres, you will generally have to think in terms of writing in the third genre. However, if one of your texts is a very particular example of a genre – such as Chaucer's poetry – then you could consider a different sub-genre of poetry.

How might you start?

From the two texts that you have studied, there may well be themes or characters which are similar – or perhaps antithetical; you could just as well exploit contrasts as similarities, and this could make your transformation more original.

However, sometimes surprising links between apparently very disparate texts may strike you, enabling you to start considering ways of combining them in a transformation. The example given here is looking at ways in which Geoffrey Chaucer's 'Wife of Bath's Prologue' and/or 'The Wife of Bath's Tale' (poetry) could be combined with either Jane Austen's *Persuasion* (prose fiction) or Henrik Ibsen's *Hedda Gabler* (drama).

'The Wife of Bath' and *Hedda Gabler*

First of all, you may want to consider the possible different interpretations of the texts.

Is Chaucer on the side of the Wife against the medieval Church's misogynistic attitudes? Some critics see her as a proto-feminist. Or is he satirising her, allowing her to reveal, unconsciously, her avaricious, lecherous and power-seeking nature? Chaucer's short poem 'L'envoi à Bukton' warns his friend against marriage, specifically advising him to read about the Wife of Bath, so it may be that Chaucer is using her as a warning to men!

And how do you regard Hedda? Is she also a woman of talent and strength, trapped by a stultifying and repressive society, and another feminist? Or is she just a cruel, self-centred and manipulative woman? Or both simultaneously?

You need to decide for yourself how you view the characters you are going to use in your transformation.

Because Chaucer has the Wife speaking in the first person, and because Hedda is a character in drama (where it is not usual to have a commentator on the action), interpretation is totally open to the reader and to the audience (though the director may well stress one interpretation in a particular production).

When you write your prose transformation, you will need to think carefully about which kind of narrative voice to use. If it is a third-person narrator, you can comment more widely on your characters' motives. If it is a first-person narrator, you will have to convey attitudes more subtly, and can – like Chaucer and Ibsen – leave your audience more leeway to choose an interpretation.

As preparation for your piece, you need to do some analysis of the base texts.

> ## Link
>
> For more information about narrative voice, see the 'Style' part of the *King Lear* transformation on p141.

Critical response activity

Make a list of:

- the qualities of character that the protagonist reveals
- the main themes of your base text
- the main events of your base text
- significant images or symbols
- any noticeable features of the idiolect used to suggest character.

Keep this list so that, if you wish, you can refer to it in your commentary.

You might then start to think in terms of comparison and contrast between the texts. For example, if you were using Chaucer's 'The Wife of Bath's Prologue' and 'The Wife of Bath's Tale' and Ibsen's *Hedda Gabler* you could draw up a table like the one below.

'The Wife of Bath'	*Hedda Gabler*
She was full of vigour and life, but is aware that the 'flower' of her life has gone.	Everything Hedda touches seems to wither and die.
She wants power over men; she wears a hat described as a 'buckler' (a shield).	She wants power over Lövborg and to know more about the world of men; her pistols symbolise this.
She has, as far as we know, no children, in spite of her justifying sexual activity as the means of procreation.	She does not want to admit she is pregnant; she destroys the 'child' of Lövborg.
She resents being read to from her husband's book. She tears pages from it.	She finds her husband's writing dull. She burns Lövborg's book.
She defies convention.	She is unconventional, but dreads scandal.
She has married three times for money and security, but later for lust and love.	She has married for security, but thinks about her previous feelings for Lövborg.
Chaucer uses features such as the Wife's gap teeth, and clothing such as her red stockings, to suggest her attitudes and behaviour.	Ibsen uses symbols such as the General's pistols and Tesman's slippers to suggest attitudes.
The Wife is deceitful, even cruel, in her treatment of her old husbands.	Hedda is deceitful and cruel with Thea and with Aunt Tesman.
Chaucer creates a vivid style of earthy speech for the Wife.	Ibsen creates particular styles of speech for his characters, especially for Tesman.
In her tale, she discusses 'gentillesse' and attitudes to rank.	Hedda is very conscious of class and status.
In the tale, the 'loathly lady' manipulates events through magic to win the knight.	Hedda is extremely manipulative, but ends up in Brack's power.
In spite of her vigour, there is a sense that the Wife has never found complete satisfaction in marriage. The ending of her tale may be wish fulfilment.	Hedda is bored, and finds no satisfaction at all in her marriage. Her suicide is her way of asserting herself.

As you can see, there are a surprising number of areas where the Wife and Hedda are similar.

There are also thematic similarities, in that both texts deal with power and women's position in society. Both have elements of feminism.

However, you will also be aware from studying these texts that the interests and backgrounds, as well as the personalities and the social status, of the Wife of Bath and of Hedda Gabler are very different.

There are also particular ways in which the writers convey their message. For example, the play – and the character herself in many instances, when referred to by others – is called 'Hedda Gabler' not 'Hedda Tesman'. Ibsen said that this was because he wanted to suggest she was more her father's daughter than Tesman's wife. Incidentally, is Chaucer suggesting something subtle when he calls both the Wife and her 'gossip' – her closest friend – by the same name, Alisoun; or is it an irrelevance? You might well consider the connotations of your choice of names for your characters.

How can you use your analysis of the texts in a transformation?

It is obvious that the Wife and Hedda would not actually meet; the Wife is from a 14th-century narrative poem with satirical elements, written in Middle English, and Hedda is from a late 19th-century Norwegian play.

If you wanted to base your transformation on an encounter between two such women, you would have to think of equivalent characters in another time and place.

If you decided to depict a present-day encounter between them – giving them different names and situations – where and how might two such different women meet? Are there any indications in the texts as they stand which might provide fruitful ideas?

For example:

■ *On a train*: the Wife likes travelling. Chaucer tells us in the 'General Prologue' that she has been to Jerusalem three times. Hedda speaks to Brack about her marriage being a journey which 'will go on for a long time yet', and Brack speaks of himself as a 'third person' who might join them on the train.

■ *At a book fair*: both the Wife and Hedda are married to men who are interested in books. Jankin insists on reading to the Wife about wicked women, and Tesman has spent most of his honeymoon researching his dull book about domestic crafts in Brabant.

On the other hand, Hedda is snobbish and moves in what she calls 'our circle'. The Wife, with her down-to-earth speech and her life as a tradeswoman, would not be eligible as a social equal in Hedda's eyes.

■ But they would not have to have a direct conversation in your transformation – and it might be better to avoid it, as you want to move away from the genre of drama. Because you are writing in prose, you could write as if you were inside the head of a woman like Hedda overhearing the Wife and some of her friends on a train, discussing marriage and their adulterous affairs. What would Hedda think to herself as she listens? What might she plan to do as a result?

■ Or could Hedda and the Wife (under the new names you have chosen for them) find themselves left in the tea tent at a book fair, and, in spite of Hedda's initial reservations about talking to the Wife, discover that they are both bored by their husbands' interests – and indeed by their husbands? How might their meeting develop? What action(s) might they take as a result of it?

Could you tell about their encounter from the Wife's point of view in the sort of down-to-earth idiolect that Angela Carter uses in *Wise Children*?

In *Wise Children* Carter tells the story of the extraordinary family of twins, Dora and Nora Chance, who are show-girls in the mid-20th century. Dora narrates her family history in an earthy cockney voice, full of lively humour, creating a picture for readers of a chatty woman of the world. The whole tone is conversational as, although Carter's work is very carefully structured, Dora appears to mention incidents just as they occur to her.

What themes would you want to deal with?

Would you introduce any symbolism, such as Ibsen's use of General Gabler's pistols or Tesman's slippers? If you were writing an exposé of society such as F. Scott Fitzgerald produced in *The Great Gatsby*, symbolism might be very appropriate to suggest a repressive society, just as he used, for example, the valley of ashes to depict a decadent one.

Once you have decided which themes and issues you want to deal with, your next task is to plan the structure of your writing.

■ Are you going to write a complete short story?

■ Would you want to introduce a twist at the end of your story, such as is found in Roald Dahl's 'The Way Up to Heaven' (one of his *Tales of the Unexpected*)?

■ Would you prefer to write a chapter – perhaps the opening one – of a novel in which issues about marriage and the feelings of a repressed woman are discussed; and where a good-hearted woman – like Ibsen's Thea Elvsted – is contrasted with a more powerful but self-destructive woman? (Hardy's *The Return of the Native* is just such a novel.)

Whether a short story or an extract, where are you going to begin? Remember that you do not have to keep to a **chronological** account: you can begin at the end, looking back over events, as Jane does in *Jane Eyre*, or you can play with time sequences as Angela Carter does in *Wise Children*.

'The Wife of Bath' and *Persuasion*

The main character in *Persuasion* is Anne Elliot. We might consider a transformation featuring Anne and the Wife of Bath. As with the Wife and Hedda, these two seem to have very little in common. That in itself might make them a good pair to bring together in a transformation.

However, there are some ways in which there are thematic – and even stylistic – similarities in these texts, however disparate they are at first sight. Some points of thematic and stylistic overlap between the texts that we are considering here are listed in Table 1 overleaf. You may well be able to think of several more – or of direct contrasts.

■ Key terms

Chronological: following a strict time sequence.

Table 1 *Comparing texts*

'The Wife of Bath'	*Persuasion*
Nobility	*Nobility*
Especially in the 'Tale', when discussing 'gentillesse', Chaucer (or at least his characters) sees nobility as a matter of attitude and behaviour rather than rank.	Austen satirises the way in which Sir Walter and most of his family insist on the importance of their rank, even though they are minor nobility.
Motives for marriage	*Motives for marriage*
Both the 'Wife's Prologue' and the 'Tale' explore the motives which lie behind marriage and the reasons for the success or failure of a union.	Through depicting a number of marriages and courtships, Austen explores the attitudes and values which are likely to lead to a happy marriage – or to the reverse.
How important is youth and beauty?	*How important is youth and beauty?*
Both the 'Wife's Prologue' and the 'Tale' examine the part played by physical attraction and youth in a sexual relationship.	By the time she meets Wentworth again, Anne is considerably older and her looks have faded, whereas Louisa is youthful and attractive. Austen explores whether these factors are important.
Narrative voice and satire	*Narrative voice and satire*
Chaucer creates an earthy, distinctive voice for the Wife. He is also satirical, attacking hypocrisy – though whether he is on the side of the Wife or not is less clear!	Austen uses a third-person narrator – but also intervenes to make her own comments at times. The objects of her satirical wit are very clear. She also allows characters such as Mary Musgrove to expose their selfishness through the way they speak.

AQA Examiner's tip

Remember to hold on to any preparatory notes you make. (If you are using a computer, remember to back up or print out your work so that it does not get lost.) You may want to refer to these preparatory analyses in your commentary.

Practical activity

Take any two texts that you know well – perhaps two you studied at GCSE – and draw up a table showing similarities and contrasts of character, theme, setting and stylistic method.

■ Does this exercise give you any new insights into the texts and the authors' approaches?

And/or

■ You could draw up a table noting any areas of (a) contrast; and (b) similarity between the two base texts you want to use.

What next?

Once you have looked at the themes and characterisation of your base texts, and of stylistic elements such as imagery and symbolism, you need to think how you are going to use this knowledge.

Chaucer's work is poetry. *Persuasion* is prose. So you are probably going to think in terms of drama for your transformation. Your next task would be to consider what kind of drama you want to create. There are 12 playwrights listed in the specification from whom a drama base text must be chosen, and this would give you 12 ideas to start with when thinking of ideas for your final transformation.

You do not have to limit yourself to these 12 when thinking about writing, only when studying a drama text. However, they do cover a good range of types of drama, including tragedy, comedy, pastoral, satire, Restoration, social commentary, 20th-century realism, feminist, confrontational, historical, **absurdist**, **existentialist**, etc.

■ Key terms

Absurdist: writing which presents us with the idea that life has no intrinsic meaning, and that it is in fact pointless.

Existentialist: writing which follows the philosophical concept that denies there is meaning to life other than what we create for ourselves.

If you wanted to write a play in which characters explicitly debate issues, there are other models for you to look at:

■ a medieval morality play such as *Everyman* – or Christopher Marlowe's *Dr Faustus* – where good angels challenge bad angels for a human soul. Shakespeare's *Macbeth* is sometimes also seen as having elements of a morality play

■ a play such as J. B. Priestley's *An Inspector Calls*, where Birling gives his opinions on the prospect of war, and where the family argue about the way employees should be treated

■ a late 20th-century play such as *Art* by Yasmina Reza which has three characters who, faced with a completely white canvas, discuss the nature of art. Reza uses comedy and monologues as well as confrontations between two, as well as all three, of her characters to consider issues of art and of friendship.

In addition, radio and TV dramas often focus on particular controversial issues, as do soap operas. You could write an episode of a soap opera featuring two characters, based on an encounter between your versions of 'The Wife of Bath' and of Anne Elliot from *Persuasion* – or between more than one character from each text.

As discussed previously, there are some links in theme and method between these two texts – but if the Wife and Anne were to discuss attitudes to marriage and loyalty, they would have very different views. And what would each of them think about the issue of trying to persuade others on the topic of love?

How to get your characters together

As we saw above with 'The Wife of Bath' and *Hedda Gabler*, the texts themselves sometimes offer suggestions for a new setting. For example:

■ *The city of Bath*: the Wife, of course, comes from Bath. It is where she has her business. Anne Elliot has to go to Bath when her family move there. Where could they meet? What business could the Wife run? Perhaps they meet at a social event, where the Wife reveals that she runs a dating agency. Caryl Churchill's play *Top Girls* might give you some ideas about women with different views discussing men and marriage.

■ *At a hospital A&E department*: the Wife is knocked unconscious by Jankin. Louisa Musgrave is knocked unconscious jumping off the Cobb at Lyme Regis. If the Wife and Anne (and perhaps other characters from *Persuasion*) met in the waiting room of a hospital, they might start discussing the results of impulsive behaviour.

■ *On a cruise ship*: we know that the Wife likes to travel. We also know that the Elliots have to leave Kellynch Hall; might they take up a last-minute deal on a cruise? Could Captain Wentworth turn out to be the ship's captain? Sir Walter Elliot would be very conscious of his class of cabin, but Anne would feel that it was unimportant. What elements of the 'Wife's Tale' and views on *gentillesse* might feature in a discussion between the Elliots and the Wife? What might happen as a result? In the 1980s there was an unsuccessful soap opera called *Triangle* set on a North Sea Ferry; you might be able to write a more successful script!

AQA Examiner's tip

Remember that *analysis* of your base texts and careful *research* and *planning* for your transformation are all-important. And remember to think all the time about how this preparation is going to be considered in your commentary.

> ■ **Think about it**
>
> You have only 1,500–2,500 words for your transformation. You may want to use some for stage directions. What functions can stage directions have? How important are they?
>
> Look, for example, at the opening of *Hedda Gabler* where the scene is minutely described; or at *Waiting for Godot* where pauses are indicated. Television and film scripts often need more indications of movement and expression than actual words. But Shakespeare probably wrote few, if any, stage directions – those that exist are usually the work of later editors.

2 William Trevor and Christina Rossetti

William Trevor was born in County Cork, Ireland, in 1928 and emigrated to England in 1954. His stories are set in both Ireland and England and they range from black comedies to tales with a political backdrop, such as the tensions between Protestant landowners and Catholic tenants. Some of his stories feature unreliable narrators, and he also uses different narrative voices to reveal the same events from different perspectives. Frequent themes in Trevor's short stories include the difficulty people have in recognising and coming to terms with truth and the mismatch between dreams and reality. Trevor's central characters are often disempowered members of society: children, old people, unmarried – or unhappily married – men and women who retreat into their own private worlds. Despite this, Trevor's stories are often tempered with a sense of the comedy that can co-exist with the disappointments of life.

Christina Rossetti (1830–94) was born in London. Her brother was the artist Dante Gabriel Rossetti, and their father, Gabriele Rossetti, was an Italian poet who came to England to seek political asylum. From the age of 14 Christina Rossetti suffered bouts of depression. She remained unmarried and her Christianity was a major influence in her life. She was a volunteer worker from 1859 to 1870 at the St Mary Magdalene 'house of charity' in Highgate, a refuge for former prostitutes. Much of Christina Rossetti's poetry concerns her yearning for lasting love and fulfilment and a desire to be released from a lonely spinster existence. In her later years her ill-health caused her to be housebound, which probably intensified her loneliness.

Although William Trevor and Christina Rossetti may not seem an obvious pairing for a transformation, there are common threads in their writing. Both Trevor and Rossetti explore and give expression to the most private fears and desires of their characters and narrators. In the case of Trevor, there is usually a more obvious separation between the writer and his characters, but in Rossetti's poems there is often an ambiguity as to whether the voice we hear is Rossetti's own or that of her created narrators.

'The Death of Peggy Meehan' and *Memory*

In Trevor's short story, 'The Death of Peggy Meehan', we are taken into the private childhood guilt of the 46-year-old narrator, a guilt that becomes a burden to him throughout his life. As a young boy he is taken to see his first movie during a summer vacation, and the fantasies that take root stay with him for the rest of his life. Nearly 40 years after Peggy Meehan's death, she continues to appear to him, even during Communion, 'in her patch of light to remind me that she never leaves me'.

Christina Rossetti's poem *Memory* is a less explicit exploration of memory, loss and guilt, but the feelings revealed would be familiar to Trevor's narrator. Rossetti's characteristic sense of unfulfilled dreams and of the associated pain are apparent in *Memory*:

> My heart dies inch by inch; the time grows old
> Grows old in which I grieve.

and in *The Prince's Progress*:

> This Bride not seen, to be seen no more
> Save of the bridegroom Death.

Compare this with what Trevor's narrator says of himself and Peggy Meehan:

> When we are old I shall desire her, too, with my shrunken evil body
> … I have a carnal desire for a shadow, which in turn is His mockery
> of me: His fitting punishment for my wickedest thought.

Critical response activity

Read both parts of Rossetti's poem entitled *Memory*, which may be found in various anthologies and on the internet at www.gutenberg.org. Print out a copy and note the references to threats, fears and worries that are unspecific, as in the first stanza, where 'it' is not explicitly identified:

> I nursed it in my bosom while it lived,
> I hid it in my heart when it was dead;
> In joy I sat alone, even so I grieved
> Alone and nothing said.

List all examples of such unidentified references and try to suggest what specific thoughts, feelings and ideas Rossetti might have had in mind. This is an act of interpretation and exploration, so do not worry about a lack of certainty about the events Rossetti was thinking about. As you interpret her words, you will inevitably be applying your own life experiences and your own thoughts, feelings and ideas to her words in order to respond to her implied meanings.

This should help you to generate much of the substance of the Trevor/Rossetti interview that would emerge in the suggested transformation idea that follows.

How can you use your analysis of the texts in a transformation?

Imagine that Trevor is going to interview Christina Rossetti with a view to turning *Memory* (either part or both parts) into a short story. Your task is to create a dialogue between the two writers. Using your knowledge of Trevor's short stories ('The Death of Peggy Meehan' in particular) and Rossetti's poems (both parts of *Memory* in particular) you will need to create the imagined dialogue between them as if Trevor is probing Rossetti's recollections of events and her present and past emotions, as any novelist or short-story writer needs to do before he is ready to plan and craft the story itself.

You will, of course, need to accept that this task is in itself a piece of fiction. In the first place, Rossetti died 34 years before Trevor was born, and even if the chronology of their lives had allowed it, there is no reason to believe that Rossetti would have wanted to allow another writer loose on her real and artistic lives! Available online is an interview between

John Tusa and William Trevor (www.bbc.co.uk/radio3/johntusainterview), which will give you an invaluable insight into Trevor's working methods.

In creating the dialogue between Trevor and Rossetti, you will need to reflect both characters on the basis of your close reading of works by each of them, but remember that writers, like their created characters, may be unreliable narrators. Their perceptions of experiences are not necessarily to be taken at face value, and one of the roles of an interviewer is to probe and challenge the interviewee, especially if the interviewee appears to become evasive when some topics are introduced.

Other transformation ideas

Role reversal

The interview could be conducted by Christina Rossetti with William Trevor as the interviewee. The Tusa/Trevor interview will be a useful model to show how an interview can be conducted, but for your transformation it would be better to have Rossetti playing a fuller part than Tusa does, so that her opinions and experiences come more into play. This gives you more opportunity in your transformation to reflect both writers' works and the connections between their experiences and their writing.

Genre transformations

A Rossetti poem becomes a Trevor short story … and a Trevor short story becomes a Rossetti poem. This is a challenging idea but it could result in excellent transformations. The success of this approach would hinge on your ability to write in the authentic style of each writer. You would need to take one substantial poem or a group of shorter poems and place yourself in Trevor's mind to work out how Rossetti's ideas and feelings could be developed and made specific in the form of characters and situations characteristic of Trevor's short stories. A major part of the challenge here would be to create a style of writing and storytelling that reflects Trevor's techniques.

Similarly, if you take a Trevor short story or novel, the question becomes: 'How would Rossetti distil the essence of the story into a poem?' Again, the success of this task would be dependent upon your ability to imitate Rossetti's style and to reflect her characteristic thoughts and feelings in a suitable poetic form. This approach would give you a wealth of fascinating material for your commentary, as you analyse the interplay between the thoughts and linguistic expression of each writer.

3 P. G. Wodehouse and William Shakespeare

The success of a single transformation which combines two texts from a pair of the prescribed author lists will often be based on the strength of the concept. Creating an idea which allows two base texts from different genres to dovetail is a difficult task. Working out the best way for themes or events or characters from the disparate pair to come together in a completely new form and style will be the product of careful planning, trial and error, and redrafting if you are to avoid long stretches of staring at blank paper.

One of the logical paths towards creating an assured, controlled and effective new text is to follow the lead of two of the base texts' protagonists. A character-based transformation will allow you to imagine how the individuals might react to the events from their fictional 'lives' in a new situation. Find a character who appears across a range of an author's work and you will be able to move away from the necessity of sticking to specific events from their life (as outlined in a single base text) towards capturing their essence as defined by a series of attitudes and behaviours which have been laid out in a series of stories. Finally, finding a distinctive genre for your new text will provide you with a model of clear conventions and proportions on which you can base your characterisation.

Seeking out texts and characters which seem totally ill-matched and even antithetical will help you to produce a distinctive new text and provide challenges that ensure you demonstrate your writing talents with a flourish.

Shakespeare and P. G. Wodehouse are writers separated by around three centuries, but both are still renowned for their skill in creating distinctive and universally recognisable characters through the subtle and elegant use of language. Scottish warlord Macbeth from Shakespeare's eponymous tragedy and Jeeves, the long-suffering valet from Wodehouse's Jeeves and Wooster series of novels and short stories, are two utterly contrasting characters from different literary contexts and genres.

How might you begin?

There is comic potential in combining the procrastinating and murderous pretender with the sophisticated and phlegmatic manservant, with Jeeves providing what Macbeth has always needed: practical common-sense answers; an anti-Lady Macbeth, if you like.

Before considering what kind of new text these two protagonists should use to retell their different stories, it is worth picking them apart to explore the juxtapositions more fully:

■ their characters
■ the methods used by their respective authors in creating them
■ what they stand for
■ which parts of their stories are ripe for transformation.

Wodehouse

| Background information |

Wodehouse and Jeeves

■ P. G. Wodehouse is a celebrated and archetypal English comic writer who is most commonly associated with **lampooning** the concerns and manners of pre-Second World War aristocracy.

■ The Jeeves and Wooster series of short stories and novels are narrated by the wealthy but feckless Bertie Wooster, a scatter-brained, idle-rich, British gentleman who unfailingly falls into a sequence of calamitous events only to be inevitably rescued by his cool and calm valet Jeeves.

■ Wodehouse's plots invariably follow the stock Roman comedy route, highlighting the ironic supremacy of the ingenious lower-class characters who extricate their masters from parlous situations without ever getting the credit.

■ Stories often began with one of Wooster's relatives making a harsh demand on him, and the complications of plot and circumstance become more convoluted and 'dangerous' as Bertie and his good-natured but buffoonish sidekicks' half-witted schemes to make things better, always go awry.

■ Key terms

Lampooning: satirically attacking and ridiculing a person, political party, writer, etc.; often light-hearted in tone.

▶

- At some point in most stories, a policeman's helmet will be stolen.
- Wodehouse's reflection of his characters' sociolect was one of his calling cards; the upper-class slang employed in the stories is a distinctive feature of his writing.
- His portrayal of the English upper class as eccentric idiots has itself become a stereotype.
- Wodehouse wrote about Reginald Jeeves's adventures in stories between 1919 and 1974. His expertise in a vast number of fields is often a source of comedy: he has the experience to shine in any given situation.
- Jeeves's understated ingenuity and firm control of any situation makes him a universally admired and respected character. The juxtaposition between his brilliance and Wooster's cluelessness is the main source of Wodehouse's comedy.
- Jeeves's dialogue is distinctively precise and elevated. His use of convoluted lexis which then needs to be simplified for his superiors' understanding is a trademark.

Grasping Jeeves's personality might seem to be a difficult task given that he appears in 11 novels and 35 short stories, but the way Wodehouse establishes a series of stock characteristics, distinctive lexical choices and generic events makes it easier. Building a profile of the valet and his customary reaction to any given situation from this vast repository of examples will provide you with a template for his character in your new text. This will mean that you will not have to try to crowbar two disparate plots from two different texts together in your transformation. The best place to start would be short story collections *The Inimitable Jeeves*; *Carry On, Jeeves* and *Very Good, Jeeves*. Tackling the novels alone (such as *Thank You, Jeeves*; *Right Ho, Jeeves* and *The Code of the Woosters*) means that it will take you longer to cover the ground.

■ Critical response activity

As you read each story, collect a list of Jeeves's quotations, mannerisms and key solutions to the most significant problems that arise. Note where they appear in each story, otherwise you will find it hard to refer back to them at a later stage.

In a separate mind map, gather together what other characters say about him. This will give you material when you come to write what his companion from your second text thinks about him in your transformation.

Almost all of Wodehouse's Jeeves and Wooster stories are narrated by Bertie Wooster. This allows extra scope to shed new light during the transformation process: Jeeves's thoughts and opinions are implied through Wooster's frequent misunderstanding of any given situation, but in a new text you can explicitly show Jeeves's feelings. To get a better, clearer impression of what Wodehouse thinks Jeeves himself would say, explore the short story 'Bertie Changes his Mind', which is the only episode narrated by the valet himself.

Shakespeare

Shakespeare's plays are not told from a single point of view and the playwright does not impose his own point of view in the same way that Wodehouse does (albeit a point of view which Wodehouse asks us to infer). Macbeth's knowledge of his own character and situation, as expressed through his dialogue in the play, is therefore as limited as anyone's in real life. What other characters are planning (for example Lady Macbeth or Macduff) or how fate may be conspiring for or against him (perhaps in the shape of the witches' plotting) Macbeth does not know, and he spends a lot of time worrying about this. Shakespeare uses language to create his characters, and with a protagonist as complex as Macbeth, this can lead to a range of interpretations by an audience. Is he a tragic hero with noble intentions, laid low by bad advice from larger evil forces? Is he a model of hubris, a warning to us all of the perils associated with an excess of ambition? Do you see him as a brave warrior, whose lifelong quality of loyalty is corrupted by his tendency to think too hard on a subject, with his conscience and imagination running riot once the witches have planted seeds of possibility in his mind?

There is evidence for all of these opinions throughout the play, and Shakespeare provides plenty of food for thought in the language he gives to Macbeth and those talking about him.

■ Critical response activity

Macbeth has a number of qualities, some of which are contradictory. He is:

- courageous
- compassionate
- loyal
- selfish
- ruthless
- generous
- tyrannous
- humble
- ambitious
- honest
- devilish
- purposeful
- a procrastinator.

Find evidence to support them all, ensuring you note where the references appear and who uses them.

What is certain is that Macbeth needs some good counsel and guidance. He allows himself to be swayed by the flattering words of the witches ('All hail Macbeth that shalt be king hereafter!' Act 1, Scene 3, line 50) and the materialistic temptations of his wife ('Glamis thou art, and Cawdor; and shalt be / What thou art promised' Act 1, Scene 5, line 14). But how would things have gone if he had access to the sage advice of Jeeves? Bertie acknowledges in the opening lines of *Jeeves in the Springtime* that 'Jeeves knows. How, I couldn't say, but he knows. There was a time when I would laugh lightly, and go ahead, and lose my little all against his advice, but not now.'

What narrative situation and genre would work for this transformation?

The transformation specification calls for a change in genre, and when you are tackling a two-texts-into-one transformation, your options for new forms become more limited. Similarly, it is obvious that a social hook-up between a medieval Scottish thane and a 20th-century manservant to the aristocracy is unlikely and impractical. Therefore, writing a comic short story or a tragic play in which Macbeth and Jeeves literally meet and interact with each other is out of the question. Placing them together in some kind of *Bill and Ted's Excellent Adventure* style pan-historical science-fiction situation will only lead to creative writing and not the sort of transformation that is required.

■ Think about it

Before deciding upon a final text genre for the transformation, it would be worth establishing what direction the basic plot of your story might take.

- ■ Select an incident, or series of incidents, from the two base texts that share a thematic thread.

- ■ Devise fresh, transformed, equivalents of these scenarios (see the examples below).

- ■ Think about how the original characters of Jeeves and Macbeth might be developed for the purposes of the new text.

- ■ Make sure you maintain links between the source and the new texts in terms of key character traits, overall style and language motifs, pattern of events.

There are many parallel events in the two texts. As *Macbeth* is the shorter text (compared to the huge range of scenarios covered in Wodehouse's stories), it would make sense to pick a scenario from the drama first.

- ■ Perhaps the arrival of Duncan at Dunsinane provides a good example of an awkward situation for Macbeth that Wooster might find excruciating: how does one deal with the unwelcome visit of 'the nephew crusher' Aunt Agatha?

- ■ Similarly, Bertie's quest to help his family claim possession of the antique silver creamer in *The Code of the Woosters* echoes Macbeth's desire to claim the mythical prize of kingship and guarantee his family's succession of power.

Melding together two clear situations from the respective base text would provide a hard and fast connection between the new text and its sources, ensuring the narrative of your transformation has foundations in your sources. All you have to do now is find a fresh equivalent that fits with your selected new genre.

■ Key terms

Picaresque: stories made up of a series of events and adventures, often loosely episodic, humorous and involving lovable rogues.

Choosing a new genre in which you can house this storyline is the final challenge. When selecting a fresh text type, see if the base texts suggest anything. If that is the case, then writing your commentary becomes much easier as there is a definite reason for your new form as opposed to merely choosing a genre for no better reason than you like it. For example, forcing together two disparate characters like Jeeves and Macbeth in a scenario that requires the former to offer support and advice while the latter wrestles with his conscience and the expectations of others might suggest an odd-couple double act. These can be found across a whole spectrum of genres, such as detective fiction (see the Dalziel and Pascoe series by Reginald Hill) or **picaresque** novels (Joseph Andrews and Parson Adams in Fielding's *Joseph Andrews* or Don Quixote and Sancho Panza in *Don Quixote* by Cervantes).

The fantasy genre often presents stories which focus around a mentor figure coaching a novice through difficult tasks (think about Gandalf's guidance of the hapless Bilbo in *The Hobbit*), while another author on the prescribed list could provide a generic template. Chaucer's framework for *The Canterbury Tales* could provide rich pickings for a new text, with a story that provides a clear moral about human behaviour, based on an aggressive lordling or businessman (Macbeth) and his travelling companion (Jeeves). Perhaps the aspiring merchant wants to usurp a more established local businessman and enlists the help of three feckless friends (in the vein of Gussie Fink-Nottle, Bingo Little and Tubby Glossop) who take the place of the malevolent witches, while his aloof and sage squire provides much better counsel.

In such cases, using the style model of modern translations (David Wright for Chaucer, Edith Grossman for Cervantes) removes the extra burden of producing an accurate piece of medieval poetry or Spanish satire.

22 Conclusion

Breaking down the transformation process

By this point you should have a clear understanding of what you need to do to produce successful transformations and commentaries. The examples of how base texts might be used for freestanding and combined transformations should have helped you to narrow down your own choices of text and your specific transformation plans. When you are ready to start work on your own transformation tasks, it will be useful to break down the work into the following series of five linked steps to help you understand the process of creating successful transformations:

- research
- analysis
- generation of ideas
- plan and first draft of transformation
- evaluation of first draft.

Table 2 *Steps in the transformation process*

1 **Research ...** texts and context	Identify the writers/base texts you are considering for your transformation(s).
	Think about possible approaches for each base text. Try to identify at least three possible approaches for each text or pair of texts that you are thinking of working on.
	Think about what the commentary might be likely to focus on in each of the approaches you outlined above.
2 **Analyse ...** your chosen base texts	Read your chosen text(s) carefully so that you become familiar with it or them and can identify significant aspects of:
	– plot and/or subject matter – characters and relationships – themes – settings – mood and atmosphere – style.
3 **Generate ...** ideas	Think about which of your earlier ideas for transformations offers the best possibilities for a successful transformation and commentary.
	Consider whether your detailed work on the text(s) has enabled you to modify your earlier transformation ideas, or even to abandon them and replace them with other, better ideas.
	Consider whether you can identify with greater confidence and clarity the most likely focuses for your commentary.
4 **Create ...** your transformation(s)	Create a plan that is realistic, bearing in mind the constraints of the guidelines of 1,500–2,500 words.
	Write your first draft and when you review it try to step back and read it as if you are seeing it for the first time.
5 **Evaluate ...** your first draft	Imagine you are not the writer of this piece and make annotations and notes, trying to be honest about both its strengths and its weaknesses. Use these notes to produce two bullet-point lists, one headed 'strengths' and the other 'weaknesses'.
	Use these lists to move on to a second draft, and further drafts if necessary.

■ Some questions to apply to your base text(s)

In studying your chosen base or stimulus text(s), your approach will, of course, need to be adapted according to whether you are studying the work of a poet, a dramatist or a writer of prose fiction or non-fiction.

Prose

Suppose you are studying a work of prose fiction by one of the 12 writers listed in the first of the three columns in AQA's specification. Use the following questions to reflect on the key characteristics of the text.

Text structure:

- How does the writer sequence the unfolding of events within the narrative?
- Is there a single narrator or are there multiple narrators?

Narrative perspective:

- Is the narrator external to the events in the story or one of the participants in the events?
- Does the narrator seem to be a reliable recorder and reporter of events?

Genre characteristics:

- Is it possible to place this text within any specific genre or sub-genre?
- How far are the language of the text and the events described specific to a particular place and time?

Characterisation:

- Does the writer tell us directly what they think of the characters, or are the readers free to arrive at their own judgements as the characters reveal themselves through their words and actions?
- Is dialogue primarily used to move the plot on or to reveal character?

Style:

- What are the main characteristics of the writer's style, as revealed through lexical choices?
- What are the main characteristics of the writer's style, as revealed through grammatical choices?

All of these questions reveal possible ways of transforming your base text. For your chosen text, ask yourself this question: what would the effects have been if the writer had made different choices?

Drama

For drama texts, most of these questions are also relevant. Any text within any genre must have a structure of some sort, which is not, of course, to say that they are necessarily tightly structured. The questions have been adapted to reflect the context of stage plays.

Text structure within drama:

- How does the writer sequence the unfolding of events within the structure of scenes?
- How do scenes relate to chronology and dramatic perspective?

Narrative perspective:

■ How does the dramatist present opposing points of view?

■ How are tensions and relationships between characters presented?

Genre characteristics:

■ Is it possible to place this text within any specific genre or sub-genre?

■ How far are the language of the text and the events described specific to a particular place and time?

Characterisation:

■ Are the characters simple individuals or do they also play some sort of symbolic role within the play?

■ Is dialogue primarily used to move the plot on or to reveal character?

Style:

■ How much variety is there in the spoken styles of the characters, as revealed through lexical choices?

■ How much variety is there in the spoken styles of the characters, as revealed through grammatical choices?

Poetry

For poetry, the analytical questions that you apply need to be tailored to the specific nature of individual texts. Some of the questions used to explore prose and drama will be useful when looking at poetry, but the sheer diversity of poetic forms, themes and voices should make you wary of applying a common analytical strategy. In the opening paragraph of her book *The Poem and the Journey* (2007), Ruth Padel writes:

> There is no secret to reading a poem, but the nearest I know is to think of it as a journey. Where are the thoughts, the sound and the feeling coming from, and where do they land up? 'Each word is a step on the road', the National Theatre's voice coach Patsy Rodenburg tells student actors learning to speak Shakespeare. To give words to an audience, she says, you have to feel 'the journey of thought' in them, the shape they make. 'Try walking', she tells the actors, 'the journey of the poem.'

This is excellent advice for reading any poem, but it is excellent advice too for trying to make sense of any written text that you encounter.

■ Transforming the base text(s): some possibilities

Here are some of the possible changes that could help to drive your transformation forward:

■ switching gender

■ beginning the story at a different point and changing the structure accordingly

■ changing the narrative point of view

■ changing the genre conventions (for example from tragic to comic)

■ foregrounding a minor character

■ switching the writer's sympathies to present a hero as a villain, or a villain as a hero

■ focusing on a scene or episode that, although potentially important, was not included in the base text, or referred to only in passing.

As you approach this unit, you need to gain the confidence to make choices that differ from those made by the writer(s) of the base text(s). In making these choices, you also become a writer, and that places the power of creation and transformation in your hands.

■ The commentary(ies)

All of these possible choices require you to make judgements about what to include in your transformation(s) and how to include it. And it is these judgements that you need to discuss in detail in your commentary(ies) . Look again at the Assessment Objectives (see p viii) and make sure that in your commentary(ies) you *analyse* (AO2) rather than merely describe the choices you made. Analysing your choices as a writer demands that you focus on your intentions as the writer of the text and explore the implications of lexical, grammatical and stylistic choices. You also need to apply your knowledge and understanding as a student of English language *and* English literature to analyse and evaluate the relationship between the base text(s) and your transformation(s) (AO3).

Avoid making anecdotal comments that describe or explain how you came to decide on a particular approach to writing your transformation(s). In the limited number of words available to you, it is essential that you focus on writing about specific details of your new texts if you are to fulfil the requirements of AO2 and AO3. When you come to reread the first draft of your completed commentary(ies), check that everything you have written is relevant to AO2 and AO3, because comments that veer away from these AOs will not help you to fulfil the task in ways that can be credited with high marks. In other words, the AOs can be used as signposts that help you to ensure that you write relevantly throughout your commentary. It is likely to be helpful for you to have copies of the AOs in front of you as you write, and the band descriptors will also help you to judge how far you have provided evidence of fulfilment of these AOs at the upper levels. The relevant descriptors can be found in the specification, which is provided on the AQA website.

■ Frequently asked questions

Some questions that are often asked about the transformation task are answered below:

1 *Can I use texts taught for other ELLB units?*
    No, to do so would result in a failure to fulfil the QCA requirements for breadth of text coverage.

2 *Can I use film or television as the source for my base text?*
    No, a published written text must be the starting point for your transformation.

3 *Can all of the students in my group use the same text and the same transformation idea for our individual transformations?*
    Although the specification does not explicitly rule out this approach, it is definitely not recommended because it would inhibit the very qualities of individual engagement and creativity that should be at the heart of this unit. The likelihood that a common text and a common approach would harness the enthusiasms and strengths of all candidates in a centre equally is virtually zero.

4 *Can all of the students in my group use the same text but different transformation ideas?*

This is acceptable, but it does raise the same question as above: is it likely that a particular text will inspire all students in your group equally well? Students' enthusiasms and abilities are likely to be better stimulated by text choices that reflect their individual tastes and ambitions as writers.

5   *Does the length of source text matter?*
Although there are no formal requirements for the length of source texts, teachers and candidates must take care to select texts that inspire strong, engaged responses. Texts chosen by candidates should be sufficiently rich and stimulating to enable them to show a critical and creative interplay between stimulus texts and transformation texts.

6   *Is it acceptable to use source texts for 'springboarding'?*
No, springboarding results in too loose a relationship between the stimulus texts and the transformations. An example would be to study *Romeo and Juliet* and then write a contemporary teenage love story that has only thematic links with the stimulus text. The transformation must in some sense cast new light on the stimulus text and springboarding does not allow this to happen, or the link is at best incidental.

7   *Does the transformation have to be in the form of a literary genre?*
No, the transformation must be in a genre or sub-genre that distinguishes it from the stimulus text but, apart from that restriction, the transformation may be in any literary or non-literary form.

8   *What is a sub-genre?*
A sub-genre is a distinctive form within one of the very broad categories used in the list of approved authors. For example, Hardy appears in the prose list; one of his novels might be transformed into a detective story in the style of Raymond Chandler and this would represent a significant (and challenging!) transformation from one sub-genre to another within the broad genre classification of prose fiction.

9   *Does the transformation need to be a complete text in itself or is it acceptable to write a section from an envisaged longer work?*
Either approach is acceptable, and the decision about what to do depends in part on the nature of the stimulus text. A short story could be transformed in its entirety into a poetic form (for example in the style of Browning's dramatic monologues), but one significant episode from a lengthy novel might be given a similar treatment. Part of a novel written by a single first-person narrator might be transformed as a series of letters written by various characters to different recipients who might not themselves be present in the stimulus text. You must remember that the 1,500–2,500 word limit imposes constraints on what should be attempted. For example, it would be a great mistake to try to shoehorn multiple plot complications and relationships between several main characters into a short story of, say, 1,250 words. A successful transformation needs to balance two equally important strands: creativity and discipline.

10 *Is it better to play safe or to be innovative?*
The answer depends on the candidate. What is likely to show the individual candidate at his or her best? An exceptionally able candidate might not exhibit his or her full potential in a safe but unstimulating task; an exacting and demanding task might be beyond what another candidate could cope with. Each candidate's teacher is in the best position to judge what is likely to be the most sensible balance between aiming high and playing safe.

Revising for the examinations

As with Unit 1, the most important prerequisite for achieving the highest possible marks in your Unit 3 examination is to enter the examination room thoroughly well prepared for what you need to do. This includes:

- knowing your set texts in detail
- understanding which Assessment Objectives apply to each question
- knowing the distinctive format and structure of the questions set in each section
- knowing the particular linguistic and literary focus for the Section A and B questions
- understanding how to apply relevant techniques so that you put all of your knowledge and skills to their most effective use.

Revision for the examinations is important but must be seen as the culmination of many months of consistent hard work. A couple of weeks' intensive revision can never be an adequate substitute for consistent application throughout the whole course of study.

Re-reading the relevant sections of this book will highlight what you need to do in the examination for each unit, but there is some general advice that can be applied to all of the examinations you will face in English language and literature.

Know the rules

Make sure that you know the following:

- How long is the examination?
- How many sections does the examination contain?
- How many questions do you need to tackle and from which sections?
- How many marks are available for each question?
- How long should be spent on each question?
- Is it an open book or a closed book examination (meaning, are you allowed to refer to an unmarked copy of a set book during the examination or must you memorise quotations and rely only on memory for making references to the book during the examination)?
- Which Assessment Objectives apply to the examination?

The A2 examination

As you know, Unit 4 of this specification is a coursework unit, so the A2 phase of the course has Unit 3 as the only examination you need to prepare for. Remember, though, that this two-hour examination counts for 60 per cent of the A2 marks, against the 40 per cent weighting for your Unit 4 coursework. The title of Unit 3, Talk in life and literature, sums up exactly what it focuses on:

- The Section A questions present you with a passage from each of the set drama texts and require you to examine the ways in which the dramatist uses literary, linguistic and rhetorical devices within crafted dialogue to create specific dramatic effects.

■ The Section B question presents you with two texts, the first being a transcript of natural speech ('talk in life') and the second a literary extract in which the writer has created representations of speech ('talk in literature'). Your task is to compare the two texts.

■ The triple T test

For all questions it is helpful to apply the triple T test. Have you understood the following aspects, which are all required for success?

■ Task
■ Timing
■ Technique

Task

Any examination is a test of what you know, what you understand and what you can do. Knowing the texts you have studied is vital, but in itself this is not enough to guarantee that you will do well in the examinations. On one level, knowing the text may simply mean that you know the plot well and can recount it faithfully in fine detail. However, your examination question will definitely not ask you simply to retell the story of a novel, a play or a poem. If that is what you do in your answer you will severely limit the credit which an examiner will be able to give your work. Knowing the text well at AS level means knowing the plot well and knowing about the writer's distinctive uses of language and structure in his or her exploration of themes and ideas.

Make sure that you understand exactly what the question or task requires you to do. The first and the most obvious step – but one that is often neglected by candidates – is to read the question carefully and analyse it in terms of what you need to do in order to produce a relevant and effective response.

Timing

You need to know exactly how much time you can afford to spend planning and writing each answer. In examinations that consist of two or more sections, it is vital that you relate the time you devote to each question to the number of marks available. Depending on the nature of the question or task, you need to spend time planning your response. In the case of questions on unseen texts, it is vital that you allocate enough time to read and annotate the text thoroughly. Refer carefully to the advice given earlier in this book about the techniques that need to be applied to particular questions in the examination.

Technique

When you write about a set text or a text encountered for the first time in an examination paper, you need to demonstrate your understanding of those aspects of the text that are relevant to the question or task. The essential strategy is to be able to identify relevant aspects of the text, to select relevant evidence to illustrate those aspects, and finally to write about your chosen evidence in such a way as to fulfil the requirements of the question. This process is shown in the diagram below.

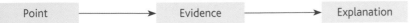

| Point | → | Evidence | → | Explanation |

If you approach your examinations with a firm grasp of this approach, you will make the best possible use of your knowledge and understanding and have the confidence that you will achieve a grade that reflects your abilities.

Glossary

A

Absurdist: writing which presents us with the idea that life has no intrinsic meaning, and that it is in fact pointless.

Accent: a form of pronunciation associated with a particular district.

Adjacency pairs: a pair of utterances from different speakers where the second speaker is controlled by the first speaker's utterance. This occurs in a question–answer format, for example, or when one person greets another.

Agenda-setting: this refers to the person who takes the initiative and chooses the topic being talked about.

Alienation: a theatrical technique developed by the dramatist Bertolt Brecht where a commonly held belief is challenged and the audience is made to reconsider its validity.

Alignment: this is indicated by repetition of a speaker's phrase.

Alliteration: the use of the same consonant at the beginning of words close together, for emphasis.

Antitheses: constructions in which words are opposed, or contrasted, but balanced, as in 'to live a sinner or to die a saint' or 'Man proposes: God disposes'.

Aptronym: a term used for stock characters whose names embody their characteristics.

Argot: special vocabulary used by a particular group and often not understood by outsiders.

Assonance: the repetition of similar vowel sounds, especially within words on stressed syllables.

B

Bathetic: anticlimactic speech or situation. It occurs when there is a change from a serious mood to a more trivial or down-to-earth mood. This often leads to humour. Bathos is the noun.

Blank verse: unrhymed verse, usually with 10 syllables to a line, with alternate unstressed and stressed beats.

Body language: gestures such as nodding or waving, or facial expressions. Body language can be used to indicate turn-taking in discourse: an inclination of the head or movement of the hand, or a direct gaze.

C

Caesura: another word for a pause or break within a line of verse. Caesuras can occur at the beginning (initial), middle (medial) or end of a line (terminal). Creating a sense of balance, they can be effective in initial and medial positions by drawing attention to a significant word.

Catharsis: the outpouring of emotions and the relief of tension that the audience feels at the climactic moment in a play.

Characterisation: how an author uses dialogue, actions and behaviour to develop a character's personality.

Choric: taking on the role of a 'chorus', and commenting and reflecting on the action.

Chronological: following a strict time sequence.

Clauses: constructions that consist minimally of a subject and a verb, e.g. 'I sang'. Or a clause may be within a larger construction and coordinated with another clause, e.g. 'I sang on Saturday and you can sing next week'. Or it can subordinate to another clause, e.g. 'they asked whether I would sing'.

Clichéd: a pejorative term for an over-used phrase that has lost all freshness. For example, 'The pirate fell to the deck with a sickening thud.'

Climax: an ascending series of events or ideas which intensify, or a moment of decision.

Colloquial: a semi-technical term for the everyday, or vernacular, form of language which is informal and may include slang words.

Comedies: plays which may include scenes of sadness and loss, but are predominantly cheerful, ending in harmony, often symbolised by a marriage.

Commedia dell'arte: meaning 'the comedy of artists', this is a form of improvisational theatre that began in Italy in the 16th century.

Commonwealth: the system of government between 1649 and 1660 after Oliver Cromwell and his Roundhead army defeated Charles I in the English Civil War. It is traditionally seen as being a time of severe, stark Puritanism, e.g. theatres were closed and mince pies were banned.

Complex sentences: sentences which contain more than one clause, linked by subordinating conjunctions (words which join clauses in such a way that some clauses are dependent on others for meaning).

Connotations: associated ideas suggested or implied by the words.

Construct: something carefully shaped and created rather than naturally occurring.

Contemporary: from the same historical time (contemporaneously is the relating adverb).

Convergence: when a speaker wants to show orientation with another speaker they may change their normal speech, perhaps by adopting a more formal or higher prestige form (upward convergence) or by adopting an informal register (downward convergence). The opposite is divergence, where a speaker wants to isolate themselves from another speaker and ensure differentiation.

D

Demotic: everyday, ordinary language. The term 'prosaic' is also used to refer to commonplace speech.

Denouement: this is when the tangles of the plot are unravelled and all is revealed and resolved.

Dialect: a variety of language where the regional or social background of the speaker can be identified from non-standard variations in their vocabulary and grammar.

Dramatic effects: effects created by the writer to evoke an emotional or intellectual response. For example, dramatic irony is when the audience knows more than the character(s) and so is made to feel helpless, anxious or tense. Suspense occurs when the audience is told something and waits in a state of dread or anticipation for the action to unfold.

Dramatic irony: this is where the character is blind to circumstances of which the audience is all too well aware, creating poignancy as the plot unfurls.

Dualism: in philosophy, this is the view that the world comprises two opposing entities such as mind and matter; in psychology, this is the view that the mind and body function separately; in theology, this is the concept that the world is ruled by the opposed forces of good and evil, and the concept that humans have two basic natures – the physical and the spiritual.

Dystopias: pictures of an unpleasant, harsh world (the opposite of a utopia, which envisages an earthly paradise).

E

Elision: the omission of a sound or syllable, usually marked by an apostrophe, e.g. 'she'd', 'didn't'.

Ellipses: the omission of part of a sentence for economy or emphasis, e.g. 'Need any help?', rather than 'Do you need any help?'

Endorsement: where a speaker wishes to endorse another speaker's view or statement to indicate solidarity by reinforcement, though it might also be used to bid for a turn such as: 'Yes, you're right there, I feel there is also …'.

Enjambement: the continuation of a phrase or unit of meaning from one line to the next without a break in a poem.

Existentialist: writing which follows the philosophical concept that denies there is meaning to life other than what we create for ourselves.

F

Face-threatening acts: Brown and Levinson use the terms 'positive face' and 'negative face'. We have positive face needs, which means we want to be liked and valued. Our negative face is a defensive one: we do not want to be imposed on or to be told what to do. Face-threatening refers to when our face needs are flouted, and in drama such flouting creates tension.

Fallacious: deceptive, misleading, illogical, wrong.

Field-specific: this refers to a particular semantic field, such as language linked with war, or with flowers, or with horse-racing; words that are connected in meaning or range of reference.

Filled pauses: vocal hesitations, e.g. 'erm'.

Foregrounded: a term used when a writer or speaker brings a topic to the foreground, i.e. emphasises it. Compare this with something in the 'background'.

Free indirect speech: a narrative method in which the actual words of a character are not reproduced, but the reported words reflect the tone of voice of the speaker.

Fricative: a severe sound created by breath forcing out the consonant 'f', in this example.

G

Gatekeeper: a person with the power to control the discourse, governing the turn-taking or the ritual.

Genre: from the French word (originally Latin) for 'kind' or 'class'. The audience will have expectations of particular genres.

Gothic literature: a genre (particularly popular in the early 19th century) which combines aspects of horror, mystery and romance.

Greek tragic model: put simply this includes the notion of a noble hero with a character flaw which leads to his/her downfall.

H

Hedge: this refers to using a softening phrase to weaken the impact of an utterance, e.g. 'As far as I know, no one has failed this course yet.' It is often a way to avoid being compromised if what you say is later proved wrong. With hedging the speaker avoids directness.

Homophones: distinct words that are spelled differently but sound the same, e.g. 'brake' and 'break'.

Hubris: a Greek term meaning arrogance and pride. In classical tragedy, a protagonist will defy the laws of the gods (a flaw of character known as hamartia), leading to an inevitable downfall. Hubris is the common example of hamartia in tragedy.

Hyperbole: exaggeration used deliberately for emphasis: 'Is this the face that launched a thousand ships?'

I

Iambic pentameter: this is the commonest blank verse metre. An iamb is a metrical foot of two syllables, short then long, first unstressed then stressed. Five of these create a pentameter.

Idiolect: an individual's particular way of speaking.

Idiomatic: speech typical of a people or place. The origin of the word is the Greek idios meaning 'one's own, peculiar, strange'. Idioms break the rules semantically and grammatically, e.g. 'jump the gun'. This cannot be understood literally, but it is a colourful idiomatic phrase.

Idiosyncratic: particular to one individual, often with the implication of quirkiness or eccentricity.

Imagery: this refers to figurative language. An image or picture can be created by imagery, but it can also be created by plainer speaking: 'The grass is green.'

Incrementum: the action or process of gradually increasing. It usually refers to lists which build up to a climax.

Interactional features: features of spoken discourse which are commonly seen when people interact, such as someone being dominant.

Intrusive commentary: the author interrupts the story to comment on, for example, the social background or related philosophical ideas.

Ironic: having a meaning or significance different from that which at first appears.

Irony: language that conveys a meaning often the opposite of what the words might literally suggest. For example, 'She was extremely generous and left all her old clothes to her sister.'

L

Lampooning: satirically attacking and ridiculing a person, political party, writer, etc., often light-hearted in tone.

Latinate expressions: words which have Latin origins and are often polysyllabic, e.g. circumnavigate, procrastinate.

Length of turn: this refers to the length of a participant's speech. The person with the higher status, because of their power or knowledge, will usually have the longest turn; but monopolising turns may well be seen as rude in a conversation when people are of roughly similar status.

Lexis: a unit in the lexicon or vocabulary of a language. Put simply: a word.

Litotes: understatements for rhetorical effect, often based on a denial of a statement, e.g. 'He is not the most generous person I know'.

Louisiana Creoles: Americans who are descended from the Colonial French settlers in Louisiana, who are a mixture of French, Spanish, African-American, and Native-American ancestry. Some Louisiana Creoles have not inherited all of these ethnic elements, and some have additional ancestries. In Louisiana, 'Creole' does not necessarily imply that an individual is of direct French and African descent.

M

Malapropism: using the wrong word, but one which sounds similar. For example, Mrs Malaprop says, 'It gives me the hydrostatics' instead of 'hysterics'.

Mediated: when someone or something has intervened in a situation, e.g. a disagreement can be 'mediated' by a teacher.

Metaphor: a figure of speech where two things are concisely compared by saying that one thing is the other, e.g. 'Denmark is a prison!'

Miscegenation: the mixing of different racial groups, by marriage or extramarital sexual relations; having children with a partner from outside of one's racially or ethnically defined group.

Misogynistic: relating to someone who hates women.

Modal auxiliary verb: e.g. can, could, might, may, shall, should, will, would, must. Using modal verbs can create tentativeness or emphasis.

Monoglot: a person who knows one language only (noun); something written in one language only (adjective).

Motif: a recurring image that gains significance from its repeated use throughout a text.

N

Narrative discourse: a spoken or written account of a linked sequence of events. In other words – a story.

Naturalistic theatre: this emphasises the naturalism of everyday speech in order to communicate efficiently. It is not to be confused with Naturalism, a theatre movement in the second half of the 19th century which purported to enact on the stage 'a slice of life'.

Nominates: chooses the next speaker, allocating them a turn in the speech. This may be a direct invitation: 'What do you think …' or by a pause and non-verbal address such as an expectant look.

O

Overlaps: where two or more speakers speak at the same time. It is a mistaken belief that overlapping suggests competitive or impatient speech behaviour; it often indicates alignment between participants to show solidarity or cooperation.

P

Paralinguistics: a broad term used to refer to aspects of talk that are non-lexical, but which convey meaning. For example, sounds made which are meaningful but are not usually recognised as words, such as grunts or affirmative noises like 'umm'. It can also refer to facial expressions or intonation which all help to convey the sense of an utterance.

Parallelism: this occurs when utterances are parallel (similar) in form, e.g. 'Our food is rotten; our beds are lousy; our clothes are torn.'

Parody: imitation of the style or approach of another writer, usually for comic or satirical effect.

Pathetic fallacy: a literary technique where the author applies human emotions to inanimate objects or nature, and uses the description of surroundings to reflect a character's mood. For example, if a protagonist is miserable then the weather will be grey, drab and raining in sympathy.

Pathos: originally a Greek word meaning 'suffering', it usually refers to feelings of sadness that a character or scene evokes.

Personification: giving human characteristics to non-human forms, e.g. 'the waves whispered'.

Phonological features: this refers to the sounds in speech: pitch and intonation, speed, stress and volume. Whispering to convey secrecy or using flat tones to suggest depression are examples of how sounds convey meaning.

Phonology: concerned with studying sounds in languages. It is a broad umbrella term. If you study phonological features you may well include a close look at stress and rhythm, which is where the definition overlaps with prosody.

Picaresque: stories made up of a series of events and adventures, often loosely episodic, humorous and involving lovable rogues.

Plagiarism: the uncredited or unauthorised copying or close imitation of another writer's words or ideas and passing them off as your own.

Plosives: sounds such as b, p, t, k; consonants which are produced by stopping the air by the lips, teeth or palate. Other sound labels include fricative (f) and sibilant (s).

Pragmatics: how we interpret the intentions of the speaker, sometimes defined as the study of 'speaker meaning' in a particular context. For example, 'watch this' can have many meanings depending on the situation.

Procrastinator: a person who puts off doing something, usually out of laziness or carelessness.

Prolepsis: in literature, this is a technique where an author anticipates events either through a character's unwitting comment, by direct narrative intrusion, or with symbolism; for example, a young Cinderella wistfully wishing she could find a pair of comfortable shoes that really fit her properly.

Proleptic irony: that irony which arises from an event, speech or thought which goes on to actually happen later in the drama.

Prosody: this is usually applied to the analysis of sounds and rhythm in poetry.

Protagonist: the main character in a play, poem or novel.

Proto-feminist: an early version of the doctrine advocating equal social, political and sexual rights for women.

Puns: word-play, usually a witty remark that relies for its humour on bringing together two words of similar form but different meaning. For example, 'grave' meaning 'serious' and 'grave' the noun; or where the different meanings of one word are exploited, e.g. cleave can mean 'cut in two' or 'to cling on to something'.

R

Realistic theatre: a movement in the latter half of the 19th century. It intended to make the theatre more useful to society in opposition to the mainstream theatre of the period, which consisted mostly of melodrama, spectacle, comic opera and vaudeville.

Register: the features that are characteristic of a particular type of language or situation, ranging from the informal register of text messages to the formal register of a legal document or a court scene.

Renaissance: (literally 'rebirth') between the 14th and 17th centuries, Europe was swept by a cultural movement which saw a revival in intellectual, artistic and political innovation and experimentation, placing a renewed emphasis on the supremacy of man's artistic achievements.

Repertoire: a person's word stock or vocabulary range.

Rhetorical: to do with the art of persuasion and effect, especially in speech-making.

Rhetorical question: e.g. 'What time do you call this?' or 'Why am I helping you?' where the intent is to make the listener reflect, rather than expecting them to provide an answer.

Romance plays: plays which move away from realism to include scenes of magic and mystery, often also introducing elements of music and dance.

S

Satire: this aims to bring about correction or reform by means of amusement or ridicule.

Schema: a set of expectations in any given situation. For example, in buying and selling there is an expected 'schema' which governs behaviour.

Secular: not to do with religion.

Simile: an explicit comparison, usually using the word 'like' or 'as', e.g. 'as thick as thieves'.

Slang: non-standard language often used to create and reinforce group identity. It is influenced by fashion and is ephemeral. Words like 'cool' and 'wicked' have replaced an earlier generation's 'hip' and 'far out'.

Soliloquy: a form of monologue that allows the character to speak their internal thoughts out loud, to offer an audience self-revelation or motive or self-uncertainty. What is said can always be regarded as the truth as it appears to that character.

Solipsism: in philosophy, solipsism is an extreme form of scepticism which holds that the only absolute knowledge is the knowledge of one's own existence.

Standard English: the 'educated' variety of English recognised in British society as the prestigious form, free of regional dialect, with uniform spelling and grammar in its written form, sometimes called the Queen's English.

Stichomythia: a device used in ancient Greek drama; a dialogue in which two characters speak alternate lines of verse.

Symbolising: made to represent something else, e.g. a river symbolising life.

Syntax: a term that refers to the order of words in a sentence: this is normally subject, verb, object (or svo) in Standard English usage. 'The dog (subject) sat (verb) on the mat (object).'

T

Theatre of the Absurd: a European theatrical movement from the mid-20th century. The plays shared a number of characteristics including a jarring juxtaposition of tragedy and comedy, characters behaving repetitively, nihilistic scenarios, cyclical plots, nonsense dialogue and a challenge to realism on the stage.

Third person narrative: this is when the author (or omniscient narrator) sees and knows everything, all actions and thoughts of the characters. The 'third person' is used: he wrote; she cycled; they danced.

Topic management: this is to do with how the subject/topic being discussed is handled, i.e. who changes the topic?

Tragedies: plays which shows the fall of a previously great character, often at least partly through their own fault, and usually ending in their death.

Tragic heroes: the main characters in a tragedy, who have great qualities but also flaws which lead them to fall from prosperity to adversity and (usually) death.

Triple structure: also known as tripling/triplets. Repeating words or longer utterances three times is a common feature in rhetorical oratory: 'Education, education, education!'

Tropes: words or expressions used in a figurative or non-literal sense.

Turn-taking: in spontaneous conversation, this is when people take turns to speak, although there can be overlaps and interruptions. Scripted turn-taking is more orderly.

Types of utterance: there are four main types of utterance – questions (interrogatives), statements (declaratives), commands (imperatives) and exclamations (though these may be couched in terms of a declarative such as 'Get away!' to indicate disbelief).

U

Unreliable narrator: a first-person narrator who, the reader gradually finds out, has been concealing material facts or being deceptive about events.

V

Verse: language in metrical form, or poetry. Verse builds discourse in a dramatic text by using recurrent syllabic patterns, imposing an order not usually found in spontaneous speech.

Index

Page numbers in **bold** indicate key terms.